AN ENGLISHMAN ABROAD

OSPREY
PUBLISHING

AN ENGLISHMAN ABROAD

SOE agent Dick Mallaby's
Italian missions, 1943–45

Gianluca Barneschi

OSPREY PUBLISHING
Bloomsbury Publishing Plc
PO Box 883, Oxford, OX1 9PL, UK
1385 Broadway, 5th Floor, New York, NY 10018, USA
E-mail: info@ospreypublishing.com
www.ospreypublishing.com

OSPREY is a trademark of Osprey Publishing Ltd

First published in Great Britain in 2019

For legal purposes the Acknowledgements on pp. 13–16 constitute an extension
of this copyright page.

A catalogue record for this book is available from the British Library.

ISBN: HB 978 1 4728 3544 4; PB 978 1 4728 3546 8; eBook 978 1 4728 3547 5;
ePDF 978 1 4728 3545 1; XML 978 1 4728 3543 7

19 20 21 22 23   10 9 8 7 6 5 4 3 2 1

Index by Angela Hall
Originated by Deanta Global Publishing Services, Chennai, India
Printed and bound in Great Britain by CPI (Group) UK Ltd, Croydon CR0 4YY

Front cover images from iStock.
Back cover: An atmospheric shot of Dick Mallaby in the late 1940s, evoking his wartime
adventures. (Mallaby family)

Osprey Publishing supports the Woodland Trust, the UK's leading woodland
conservation charity.

To find out more about our authors and books visit **www.ospreypublishing.com**.
Here you will find extracts, author interviews, details of forthcoming events
and the option to sign up for our newsletter.

Dedication
This book is dedicated to all those who, at least once in their life (just like the author),
have shown courage (despite a dying father and a dishonest woman).

Given that its subject matter comprises the adventures of an Englishman, the author
wishes to remember, affectionately and nostalgically, another Englishman whose (quite
different) deeds are very dear to him: Keith John Moon, an enormously talented young
man, who 'hoped to die before he got old'. He succeeded, but his self-destruction took
place amidst the indifference of those who should have and could have helped him.

CONTENTS

FOREWORD

A writer of spy novels like Ken Follett would certainly enjoy the story narrated in this book by Gianluca Barneschi, a forensic and committed researcher into the dark and controversial aspects of a dramatic moment in recent Italian history – the events immediately preceding, accompanying and following the 8 September 1943 armistice. For years, Barneschi has been trawling through public and private archives and collecting source documents and accounts, largely unpublished, seeking to shed light on the mysteries, misunderstandings, ambiguities, and acts of cunning or indolence that, as a whole, marked this event. The latter has been transformed into a symbolic milestone, widely discussed in historiography, marking the 'end' or rather the 'rebirth' of the nation.

The story of the British special agent Dick Mallaby is the distillation of this long research, one piece of the puzzle that Barneschi is attempting to patiently and scientifically put together. Such details usually escape the attention of macrohistory, but, on closer inspection, this piece turns out to be important in creating a more coherent and broader depiction of events.

In most studies dedicated to the dramatic Italian crisis of September 1943, the figure of Mallaby does not appear. At best, Mallaby appears only in passing, and unnamed: a handsome polyglot Englishman seen disembarking, on the afternoon of 10 September 1943, in the port of Brindisi from the corvette *Baionetta*, which – bearing King Vittorio Emanuele III, Marshal Pietro Badoglio, and several other members of the Italian royal family and retinue, both military and government – had arrived under the escort of the cruiser *Scipione*.

Whilst the presence of Mallaby on board the *Baionetta* failed to arouse the curiosity of many scholars, who set it aside as an unimportant or secondary fact, it led Barneschi to research both this Englishman and the reasons why he was accompanying the Italian king and head of government following their flight from Rome in the aftermath of the proclamation of the armistice.

From this curiosity Barneschi's research was born. With great patience, he has pored over historical works and accounts, rummaged through Italian and foreign archives, traced Mallaby's surviving relatives, gaining their trust and overcoming their doubts and reticence, and tracked down and interviewed eyewitnesses.

The results are to be found in this book, which, for the first time, reconstructs secret agent Dick Mallaby's background, and his first mission in Italy. It makes for an exciting tale, if only for the fact that – due to a strange ensemble of circumstances (so often a determining factor in historical events) – the protagonist became, in spite of himself but to his good fortune, a key player in the relations between the Badoglio government and the Allies. Captured by the Italians after parachuting into Lake Como under a full moon on 14 August 1943 on an intelligence mission, the British agent avoided the customary fate of enemy spies caught in the act – the firing squad – because his very capture proved useful to the armistice negotiations that Italy was conducting (via Brigadier-General Giuseppe Castellano) with the Allies. Mallaby, with British approval of course, became, by means of wireless communication, the conduit of dialogue and negotiation between the Italian Supreme Command and the Allied Force HQ in Algiers.

With both care and efficiency (just like in his previuous work *Balvano 1944: Indagine su un disastro rimosso*), Barneschi has analysed the incoming and outgoing radio communications, and compared their contents with both the accounts of those who took part in the armistice negotiations and historical research. The result is a fresh reconstruction of events that will certainly find a following in future works.

An identical approach – with identical results – has been used for Mallaby's second Italian mission. By analysing the same sources, Barneschi manages to reveal, after 70 years, new aspects of a key moment in World War II, further demonstrating that macrohistory is made up of (what appear to be) multiple microhistorical events.

Above all, the whole allows us to grasp the often fundamental importance of the contribution that men like Mallaby have made, consciously or obliviously, to history.

Francesco Perfetti
Professor of Contemporary History
Faculty of Political Sciences
LUISS Guido Carli University
Rome

PROLOGUE

The credit of success is claimed by all, while a disaster is attributed to one alone.

Tacitus, Agricola (27)

Life is like a play: it is not the length, but the excellence of the acting that matters.

Seneca, Moral Letters to Lucilius (77)

Lake Como, 14 August 1943 – a full moon night.

'Who are you, then, eh? A fisherman?'

With threatening sarcasm typical of those who have caught their prey, a small group of Italians was taunting a soaking wet, helpless young Englishman who had just been picked up.

The young man was thinking hard, trying to come up with something plausible and useful. His first special mission had ended in immediate failure. There was no means of escape and the most likely next step was, at best, to be shot, after a summary process – providing that some Italian hothead did not exact rapid revenge for some recent air raid by the young man's compatriots – not to mention the prospect of torture.

At this point, the young man was focusing solely on continuing to live beyond his 24 years; even a lengthy prison sentence seemed like a dream outcome.

Cecil Richard Dallimore-Mallaby (known as Dick) could never have imagined that, thanks to several fatal but favourable coincidences, in a few days he would be the right person, in the right place, at the right time, and instead of staring death in the face, would be granted full protection. Moreover, the young Englishman could have no idea of his imminent role as actor in and witness to the greatest institutional tragedy in the country where he had grown up, and where he would later return to live, and end his days.

ACKNOWLEDGEMENTS

The publication of a book in English written by an Italian amateur historian is something of an achievement and almost makes for a case study. When I began my research, I had little idea of what I would go on to discover. The various difficulties encountered along the way never failed to deter me, given that those things that are hardest fought turn out to be the most satisfying; the results speak for themselves now, and offer an invitation to continue.

Although our protagonist Dick Mallaby was sadly unavailable to me in my 20 years of research, I have met many of his wonderful relatives.

Dick's son Richard 'Vaky' Mallaby opened up the entire family archive to me. Christine Joyce Northcote-Marks Dallimore-Mallaby, Dick's widow, was kind enough to allow me to interview her and after 70 years she finally felt able to speak freely about her husband's wartime activities. I would also like to thank Dick's daughters, Caroline and Elisabeth, for their kind collaboration; Alessandra Mallaby, Dick's niece, for allowing me to visit Poggio Pinci, where Dick lived and rests; Pia Teresa Mallaby; Nicola and Francesco Barresi; Elettra Mallaby; and Neil Chapman.

My son Pietro accompanied me on a research mission that ended with him dropping into Roma Termini station. He also maintained the 'most secret' status relating to the publication of this book with 'Mami', sharing my sufferings. I hope he enjoyed it and is proud of his father (who adores him, even if he doesn't make as much a fuss of him as he sometimes should). As regards to my Antonella, I must thank her again for these 32 years of emotions, love and complicity. She is the other half of 'the last couple left', in this brilliant and strong enduring *ménage à deux* that looks so much like us. But even considering that she was unaware of my project, moving all the papers for this book in a crucial moment was not a useful move. My mother Fatima helped check the text, especially for details about the House of Savoy, continuing her almost 60-year-long role as a loving mother. My sister Cristiana and her husband, Ramòn, helped with the translation of some far-from-Shakespearean passages, and gathered documents in the United States. My cousin and brother-in-law Lorenzo Dianzani was a skilled and patient consultant.

I thank the following academics and experts: Elena Aga Rossi; Roderick Bailey (he may regret ever meeting me); Mireno Berrettini; Giuseppe Parlato; Francesco Perfetti (for the flattering Preface and insertions in *Nuova Storia Contemporanea*); Michele Sarfatti (for details of his father Giacomino's activities); Marco Zaganella; Professor Aldo G. Ricci; then Franco Nudi at the Archivio Centrale dello Stato; Alessandro Gionfrida at the Ufficio Storico dello Stato Maggiore dell'Esercito;

Giancarlo Montinaro and Massimiliano Barlattani at the Ufficio Storico dell'Aeronautica Militare; and Herb Pankratz of the Eisenhower Presidential Library in Abilene, Kansas.

Well deserved thanks are also due to Fabio Andriola, for promoting my book in the magazine *Storia in Rete*; Armando Ferracuti, Alessandro Tuzza, Laura Vivio and Dana Lloyd Thomas, for their archival research; and Mauro Taddei for allowing me to consult Henry Boutigny's unpublished diary.

I am grateful to the following eyewitnesses to the events described in this work: Don Giovanni Barbareschi; Tommaso D'Antuono; Fabio and Lorenzo Magi; Ina Elisabeth Mann; and Anna Maria Rusconi. Thanks are also due to the following for their contributions: Saverio Addante; Antonio Albanese; Gregory Alegi; Francesco Arcieri; Giovanni Enrico Arcieri; Manuela Baldi; Claudia Banella; Roberto Barzanti; Paolo Bertoia; Loriano Bessi; Stefano Bodini; Aloisio Bonfanti; Francesco Valerio Caltagirone; Laura Cancellieri; Luca Caneschi; Corrado Chiariello; Pasquale Coppola; Maria Costabile; Francesco Crispino; Alda Dalzini; Augusto Dami; Angelo De Nardis; Mario De Vita; Renato Dionisi; Margherita Di Rauso; Silvia Franceschini; Mimmo Franzinelli; Francesca Garello; Emilio Gin; Marco Tullio Giordana; Antonella Grossi; Guariente Guarienti; Marco Imbimbo; Tom Kington; Maria Kisseloff; the youthful but nigh-on-100-year-old Sergio Lepri; Marco Lungo; Roberto Marabini; Guglielmo Marchionno; Stefano Mencaroni; Aldo

Minghelli; Alberto Montalbani; Franco Morosini; Massimo Mortari; Giuseppe Ludovico Motti Barsini; Mauricio Negrao; Corrado Ocone; Roberto Olla; Angelo Ottavianelli; Emilio Pappagello; Ivano Patitucci; Cesare Pellegrini; Federico Piana; Maurizio Pini; Gloria Provedi; Giuseppe Quilichini; Susanna Sala; Raimondo Sancassani; Anna Savini; Carla Scarozza; Vito Scelsi; Renato Sorace; Paolo Spiga; Nick Squires; Giacomo Steiner; Alberto Tabbì; Paolo Torino; Simona Trevisi; Lelio Triolo; Maria Giuditta and Maria Rosaria Valorani; William Ward; and Roberto Zanella.

For the events of 23 September 2016 in Asciano, I thank Mayor Paolo Bonari, Deputy Mayor Fabrizio Nucci and Counsellor Lucia Angelini, as well as Pierluigi Puglia and Colonel Lindsay MacDuff of the British Embassy in Rome.

Moriano Micheli took care of editing the movie for the book's presentation, *comme d'habitude* at nighttime.

The dependable Maria Maddalena Trina carried out numerous complicated activities with customary calm and resignation.

For this English edition, I would like to thank Nikolai Bogdanovic, Marcus Cowper, Gemma Gardner, Nigel Newton, Adriano Ossola, and Richard Sullivan.

G. B.

PREFACE

> For the time will come when they will not endure
> sound doctrine; but after their own lusts shall they
> heap to themselves teachers, having itching ears;
> And they shall turn away their ears from the
> truth, and shall be turned unto fables.
>
> Second Epistle of Paul the Apostle to
> Timothy, 4:3–4

> I help the old to remember and the young to
> understand.
>
> Gervase Cowell, MBE (1926–2000)

> Tradition is the handing down of the flame and
> not the worshipping of ashes.
>
> Gustav Mahler (1860–1911)

For the past 30 years, I have been studying and
analysing the events of summer 1943 in Italy with the
firm conviction that the consequences continue to this
day, and, above all, that there is still much to discover
and make known.

What follows is a tangible demonstration of this.

The study of sources and documents, both Italian and foreign, relating to the events surrounding the unconditional Italian surrender to the Allies (which culminated in the unexpected arrival in Brindisi, on 10 September 1943, of the Italian king, queen, crown prince, head of government, chief of the general staff and many other VIPs) offers up brief mentions of a certain Dick Mallaby, who is sometimes described as an Englishman, at other times – in erroneous sources – as an American.

What resulted was thus a logical, embryonic question: who was Dick Mallaby? Following further analysis and research, the question became: what was he doing there, and why was an Englishman part of this elite group, composed of members of the Italian royal family and political–military leaders, which had travelled from Rome to Brindisi?

David Stafford, in his book *Mission Accomplished: SOE and Italy 1943–1945*, succinctly summarized the object of my curiosity:

> Among those disembarking from the *Baionetta* was a blond young man in his early twenties. Despite his fluent Italian, he was a member of neither the government nor the Supreme Command. In fact, he was not even an Italian. He was an Englishman, and his name was Cecil Richard Mallaby.[1]

This initial curiosity on my part has resulted in a 20-year-long investigation, the substantial results of which are presented in this volume.

The 70-year-long absence of in-depth research into, and general interest in, Dick Mallaby's two war missions is astonishing.

Having uncovered very important papers in Italian, US and British archives; having acquired key documents, kindly made available by the Mallaby family (after five years of asking, finally breaking the chains of secrecy); and having interviewed Mallaby's wife and son, as well as eyewitnesses, it has been possible to accurately reconstruct, for the first time, not only how and why in September 1943 Dick Mallaby came to be in Brindisi, but also how in 1945 he managed to negotiate with the Supreme Commander of SS forces in Italy, Karl Wolff, and to do it in such a way as to confuse historians for decades.

In short, I discovered a highly distinctive character, who was the protagonist in and witness to historical events, the details of which remained largely unknown.

Having spent years analysing Mallaby's missions as part of SOE, it seems that he certainly could have been, and perhaps was, an excellent source of inspiration for many fictional characters such as James Bond. His first mission in 1943 was among the first ever to involve parachuting into water at night, bearing cryptographic codes and special technology, and, lacking any clever disguise or means of concealment, he attempted to carry out a risky operation in full enemy territory with the near certainty of being killed if captured. Even his second mission in 1945, which featured a humbler opening scene comprising a hard march over the snow-covered mountains, featured highly dramatic moments.

It is therefore somewhat surprising that in Mallaby's native Great Britain, his heroic deeds and the events which he witnessed and in which he played a key role were neither the subject of more extensive research, nor more widely disseminated.

This is, perhaps, an indirect consequence of a disinterest in (or contempt for) all things Italian among some of Mallaby's compatriots, as a form of payback for the events that took place between 1922 and 1945. David Stafford, in his previously cited work, confirms this, in the context of his broad and balanced reasoning referring to myths, embellishment and posthumous distortions relating to the resistance movements in Italy.[2] The narrow-minded attitudes of the time demonstrate an ignorance of not only all the positive and brave achievements of the Italians, but also, and above all, the considerable historic achievements in Italy that can be credited to the British operatives there.

As a partial justification, it should be noted that the part played by SOE in the historical events which featured Mallaby was kept secret for a long time; even the very existence of SOE was officially denied for several decades.

In my first published work, *Balvano 1944*, I dealt with a terrible, little-known event; in this work, it is the turn of the little-known deeds of a man who deserves wider fame.

Dick Mallaby's story is one of a man who, although called upon to improvise difficult and important actions – far greater than those initially foreseen – completed his missions in an excellent and fruitful way, becoming the right person, in the right place, at the right time, and proving how the reality of the situation can surpass one's wildest imagination.

He was twice destined by chance to be in the right place, at the right time, but he also knew how to use his courage and his intelligence to improvise in the right way.

In the 21st century, equally by chance, the task of disclosing the achievements of Cecil Richard Dallimore-Mallaby to public attention fell to the present author, a lawyer born in the 'Eternal City' of Rome, who is passionate about history, and seeks to apply the same bespoke approach to research as he does to his professional activities, and whose family roots, by chance, lie within a few miles of the places which Mallaby liked the most, in which he spent his childhood, and in which he now lies at rest.

So, if, after more than 70 years, the reader wishes to find out what really happened in the summer of 1943, in the ambiguous and controversial matter of the Kingdom of Italy's unconditional surrender to the Allies, and how, in 1945, a cessation of hostilities in Italy was agreed between the German and Repubblica Sociale Italiana (RSI) forces and the Allies, my advice is to continue reading.

The original subject matter for my second book was supposed to be a controversial World War II Italian general; but at the conclusion of many years' work on this topic, despite having uncovered some startling results, a certain spark was missing. As a result, this biography of Dick Mallaby happily got the upper hand, like a wild plant triumphing over what has been sown (and eradicated) by the gardener.

My work here is based on in-depth research to the extent of appealing for help on local radio stations around Lake Como; has taken 20 years of, at times, quite maddening study and analysis; is not based on inference; features a self-imposed limit on the use of personal evaluations; and has been written in a style to render it as readable as possible.

The reader must now judge if the process has been successful, considering that what follows was mainly written in the small hours, and at very low temperatures.

Do not ask me why and how I managed to do it.

I currently find myself living through a phase succinctly described by my favourite musician, the West Londoner Peter Dennis Blandford Townshend of The Who, in which I am 'too old to give up, but too young to rest'.

And so I am trying to make the best of my increasing experience and of my as yet unwaning strength.

It is enough to force oneself to do, and remember, everything, all of the time.

Even if this is ever more tiring, often frustrating and ever less appreciated.

G. B.

From La Castolina, Laviano, Perugia Province
25 October 2018

LIST OF ACRONYMS

ACC   Allied Control Commission

ACS   Archivio Centrale dello Stato (Central State Archive, Rome)

AFHQ   Allied Force Headquarters

AMGOT   Allied Military Government for Occupied Territories

AUSSME   Archivio dell'Ufficio Storico dello Stato Maggiore dell'Esercito (The Italian General Staff Archives)

CLNAI   Comitato di Liberazione Nazionale Alta Italia (Committee of National Liberation for Northern Italy)

CVL   Corpo Volontari della Libertà (Volunteer Freedom Corps)

EIAR   Ente Italiano per le Audizioni Radiofoniche (the public service broadcaster in Fascist Italy)

FANY   First Aid Nursing Yeomanry

GS(R)   General Staff (Research)

MI(R)   Military Intelligence (Research)

NARA   National Archives and Records Administration

ONB	Opera Nazionale Balilla (a Fascist youth organization, 1926–37)
OSCAR	Organizzazione Scout Collocamento Assistenza Ricercati (an organization dedicated to the expatriation from Italy to Switzerland of former prisoners, dissidents and Jews after 8 September 1943)
OSS	Office of Strategic Services
OVRA	Organizzazione per la Vigilanza e la Repressione dell'Antifascismo (Organization for Vigilance and Repression of Anti-Fascism)
RSI	Repubblica Sociale Italiana (Italian Social Republic – also known as the Republic of Salò)
SD	Sicherheitsdienst (the SS intelligence agency)
SID	Servizio Informazioni della Difesa (Defence Information Service)
SIM	Servizio Informazioni Militare (Military Information Service – Italian military espionage and counterespionage)
SIS	(British) Secret Intelligence Service
SOE	Special Operations Executive
TNA	The National Archives, London
UPIDA	Ufficio Protezione Impianti e Difesa Antiparacadutisti (Office for the Protection of Infrastucture and Anti-Parachute Defence)

I

Mallaby's Early Years,
1919-39

There are people who express contemptuous
amazement at the time sacrificed by some
scholars in composing such works and by all
the rest in familiarizing themselves with their
existence and use.

Marc Bloch, *The Historian's Craft*

Cecil Richard Dallimore-Mallaby – known as Dicky,
Dick, or in the Tuscan dialect as Gnicche, Dicche, or
Signorino Dìcche – was born in Nuwara Eliya, a city
known for the growing of tea and known by many as
'Little England' for its cool, humid climate, in modern
Sri Lanka (then Ceylon) on 26 April 1919 to Mary
Beatrice Schofield and Cecil-Dallimore Mallaby, who
had married on 24 December 1918. Cecil, who had been
born in Hyderabad on 21 February 1886, was the son
of Florence Maud Dallimore and Cecil Ridley Mallaby,
a British Army captain and subsequent member of the
colonial police in West Africa.

At the time of Dick's birth, the Mallaby family lived in fairly comfortable conditions in the town of Naseby, Ceylon, where his father was employed by the Anglo-American Direct Tea Trading Company and was responsible for the extensive tea cultivation in the area.

According to the Mallaby family diary, which Dick's parents began to keep with the arrival of their firstborn, in the phase following the happy event, his mother began a long convalescence from childbirth; it also records the regular, pleasing growth of the newborn.

His father's comments on the first moments of Dick's life were both somewhat peculiar and typical of the 'new father':

> 26th Saturday. At about 2 AM the child is born a son, as I hear the nurse tell Mary – then, to my horror I am called in to assist. I do not see very much as I keep my eyes fixed on my baby lying on the bed looking rather like a skinned rabbit but still quite sufficiently unpleasant for a young husband to experience.[1]

However, almost immediately Cecil Mallaby was obliged to show how affectionate and attentive a father he could be.

In the days that followed, the couple's affectionate writings demonstrate a rediscovered serenity, after the worries and sufferings of pregnancy and the immediate period following the birth. What also comes through is the joy (sprinkled with the typical anxiety and concern) that every worthy parent feels following the birth of their first child – for a number of years, Mallaby senior even noted down the age of his son in days.

But fate began almost immediately to turn the development of Dick Mallaby's existence away from the norm. On 2 June 1920 his mother died in hospital, aged 38, from complications relating to her second pregnancy.

Cecil Mallaby, who had himself lost his father aged nine, was left alone to write the family diary. In the midst of his immense suffering, he wrote his first entry only on 16 June, following on from the last lines composed by his wife on 15 April, before the onset of her illness. His first thought was for his son Dick: 'This poor little boy will never know the loss he has suffered of his sweet mother's love and wisdom. Only with the aid of infinite divine mercy will I be able to make up for this in some small way.'

Across six pages, Mallaby senior recorded the events for future memory, describing to his son the details of the last days of his mother's life, reminding him who took care of them in those terrible moments and revealing that, on his wife's death bed, he promised her to always do his best to help their only child.

The last moments of his wife's life were described as follows: 'Her breathing became more and more difficult, and at the end, around 5.30 in the afternoon of Wednesday 2 June 1920, she drew her last delicate breath and her spirit passed. Also towards you, my son.'

Cecil Mallaby would commemorate the anniversary of this tragedy every year, and, for a long time after, every Wednesday would note the weeks passed since his wife's death.

The upheavals of that period brought Cecil Mallaby to religion: he was baptized on 28 August 1920, St Augustine's day, at the Church of San Filippo Neri in Petiah district, Colombo. The curious thing is that the family documents reveal that Cecil Mallaby had married according to the Catholic rite two years before. Evidently, the Mallaby family already had some kind of karma for peculiar and extreme exploits.

But, in light of subsequent events, the above appears to be a fateful step towards both Cecil Mallaby's arrival and settlement in the capital nation of world Catholicism, and his second marriage to a committed Catholic.

Indeed, shortly after, fate offered some slight compensation for the devastating loss suffered by Cecil and Richard Mallaby.

On 28 February 1921, a telegram arrived in Ceylon, sent three days earlier by the notary Guglielmo Rossi in Asciano, a district located some 30km south-east of Siena, Italy. It read: 'This morning Marquise Elisabeth Mallaby died leaving you heir.'

Many would have rubbed their hands with glee at this point, given the material benefits of this inheritance, but Cecil Mallaby's comment reveals the nobility of his soul: 'Another who loved us has left us, as all those who love Dicky and I seem to abandon life, leaving only the indifferent, or our enemies! Poor little Dick, it seems likely he will grow up a lonely boy. I hope I'm not an old boring dog for him, but his best companion.'

Mallaby senior's mood failed to improve when, a few hours later, a final, affectionate letter arrived from his now deceased Aunt Elisabeth.

Italy, and Tuscany in particular, was about to play a key role in the lives of this British family, which for several generations had lived beyond the borders of their mother country. On 13 May, Mallaby senior left Colombo aboard the *Orvieto* and arrived in Asciano on 8 June.

There, almost at once, he met Countess Maria Luisa Bargagli-Stoffi. The countess, born in Asciano in August 1888, was of English origin on her mother's side, and was involved in managing Elisabeth Mallaby's estate.

Having settled matters relating to the estate and appointed Countess Bargagli-Stoffi as his attorney, Cecil Mallaby departed from Naples on 29 August aboard the *Ormonde*. On 14 September, he was reunited with a slightly thinner-looking Dicky, who, in his absence, had been cared for at a monastery.

The following May, Mallaby senior set off for London once again, this time accompanied by the infant Dick, for whose safety during the sea voyage he had purchased a pair of reins. After spending a few months in England, the pair reached Asciano on 20 December 1922.

Having returned to Sri Lanka once more, their next journey was to be a permanent one. The Mallaby family changed not only their place of residence, but also the continent, returning to Europe – but not England.

The tea plantations were swapped for fields of wheat, surrounded by the olive trees, cypresses and evergreen oaks of the beautiful Crete Senesi region in Tuscany.

On 1 June 1925, the older and younger Mallaby arrived in Venice; two days later, they were in Asciano, residing at the villa Il Campo.

On 27 November of the same year, his father Cecil and Maria Luisa Bargagli-Stoffi were married, and all of them lived at Poggio Pinci, another of the family's dwellings. Cecil Mallaby's second marriage led to the arrival of Carlo Alberto in 1926 and, in 1928, Pia Teresa.

According to those who knew him, Dick Mallaby was a handsome boy with striking blue eyes, light hair and fair skin, who spoke with a strong Tuscan accent and spent his days furiously pedalling along the roads that connected Poggio Pinci and Il Campo.

The young Mallaby already had a reputation for daring enterprises: the most common was cycling along the parapets of bridges. Fearful local mothers would warn their children not to hang around with, or at the very least not to copy, this dangerous stranger, whom not even his father's punitive lashes could completely tame.

As the years went by, Dick also developed a precocious interest in the opposite sex, which led him on one occasion to steal a precious family object which he then gifted to one of his girlfriends. His reputation in Asciano was such that he was, albeit affectionately, nicknamed 'Gnicche' after a famous 19th-century brigand from Arezzo.

Fascism was in full flow in Italy during this period, and even the Mallabys conformed to the customs of the time despite their British citizenship; the black fez of the ONB (Opera Nazionale Balilla – a Fascist youth organization), which Dick was given, is one of the family's heirlooms, although now deprived of its *fascio littorio* badge – a symbol of Italian Fascism.

From 1925 to 1928, Dick Mallaby attended the Asciano elementary schools, reluctantly but with average results; then, from 1928 to 1931, he was a pupil at Panton College in Lincolnshire, UK, which was run by Franciscan friars.

Back in Italy, from 1931 to 1935, he boarded at the Nobile Collegio Convitto Nazionale Celso Tolomei in Siena. Between 1935 and 1939, he was a student at the scientific high school at the Collegio San Carlo in Modena. Mallaby intended to study engineering, and was awarded a place at university, which he was unable to take up due to the outbreak of war.

The subjects Mallaby studied undoubtedly served him well during his wartime activities, for on leaving school, in addition to English and Italian, he could speak and understand German and French.

In Europe, meanwhile, as Mallaby passed through childhood and adolescence, the first signs of the new world war were beginning to show. In the portentous summer of 1939, on the outbreak of hostilities, young Dick, despite having spent most of his life in Italy and being an Italophile, without the slightest delay decided to enlist in the British Army.

After an emotional conversation with his father, Dick Mallaby decided to head to Britain as soon as possible. Having said goodbye to his best friend Bernardo and the family cook Adele, without further disclosing the news of his imminent departure he went to Florence, accompanied by his father, where they met with the British consul with unsatisfactory results.

In his private memoirs, Mallaby confided that en route to Florence he had even felt 'a little excited' about what lay ahead, in contrast to his father. Evidently, adventure and risk were part of his makeup.

The two Mallabys continued on to Milan, in time to allow Dick to reach Britain by train across Switzerland before any restrictive measures could impede him. The date was 1 September 1939, the day World War II broke out. Dick Mallaby had avoided getting stuck in Italy, which was not yet at war.

In Milan, the long journey and the wait before departure allowed tiredness to prevail over the excitement, and Dick Mallaby began to reflect on what he was leaving behind.

Cecil Mallaby said goodbye to his young son with understandable emotion, hoping to see him again, with these words: 'Dick, I know you'll think me an old bore, but don't forget what I told you, it always pays to be honest and straight, though other ways may seem easier, and keep your chin up.'

On the train bound for Britain, Mallaby found himself travelling with many British and Americans fleeing Italy. In his compartment was an elderly man with his family who had evidently been plucked from hospital, as he was still wearing his pyjamas under his coat.

Dick Mallaby's movements did not escape the efficient Italian information-gathering network, which immediately knew about them. Thereafter, there would be plenty of reports by the Italian information services on Mallaby, his family and his activities.[2]

Within a few days, the situation in Europe had deteriorated. When Dick left Italy, Germany had just invaded Poland, but when he arrived in Britain, war had been declared. News of the latter, which came through during a stop at a small French station, helped bind together Mallaby and his travelling companions on this long journey.

On 3 September 1939 – the day the United Kingdom, together with Australia, New Zealand, India and France, declared war on Germany – Mallaby arrived in Britain, having managed to board one of the last available ferries.

At the Dover border check, he was asked the reason for his journey to Britain. The 20-year-old Dick Mallaby replied: 'I have come to join up.' The clerk looked at his colleague and said: 'This man has come to join up.'

'Man!'

With a mixture of excitement and emotion, Dick realized that his adolescence was officially over. He was 20 years old, he had been officially declared a grown man, and his duty was to defend his homeland.

During his first night in Britain, Mallaby experienced an air raid alert and a blackout. The next morning he formally submitted his request to join the armed forces, but bureaucracy immediately intervened to frustrate his attempt: his age group had not yet been called up, and no voluntary recruitment was planned.

Dick Mallaby decided to join his aunt in Sidmouth and find a temporary job, but five weeks later he managed to succeed in his original intent.

On 18 October 1939, Private Cecil Richard Dallimore-Mallaby was enlisted in the 8th Battalion, The Devonshire Regiment, in Exmouth. Three months of basic training on Dartmoor were followed by several weeks in the Signals Section.

In March 1940 Mallaby was still in Britain, engaged in coastal defence duties in Sussex, which he found less than satisfying. In an attempt to get nearer to the action, he volunteered for a parachute course, which led him to join the elite No. 2 Commando and undergo gruelling training at Largs and on Arran, in Scotland.

By chance, or by choice, Mallaby had taken the first steps that would give him the skills to perform his breathtaking missions. In January 1941, he was assigned to the training centre for No. 8 (Guards) Commando in Scotland, under Robert Laycock's command.

Clearly, whoever was responsible had not properly checked Mallaby's background; even at that point, he could have been employed more productively.

Mallaby's quality shone through, and in February 1941 he left the United Kingdom for destination unknown in the ranks of No. 8 Commando, part of the 'Layforce' special unit. Layforce was heading for

Egypt, but to get there Mallaby and his comrades had to circumnavigate Africa, and they arrived only on 13 March 1941.

The following summer Mallaby fought against the Axis forces at Tobruk, but then contracted dysentery and was forced into a long convalescence. Keen to return to action, Mallaby returned to base after forging his medical clearance certificate. There he found that his unit had been dissolved, and realized that he was still not fully recovered. Having gathered his strength, his requests to enlist in the Special Air Service, Special Boat Service and Arab Legion were rejected.

Mallaby was promoted to corporal, but turned down the chance to become an officer and assume a leadership role. He wanted action, but his duties consisted of nothing more than dull stores work and the supervision of Italian prisoners engaged in building camps and latrines. And thus 1941 drew to a close.

Since his intimate knowledge of the Italian language and situation had not yet been evaluated, Mallaby himself put these to good use, amusing himself by putting the wind up any Tuscan prisoners, flaunting his perfect knowledge of their localities, not to mention their vernacular.

Eventually, the two predestined parties joined together. Mallaby (fortuitously or not, we shall never know) came into contact with Special Operations Executive (SOE) and was immediately recruited at its Cairo station as 'Conducting NCO and Interpreter'. The date was 15 January 1942.

Dick Mallaby recalled this crucial moment in his personal diary in this way: 'I was told that a mysterious organization called M.O.4 in Cairo wanted my assistance'.

The breakthrough moment had come.

This is an opportune moment to pause Mallaby's story, and to provide the essential context on SOE and its missions in Italy and elsewhere during World War II.

Special Operations Executive

Success in war, like charity in religion, covers a multitude of sins.

Sir Charles Napier (1782–1853)

[The] secret history of a nation [...] is often so much more intimate and interesting than its public chronicles.

Sir Arthur Conan Doyle (1859–1930)

Special Operations Executive was a secret organization that was officially created on 19 July 1940. At its peak, it comprised c. 13,500 members, of whom 5,000 were operational agents. It should be recalled that at the time of its founding, Great Britain was the only European nation offering any resistance to the German and Italian armed forces.

In illustrating any aspect even indirectly connected with SOE, any categorical statement should be avoided, given the secrecy of the structure – its existence was only first officially acknowledged in the 1980s. Put very briefly, this secret organization was tasked with carrying out a wide range of activities such as sabotage, support for clandestine movements, terrorism, all prohibited by international conventions, wherever local circumstances would allow.[1]

Many SOE operations were carried out by single agents acting autonomously and independently, beyond the constraints of any military framework, but deprived of relevant protection. At the operational level, this constituted the most significant difference compared to the *modus operandi* of other special units, such as the Commandos.

It should be further clarified that the men and women of SOE did not operate like regular soldiers, nor did they have much in common with espionage and counterespionage operatives, even if SOE activities sometimes involved aspects of espionage.[2]

All those who worked for SOE were special agents, belonging to a special service. Their life expectancy on missions was statistically quantified in weeks, partly due to the fact that, according to international convention, execution was legitimized in the event of capture in enemy territory without uniform.

The structure of SOE was conceived by two senior politicians of the time: the Conservative Prime Minister Winston Churchill and Labour member Hugh Dalton, Minister of Economic Warfare. Although from different camps and mutually unsympathetic, they pragmatically joined efforts to create this secret organization, the necessity of which was clear to them.

From a strictly administrative point of view, the foundation of SOE and even its naming were among the last executive acts of Neville Chamberlain.

Curiously, the principal stimulus in creating this secret organization was based on erroneous supposition. In the looming panic that followed the overwhelming initial German military successes, it was wrongly thought that one of the main reasons for these successes was the presence of unconventional units in these territories that favourably predisposed the local populations towards an invasion. It was therefore decided to create a structure that could coordinate guerrilla activities should Britain be invaded, and could also operate secretly in enemy territory and in countries occupied by Axis forces.[3]

However, both of these initial purposes were soon left behind. SOE's fundamental activities came to comprise the following: infiltration into enemy-occupied areas; the organization of and support for clandestine guerrilla movements and sabotage; the training of committed volunteers ready and able to destroy roads, railways and strategic infrastructure; the distribution of weapons, ammunition and explosives, as well as communications equipment; and the development of unconventional strategy aimed at supporting military action.

In more official terms, SOE was to coordinate all kinds of action against the enemy (initially in Europe and later, after Pearl Harbor, around the globe), whilst also supporting local resistance movements.

At the time of its operation, SOE was also known as 'Churchill's Secret Army', the 'Baker Street Irregulars' or the 'Ministry of Ungentlemanly Warfare'. Churchill used to call SOE's activities 'naughty deeds'.

Some of the details of SOE's particular administrative structure are noteworthy: from the outset, it was financed by secret funds, it was free from parliamentary and military control, and as officially it did not exist, it was legitimate to deny its existence.

SOE resulted from the union of three pre-existing departments, created in the immediacy of (and fear provoked by) the outbreak of war: the department known as CS (after its head, Sir Campbell Stuart) or EH (after its Electra House location) at the Foreign Office; Section D of the Secret Intelligence Service – SIS, also known as MI6 – tasked with propaganda and counter-propaganda, sabotage and unconventional warfare; and General Staff (Research) – GS(R), subsequently retitled Military Intelligence Research or MI(R) – at the War Office.

The activities of these three departments had been very limited, not least because of poor leadership and the scarcity of resources, and often overlapped; thus it was decided to merge them into a single entity.

With great pragmatism, and without qualms, one of the models adopted for operational use was that developed by the Irish Republican Army (IRA) during its struggle for independence against the British. Moreover, Scotland Yard's reports on the most successful burglars' tricks of the trade, and the guerrilla manuals used by communist fighters in the Spanish Civil War, were also carefully studied.

Another somewhat surprising fact relates to the non-military backgrounds of the chiefs who led SOE (codenamed CD). The first was Frank Nelson, who had a commercial and diplomatic background. He was followed in 1942 by Charles Hambro, head of the eponymous influential bank. The last head was a soldier at least, Colin Gubbins. He was appointed in September 1943, at the height of three key events in World War II and SOE's history: the Italian surrender, the Allied Salerno landings and Dick Mallaby's first mission. Gubbins remained in post until the winding-up of SOE. He at least could offer a background more specifically related to his duties, being a polyglot who had written several manuals on guerrilla warfare and had previously managed and taken part in covert special operations, which varied in nature.

In accordance with the service's style, the heads of SOE chose their personnel with great pragmatism, not favouring any particular category. Failure to supply a blank criminal record did not constitute an impediment to entry; on the contrary, in relation to specific missions and sectors, especially deception and counterfeit work, such experience was even considered more relevant than an international background.[4]

The executive also turned a blind eye to discriminations of the time: homosexuals, communists and even anti-British nationalists were recruited without qualm. A significant percentage of its personnel also came from the ranks of exiles and prisoners of war from countries invaded by Axis forces.

All this helps us see that SOE agents generally operated beyond the limits of international convention, which also meant that they could be condemned to death and liquidated straight after capture.

In fact, the international agreement governing war (the 1929 Geneva Convention, a development of the 1907 Hague Convention) allowed a certain discretion with regard to the treatment of spies and saboteurs disguised in civilian clothes or friendly uniform, thus implicitly legitimizing their elimination. However, the 1907 Hague Convention also established that no agent, even if caught in the act of spying, could be punished without first being subjected to trial (Article 30).

The statistics of how many SOE agents were deliberately killed on active service are revealing: the total amounts to 'only' 850 (about 20 per cent), in 36 different countries, and in many cases death followed or resulted from torture.

Overall, despite the unorthodox recruitment parameters, this heterogeneous group of military personnel and civilians produced positive results, even if there were cases of infiltration by enemy counterintelligence elements, and of desertion too.

Infiltration was the nightmare scenario for any such organization – and the one that materialized in Italy, which affected Dick Mallaby's first mission, remains quantitatively and qualitatively unsurpassed, and perhaps for this reason its details have come to light only in recent years. No such incidents were recorded on British soil, despite the presence of several dubious figures, and the fact that, for a year, among the SOE instructors was a certain Kim Philby.[5]

The nature of SOE's activities and the ever-present competition between special units meant that its relationships with the other military and government bodies were neither idyllic nor constructive throughout the course of the war. One can thus state, without much difficulty, that SOE's main enemies were (in order): the Foreign Office, the military leadership, and the other special units.

These difficult relationships would lead to the resignation of Charles Hambro, the head of SOE in September 1943, and even saw the continued existence of SOE as a separate organization threatened.

The original plan was that every special operation should receive preliminary Foreign Office approval, though this agency often favoured its own creation (i.e. SIS) to the detriment of SOE. However, on occasion SOE's activities did provoke clashes with the exiled representatives of Axis-occupied countries due both to their lack of involvement and reprisals against their civilians. One such example is the 27 May 1942 attack on the governor of the Protectorate of Bohemia and Moravia, and eminent SS member, Reinhard Heydrich. This is perhaps the most famous SOE operation, and was certainly the most prominent target in its history. Although it succeeded and Heydrich died on 4 June, it provoked violent and bloody German reprisals against the civilian population.[6] Apart from the odd clash caused by reckless behaviour of some

SOE agents (such as the ones operating in Hungary who hid large quantities of explosives in the cellars of the British diplomatic headquarters, without permission of course), the contrasts between SIS and SOE were chiefly visible in their differing *modus agendi*, notably during operational overlaps.

SIS favoured the acquisition of confidential information via carefully cultivated high-level personal contacts that was coherently developed across a long-term perspective. SOE, pragmatically and cynically, tended to provoke and use violence, sabotage and subversion, dealing (sometimes highly recklessly) with anyone who proved useful at that specific moment to its objectives (including communist groups, whose post-war aims were the antithesis to those of the British government).

SOE was commonly and typically branded in a dismissive and haughty manner as producing no real advantage in general terms in operations against the enemy.

Setting aside the prejudice and poor analysis, the above was a result not only of the restrictions of secrecy (even at the very highest level), but above all of the intangibility of the results of SOE operations (and thus, their contentiousness). The results of an aerial bombardment were immediately evident; those of an infiltration that lasted for months almost never were, compounded by the fact that they could rarely be disclosed. This secrecy was also almost total in the case of Dick Mallaby's two missions, as we shall see.

One of SOE's most undervalued contributions was its involvement in a wide range of covert propaganda activities, mainly delivered via the media, aimed at securing the United States' entry into the war. The men and women of SOE were also tasked with nurturing the embryonic structures of the American Office of Strategic Services (OSS).[7]

The training of SOE agents (who were usually grouped by nationality) was onerous and included – in addition to standard weapons training – sabotage, unarmed combat, survival and navigation techniques, silent killing, how to resist interrogation and torture (both physical and psychological), parachuting, radio-telegraphy, and the study of the specific nations in which operations were planned in order to achieve perfect cover.[8] SOE instructors were also able to introduce innovative techniques, later widely adopted: for example, shooting from a kneeling position, with both hands on the pistol.

The 'graduation test' at the conclusion of training courses held in Great Britain is worthy of note. Each agent was instructed to carry out a particular crime, with the aid of identified accomplices, in areas where the police had been alerted. Naturally, those who 'graduated' were not subject to prosecution; but the principal aim was to evaluate the creativity and self-discipline of the agent when faced with sudden and unexpected danger.

As has often happened, the seeds planted rapidly by special services to serve their immediate tactical needs – in some cases, in particular times and locations – have borne poisonous fruit. According to many experts and analysts, the terrorist guerrilla warfare put into practice and instigated by SOE in World War II served as a model for many subsequent terrorist formations, and not only in the immediate post-war period.

According to the forthright, non-PC opinion of the historian John Keegan, quoted in *The Irish War* by Tony Geraghty:

> We must recognise that our response to the scourge of terrorism is compromised by what we did through SOE. The justification ... that we had no other means of striking back at the enemy ... is exactly the argument used by the Red Brigades, the Baader-Meinhoff gang, the PFLP, the IRA and every other half-articulate terrorist organisation on Earth. Futile to argue that we were a democracy and Hitler a tyrant. Means besmirch ends. SOE besmirched Britain.

Such evaluations, which are not unusual in British historiography, contrary to what some might expect, stand opposed to the Machiavellian (and frequently misinterpreted) maxim of 'The end justifies the means'.

A fundamental requirement for SOE agents was an intimate knowledge of the language and customs of the country in which they were destined to operate, even better if they were of dual nationality – although this could prove to be a mixed blessing where the counterintelligence services were particularly thorough and efficient, as in Italy.

This holds true, since 'blind' missions (i.e. those without a reception party at the point of entry) were not uncommon, and led to the recruitment not only of numerous exiles, but also of deserters.

SOE's internal organization was based upon the countries it was involved in. The size and subdivision of individual departments was proportional to the amount of operations in each country. France, for example, was the country with the largest number of sections (six). After France came Yugoslavia, Greece and Italy.

SOE headquarters, after some provisional moves, was established on 31 October 1940 at 64 Baker Street, London, where officially they occupied the offices of the phantom organization ISRB (Inter-Services Research Bureau); after a few months in which the organization grew, it came to occupy a good number of the buildings on the west side of this famous street, as well as in the surrounding area.

SOE had numerous branches and training centres within and outside of London, with the degree of cover relating to the secrecy of their function. In addition to creating a full spectrum of false documents, ration cards, clothes and outfits, SOE developed and tested cutting-edge technology, weapons and special devices. With regard to its foreign branches, the famous (or infamous, on account of various fiascos and its erratic management) Cairo station initially coordinated operations in the Mediterranean, the Middle East and the Balkans.

In the closing weeks of 1942, the famous base codenamed Massingham (Inter-Services Signals Unit 6, or ISSU 6) came into operation near Algiers. This station played a key role in the secret operations that took place in Italy and the Mediterranean in the period that followed, as we will shortly see.

After the Italian surrender in 1943, numerous bases were established in Apulia, specifically intended to support the missions executed in German-occupied central-northern Italy, as well as those in Yugoslavia, Albania, Greece, Bulgaria, Romania, Hungary and Austria. As the front line pushed northwards, in February 1945 almost all activities were transferred to Siena. Other wartime stations were established in India, Ceylon, Singapore and New York.[9]

For SOE's activities, special weapons and explosives were its bread and butter, both on operations and in study and research. There were numerous instances where SOE's inventions and developments were adopted by competing services.

Among Dick Mallaby's surviving documents is a notebook (neatly handwritten and beautifully illustrated) dated 12 February 1942 of the 'Explosives and weapons course' that he completed during his training. If this notebook had been found during a house search in the post-war period after Mallaby's death it would have made for some awkward moments for his wife and children, given the detailed instructions on how to make explosive devices and how to attack the railway infrastructure.

Much of the technology developed during World War II was later applied for more peaceful purposes, before the advent of the digital age. Many of the devices, including some technologically sophisticated ones that later became relatively common, had their origins in less peaceful inventions and/or special development work by the designated SOE department (Station IX, or Q – as imaginatively represented in the James Bond films). Many deserve to be remembered as the products of creative minds seasoned with a pinch of high spirits.

In terms of transport methods, in addition to the Welbike (a foldable minibike), SOE created an electric-powered submersible canoe, dubbed 'Sleeping Beauty', and the Welfreighter midget submarine, the existence of which was revealed only in the 1990s.

Among the weapons used by SOE agents was the simple but powerful Sten gun, but also foreign-made items. SOE helped pioneer the use of plastic explosives (the name, which stuck, derived from the habit of SOE agents of packing the soft explosive *matériel* inside plastic). Other innovative creations that made it through testing included magnetic ('limpet') mines, a folding canoe and timed detonators.

One of the most creative inventions, however, was the 'explosive rat'. Dozens of rodents (officially acquired for laboratory experiments) were skinned, filled with plastic explosives and stitched back together. These stuffed rats would be left near boilers: the instinctive reaction of those who found them would be to toss them into the fire, resulting in a devastating explosion. The results were positive, although unexpected. A delivery of these 'weapons' was intercepted by the Germans, and the discovery triggered an explosive rat hunt that wasted precious energy and created a threat that was greater in the mind of the enemy than any damage that the stuffed rodents could create, demonstrating that creativity pays, even if unexpectedly.

The SOE laboratories also developed radical reworkings of older weapons, such as a repeating crossbow which fired incendiary darts. But the fundamental operational need that its technicians were called upon to respond to was, obviously, the concealment of weapons, quartz crystal oscillators, codes, money and maps. To this end, all manner of objects and *matériel* were exploited and utilized.

In addition to certain objects that later became classics for secret agents and terrorists, such as explosive soaps and mines in the form of fake cowpats or elephant dung, the exploitation of everyday objects included adapting books, packs of cigarettes, cans of food, shirt buttons, sponges, tubes of toothpaste and shaving soap – often featuring labels from the places where they were to be used. In order to conceal two-way radios, explosives and other items, fake fruit and vegetables (such as the beetroot grenade carrier), piles of wood and explosive coal (in hundreds of different shapes, precisely because each piece of coal is different) were created.

As far as creative weaponry is concerned, the list includes itching powder (which, according to the instructions, was best applied inside underwear); a special paste, contained in a tube of toothpaste, which when applied to vehicle windscreens formed a layer that obscured visibility from the inside; a highly useful deodorant, which covered the wearer's scent to dogs; and stink bombs.[10]

One particular application created for use in Italy was a fake bottle of Chianti. This comprised a perfect celluloid flask, complete with labels and signature straw basket, divided into two parts: one containing wine, and the other a detonator and explosive charge.

With regard to combat knives, research focused on concealment. One of the best products created by SOE's experimental departments was a small combat knife, which could be stored in a boot heel or coat lapel.

As for the supply of resistance movements, SOE's extremely pragmatic approach to operations clearly comes through. Consignments almost always consisted of light arms (being easier to transport, parachute in and use) and were usually sourced from war booty.

The famous cyanide pills – which, despite the legends, few were happy to equip themselves with, and perhaps nobody ever used – were intended for rapid suicide in a dead-end situation. They were normally hidden in the buttons of overcoats. A particularly sophisticated version was covered with a hard casing; it could be hidden between the teeth and, if necessary, crushed, using strong pressure.

Although SOE had great success with its developments in weaponry and technology, there were problems to be faced in other areas. A considerable issue was transportation, for which SOE was dependent, at least initially, on the availability of regular service units. The Royal Navy was always reluctant to allow the use of its submarines and other means for transporting agents and materials, due to the dangers inherent in approaching enemy coastlines too closely.

SOE also had problems with air transportation, especially in the face of firm opposition from Air Marshal Arthur 'Bomber' Harris to offering RAF assets. In time, matters improved, but a lack of aircraft continually affected SOE activities and caused friction with various clandestine forces due to the favouring of certain operational options at the expense of others.

SOE agents thus often infiltrated using fishing vessels and other small boats, frequently steered personally by SOE personnel. SOE also developed another futuristic vehicle: the Witch, a two-seater submarine, which featured a handy timed and programmable diving and emersion function.

Given SOE's particular requirements, purpose designed and built aircraft would have been ideal, but some compromise was required here. The typical airframes used for SOE missions, both for agent transport and for recovery and rescue from enemy territory, were the Westland Lysander (a small aircraft, the chief benefit of which was the ability to land and take off in little over 300 metres, even on unprepared runways), the Lockheed Hudson and the Douglas DC-3 Dakota.

For parachute missions, SOE generally used bombers: initially, the Armstrong Whitworth Whitley, and then the Handley Page Halifax and the Short Stirling. Parachuted *matériel*, the delivery of which was just as important as the missions of SOE's agents, was dropped loose, or in special cylindrical containers, some of which could be broken up into pieces to simplify ground transport.

For marking a drop zone, or rendezvous site, the usual method was somewhat primitive: the site was illuminated with bonfires or bicycle lights. However, this required excellent visibility, in part to ensure the correct site was targeted.

Over time, and in order to facilitate these difficult operations, SOE's technicians developed a small, portable wireless telephone called the S-Phone and even a portable radar.

All this technical work was paralleled by careful research into the culture and customs of the nations in which operations were planned, including analysis of current clothing trends.

In training, particular care was taken in analysing the psychological makeup of agents and evaluating their reactions in the kinds of tricky situations in which they might find themselves. In addition to specific courses on resisting interrogation and torture, SOE instructors focused heavily on getting agents to process radio-telegraphic messages briefly and concisely, and on security issues; the latter was with particular reference to the destruction of cryptographic codes, which, it was realized, agents had a surprising tendency to avoid doing.

A fundamental aspect of an SOE agent's work was cryptographic radio-telegraphy. Encoding and decrypting transmissions were not automatic processes, but instead relied on cyphers and special devices. Anyone tuned to the wavelength of a certain transmission could receive a message tapped out in Morse code, but they would be unable to understand it if it was encrypted. Thus the composition, security and usability of the cyphers were essential aspects, as was the ability and speed of the person transmitting.

Radios featured interchangeable mini-quartz crystal oscillators, the size of a stamp (usually hidden inside small boxes), the characteristics of which determined the transmission frequency.

Initially the portable radios used by SOE were supplied by SIS, but these turned out to be quite unsuitable, being cumbersome, heavy (at 20kg) and power-hungry to operate.

Improvements in SOE's transmission activities were thanks to the work of Polish technicians in exile who helped create models specifically designed and made for the needs of SOE operatives. At the height of their development, radios came to weigh (complete with batteries) just over 4kg and, despite being much smaller in size, were able to handle transmissions receivable up to a range of several hundred kilometres. Radios for use in permanent sites were naturally different.

For the transmission of a secret message, composition using secure codes is only part of the task: in addition to preventing the enemy from understanding its contents, it is just as important to prevent him from identifying the transmission's point of origin using radiolocation.

To prevent the identification of a transmission site, there is only one fail safe method: spend as little time as possible transmitting on the same frequency. This is achieved by avoiding verification and recognition transmissions, and by varying transmission frequencies, thus making scanning more difficult.

At the outset of SOE's activities, its results in this area were less than satisfactory, due to the clumsiness of secret message composition. After several failures, notably in the Netherlands which involved the capture and often death of operatives, and their replacement by German imposters, with obvious consequences, things only improved when SOE decided to adopt its own cyphers and introduced safer, improved operating procedures. At the same time in order to make it harder to identify transmission sites, it imposed a limit on each transmission of five minutes; this meant that unavoidably lengthy messages were relayed across multiple transmissions (with some extreme examples split into more than 90 separate parts). No operator was ever captured as a result of failures in code security, and the only incidents were the consequence of failure to respect the rules.[11]

SOE created an autonomous Italian section (Department J) only in October 1941, with

Lieutenant-Colonel Cecil Roseberry at its head. Roseberry had no knowledge of the Italian language or issues relating to the country, and only one assistant.[12]

SOE's operational activity in Italy was initially executed in very limited ways. Until August 1943, SOE's lack of success in Italy was due to a scarcity of Italian volunteers, the remarkable efficiency of Italian internal security services, and an almost total infiltration by Italian counterespionage assets of the network organized and run from the base in Bern, Switzerland. The entire leadership was also paying the price for an overly optimistic assessment at the top of British politics regarding the number of effective and exploitable anti-fascists.

The invasion of the Italian peninsula, the defenestration of Mussolini and the beginning of the collaboration of that part of the army still loyal to the king saw the beginning of a series of operations, remarkable in both scope and number, in support of the Italian resistance in the areas under the control of the Repubblica Sociale Italiana (RSI)[13]. In many of the principal operations in the 1943–45 period, SOE agents acted not only as instructors, but also as liaison officers.

The fundamental strategic aim of this support activity was somewhat incongruous: to keep the German forces in the Italian peninsula, to prevent them from being used in other theatres. This, along with the dismissive attitude of British politicians and military leaders towards a former enemy whose institutional representatives lacked competence and cohesion, introduced further elements of ambiguity and complication into SOE's activities. This was problematic because, given the particular nature of its activities, SOE required effective and assured collaboration both operationally and politically, not least because operational dynamics and the demands of resistance and guerrilla movements do not always go hand in hand with those of general military operations, nor with special operations, espionage or counterespionage. The memories of Italy and the Italians preserved by the men and women of SOE are varied and witnessed in different ways.[14]

The observations of Raimondo Craveri, a top figure in the Italian resistance movement, appear rather timely (and not entirely positive):

An English colonel told me one day how much the Italian people remained incomprehensible to him. According to his experience, Italians lived in peace and good harmony only in the absence of all constituted power. But in Italy this absence did not result in anarchy, with all that anarchy entails. The lack of all constituted power joined us together, instead of unleashing us in a war of all against all. When a village stays in no man's land for weeks, between our lines and those of the enemy, people do not steal and do not kill each other, but they help each other in an incredible way. All this is both absurd and marvellous. We arrive, and we institute the vital offices and services of the AMG (Allied Military Government) and the

Italians immediately split apart, squabble, fight over trivialities, denounce each other. The prior harmony dissolves into feuds and all manner of vendetta. It is truly incredible.[15]

When the war ended, an institutional conflict broke out: the presiding minister, Lord Selborne, proposed continuing the service while ending its almost complete independence (it would become a department of the Ministry of Defence), and tasking it with dealing with Communist Bloc countries and the Middle East. The Foreign Office wanted to reclaim control over it, based on the premise that SIS was also under its control. Selborne observed, caustically, that 'Having the SOE managed by the Foreign Office would be like inviting an abbess to manage a brothel.'

Churchill made no decision on the matter, and, following his July 1945 electoral debacle, the issue was addressed by the new Labour Prime Minister, Clement Attlee, in an extremely brusque and sharp manner. Faced with the insistence of Selborne, who also described SOE's worldwide network of agents and radios at its disposal, Attlee replied that it was not his intent to run a British Comintern and authorized its termination, giving it 48 hours' notice.

Special Operations Executive officially ceased to exist on 15 January 1946. Most of the staff returned to their previous occupations, civilian or military. Only a small number (fewer than 300) of SOE personnel were transferred into SIS's Special Operations Branch.

During SOE's operational lifetime, even its leaders remained unknown to most and were not identified by name. Those allowed to contact them referred to them by codename, of which there might be more than one depending on the interlocutor, with obvious correspondence confusion resulting.

The decision to make payments to all SOE members tax-free was also a result of the desire to retain anonymity.

This curtain of secrecy was retained after the war not because of SOE's mistakes, but because of its achievements. Revealing SOE's involvement in some of the historic successes which led to victory would have overturned the widely accepted version of events presented at the time.

The secrecy that has surrounded SOE's activities during and after the war has clearly affected the amount of useful documents available to researchers. The weighty study *The Secret History of SOE*, written by the historian William Mackenzie at war's end and sanctioned for internal use only, is emblematic of this. Completed in 1948, this book was only finally released for wider publication in 2000.

Moreover, the nature of SOE's activities not only greatly hampered the availability of archival material, but also clearly led to the 'sanitization' and suppression of documents at a much higher rate than for those relating to less clandestine topics.

With regard to the 20-year-long research presented in this work, I consider myself to have been fortunate.

Although a series of mysterious fires in 1945 destroyed a lot of material in SOE's archives, the (some only recently) declassified documents relating to Dick Mallaby's missions appear both complete and plentiful. Among the papers examined for this work, some 'cleansing' and blacking out is evident, but thankfully rare.

And, as usual, sometimes it's useful to read between the lines...

Operation *Neck*,
14 August 1943

The First Mission

(Or: how agent Dick Mallaby is thrown into the fray and parachutes into Lake Como; swiftly captured in an unfortunate sequence of events, he manages to escape the firing squad.)

> It is not enough that we do our best; sometimes we must do what is required.
> In wartime, truth is so precious that we must always protect it with a curtain of lies.
>
> Sir Winston S. Churchill (1874–1965)

Dick Mallaby was a perfect candidate for SOE: besides being young, reckless, sporty and multilingual, in the course of his military career he had also qualified as a paratrooper and was a skilled wireless operator. And he had grown up in one of the countries which Britain was now fighting.

While the Italian state security services had placed Dick Mallaby and his family under surveillance from the outbreak of war, in Britain, Special Operations Executive had not immediately spotted his potential.

It is fair to say that the trump card on Mallaby's CV – the fact that he had lived in Italy for a long time, and had a perfect knowledge of its language, customs, transport network and geography – was not immediatley relevant, given that, apart from Allied bombing raids, in the opening years of the war events were played out far from the Italian peninsula. However, from the point of its creation SOE had attempted to carry out missions in Italy, and, even at the highest level, it was wrongly believed that beneficial subversive and guerrilla activities could be stirred up in Mussolini's homeland.

However, at the end of 1941, in the wake of events in Africa, the theoretical number of Italians available for missions against their homeland increased, as did the need for Italian-speaking Brits to run them. So, the military situation became more favourable for someone with Dick Mallaby's skills.

Dick Mallaby, as already noted, officially joined SOE on 15 January 1942 as an escort officer, translator and interpreter. Having completed his training, he was sent to Suez to work with a group of Italian volunteers, including both prisoners of war and civilian internees.

Mallaby was tasked with escorting the most promising volunteers to Haifa, Palestine. Whilst there, he took the opportunity to take parachute and radio-telegraphy courses at SOE's Mount Carmel training camp. But something much more interesting was beginning to take shape.

During the first months of 1942, SOE had planned to set up a radio in Italy, and it was decided that the Trieste area, a strategically important part of enemy territory, would be the ideal location. SOE's Cairo headquarters conceived a special operation (codenamed *Pallinode*) aimed at infiltrating an agent to make good use of this device, and from October 1942 began to train Italian volunteers for such a mission.[1]

It was a risky operation even by SOE standards, considering its use of an Italian on a mission against his own country, against standard operational norms.[2]

Efforts focused on Bruno Luzzi, a 30-year-old Tuscan from a moderately socialist family, recruited in 1941 by SOE in Addis Ababa, where he had been working for the past six years in aviation. Luzzi was given the codename Kelly (or D/E 42).

In November 1942, Kelly learned the details of his mission and was placed in the hands of Dick Mallaby for specialized advanced training, which took place in Haifa and Cairo. The plan was for Kelly to reach Trieste with the help of SOE's Slovenian branch, by first parachuting into Yugoslavia and then boarding a merchant ship.

Once in Trieste, Kelly was to hook up two local agents working for SOE (codenamed PSI and agent 900) and keep each in contact with SOE by means of a radio (sent from London via Bern, Switzerland), in order to communicate operational needs, agree details of subsequent missions and provide all sorts of useful information.[3]

Agent 900 was in fact Eligio Klein (alias Almerigotti, alias Giusto), an Italian double agent from Trieste whom the Servizio Informazioni Militare[4] had already turned with great success and without arousing British suspicions.

According to John McCaffery, SOE's head of Bern from February 1941 who also managed Italian affairs, Klein was a 'first-class agent on which everything could be waged', given that 'we will never have a more able man in our pay'.

Klein claimed to be Jewish, a fact that should have raised British suspicions given the race laws in force in Italy, and had passed himself off as a former army officer who headed an anti-fascist organization called Comitato d'azione (Action Committee), comprising 1,500 members. Despite the clumsiness of all this, Klein was blindly trusted by SOE; ignoring basic precaution, he was even put in touch with other agents operating in Italy.

Cesare Amè, head of SIM until 18 August 1943, describes the operation in his book *Guerra segreta in Italia* (*Secret War in Italy*):

> Every week or so the British sent a suitcase to Italy containing 30–40kg of various sabotage materials which, through our agents, regularly fell into our hands ... It was necessary for the agents to demonstrate the use made of the material. SIM carried out a detailed study of all unrelated incidents of and

facts related to sabotage that took place in Italy, in all their variations, to appropriately inform the agents so that they could transmit the results to the British as evidence of their alleged work ... From October 1942, sabotage material intended for the network of agents, which in the meantime had spread to Southern Italy and the Italian islands, was delivered in *c.*150kg bidons which British submarines deposited at certain points on the Tyrrhenian coast or was parachuted onto lakes Viverone, Lesina, Varano. Since the choice of location, day, time etc. had previously been agreed, the material was picked up by SIM's elements, who were aware of everything.[5]

Agent 900 was considered a fundamental element within SOE's Italian organization, so much so that he received funds worth millions of lire and from December 1942 was in possession of a radio. It also meant that his purported exploits were highlighted among SOE's major successes, and even included in reports sent to Churchill himself (who was delicately made aware of the subsequent discoveries).

Among the *matériel* that was intercepted by the Italians in those years was a packet of suicide pills that they promptly replaced with harmless substitutes, in order to exploit the possibility of interrogating anyone considering such a macabre shortcut, as well as to develop an antidote.

Klein's true role was discovered by the British only in November 1943, when this serious infiltration was revealed by SIM personnel who had begun to collaborate with the Allies in southern Italy.

Thus a dismayed and terrified SOE realized that most of McCaffery's most important agents were working for SIM (and initially also for the Organizzazione per la Vigilanza e la Repressione dell'Antifascismo – OVRA – the Organization for Vigilance and Repression of Anti-Fascism, the Fascist intelligence organization) and also that all the safe places indicated by agent 900 within Italy were run by SIM itself.[6]

Attempts were made to gloss over this embarrassing affair, above all towards the political–military leadership. That was successful and became the official line in post-war authoritative accounts and works about SOE, generating erroneous but persistent reports and statements.

In fact, in 1945, when the unmasked Klein was questioned, the resulting report tried to portray him as a skilled and keen double agent actually working for the British. This version obliterated the fact that even the person who acted as a courier and link between McCaffery and Klein – Elio Andreoli – was a SIM agent, who not only had the opportunity to intercept all the shipments of money and *matériel*, but also to verify the correspondence and evaluate the behavior of Klein. The cross examination of British, American and Italian secret papers reveals that SIM agents, shrewdly, did not trust Klein as much as the British.

It is no wonder that the Italian secret services were the only functional apparatus of the Kingdom of Italy to receive consistent praise and attestations of superior skills from the British military and historians.

William Deakin (who, besides being a friend and 'literary assistant' to Churchill during the war, was an SOE agent prior to dedicating himself to the writing of history) praised the Italians as Allied intelligence's 'most brilliant professional opponent operating in any European country'.[7] Churchill himself on several occasions expressed the belief that SIM formed the most efficient part of the Italian armed forces, even stating that 'SIM did not lose the war'; Erwin Rommel confided to a SIM agent that he trusted the Italian information services more than the German ones, an opinion based on the amount of strategic and secret information given to him, which proved enormously useful for his initial successes in North Africa.

It has taken until the 21st century for a more critical approach to finally be offered, with Roderick Bailey correctly stating: 'the Second World War was not the heyday of British secret service vetting'.[8] In no case was this more obvious than in McCaffery's blind faith in agent 900, a faith so extreme that it was not shaken even when he was informed by other sources that agent 900's network was a creation of SIM.

Returning to *Pallinode*, a detailed picture of its continual, drawn-out deferments and operational modifications emerges from secret documents in the British and American archives. The first documentary evidence, dated 8 August 1942, reveals that SOE's Cairo branch was informed that the planned operation was to deliver an agent (possibly an Italian) into north-west Yugoslavia, who was then to be taken into northern Italy. Three days later, in reply to this, it was pointed out that the usefulness of an agent without a radio was very limited; as a consequence, the Bern station became involved, both to guarantee safe houses through the groups operating in Trieste, and to arrange the dispatch of a radio.

The response from Bern was positive and SOE's leadership speeded up preparations, giving notice on 24 August that the operation was in 'an advanced state of planning'. However, almost a year passed between planning and execution.

A top-secret message dated 30 September stated that a cryptographic code plan called Maraschino had been set up for the mission, while on 7 October the Bern station announced that the safe house in Trieste was Flat B on the third floor of No. 14 Via Diaz, belonging to Mrs Maria Pitacco (the pass phrase was: 'I am the friend of Mr Remo Dussi, who made arrangements for the room with you').

On 16 October, Cairo reported that agent Kelly could not enter action before 19 November, with the prior consent of the 'welcoming committee' in Yugoslavia; the communications of that time reveal there were also major problems with the required false papers.

Four days later, a message from London expressed satisfaction that Kelly had not 'gone off', given that 'this would have been particularly frustrating since we set up the Trieste base – something that was not easy to do – and our reputation among our people in Italy would have suffered if we had not been able to do our part of the job'.

From this long message it emerges that agent Kelly was meant to keep a low profile initially, avoiding any risks, transmitting messages for only a few hours a week and seeking to improve clandestine links to and from Yugoslavia. The note ended by pointing out that via the Bern station, agent 900 (the 'head of the Italian group') was asked to assist Kelly. Thus, Italian counterespionage became aware of the *Pallinode* operation almost immediately, thanks to the engagement of agent 900's services.

According to a specific memorandum, *Pallinode*'s objectives were to assist the groups with which SOE was interacting in northern Italy with communications, guerrilla strategies and sabotage. In addition, the agent was to carefully monitor these groups' activities, without arousing suspicion. With regard to transmissions, the agent should proceed without too much involvement from local groups, making sure that information was always carefully chosen, and giving priority to that of a political and military nature. They should also execute false transmissions as a precaution, especially where the duration of the broadcast had gone on too long.[9]

Although branch work focused on such security details, the whole operation was doomed from the outset because of SIM's successful infiltration of SOE. This is confirmed by the confidential directives dated 22 October 1942, in which it is clear that SOE's leadership placed complete reliance, without reservation or suspicion, on agent 900's group, to whom the entire management of the mission and of the agent was delegated following his arrival in Trieste.

It was pointed out to Kelly that his security depended on the protection of agent 900's group, which was:

> doing useful work and expanding. With a W/T man to maintain contact with us they should go still ahead. There will come the time when we may need to take control over what is done there, and it would be one of Kelly's jobs to assist in the reception of additional agents. His future usefulness will depend almost entirely on his ability to establish himself well in the confidence of 900 and prove his ability. 900 has an affiliated group at Venice (our own name for this group [is] 'The Cubs') and it is quite possible they may wish to pass Kelly on to Venice.[10]

In the following days, the relevant departments worked hard to produce the necessary false documents and to improve the cryptographic package and the supply of Italian currency. However, there were concerns about delays in organizing the Yugoslav assets to provide the agent's reception, leading to the prospect of using submarines stationed in Malta. The mission start date was postponed to January, which added the further complication of the looming winter weather; however, another more fundamental complication arose.

Agent Kelly had already caused a few problems and proved to be somewhat slow on the uptake. As a result, SOE's leadership assigned him to the personal care of instructor Dick Mallaby in an effort to bring him up to an acceptable standard in vital Morse and radio-telegraphy skills.

Dick Mallaby's name pops up for the first time in a secret dispatch of 7 November 1942, which states that the hesitant agent Kelly was to start an additional course of radio-telegraphy under Mallaby himself (who had been promoted to sergeant from 1 September).

The secret documents suggest that Mallaby was primarily a sort of guardian angel for Kelly (the instructions were for Kelly to be under constant watch and to have no contact with the outside world). In this period, the two of them resided between Jerusalem and Haifa.

Despite 'Mallaby's medicine', the patient did not improve. Kelly, whilst a volunteer, definitively lost heart and gave up when informed of the imminent launch of his mission (especially on account of his fear of parachuting).

Commenting retrospectively on this key episode, Mallaby, expressing regret and then disappointment, consigned to posterity a phrase which, above all, reveals a great ability to identify the attitudes of Italian people: 'There is no better fighter than an Italian, if he has faith in the cause for which he is fighting.'

Mallaby's superiors found themselves greatly embarrassed before the London leadership for this premature failure, and over the course of many weeks in their communications continued to use Kelly's name as if nothing had happened. They then turned to Dick Mallaby to see who was the next candidate among his students. Without delay, Mallaby proposed himself. Faced with the objection that the agent should appear Italian in all respects, he pointed out that, beyond his appearance, which was clearly not Mediterranean, his Italian was better than his English.

SOE's current practice at that time was to train agents from the nations in which the missions were to take place, and not to send its own men. This was partially changed in Italy after September 1943, when many SOE men were sent to the various mission areas as heads of mission, instructors, or as communications specialists.

Mallaby's offer was much appreciated. Cecil Roseberry emphasized that volunteering to replace someone who stepped down through fear required rare determination.

The Mallaby option presented overlapping risks. Although in Italy, even in the south, there are more men with blond hair than is commonly assumed, undoubtedly blonds stand out, leading to a violation of rule number one for every secret or special agent: avoid being, or appearing, different from the local population in the mission area.

On 16 November 1942, a top-secret report set down the formal record of events, stating that agent Kelly's training had not yielded good results because of 'a lack of intelligence and memory in the same' and Mallaby (officially an officer training cadet) had volunteered.[11] A week after his volunteering, Mallaby was called to Cairo to begin a further course of specific training.

To mark the occasion, Dick Mallaby, with due reserve towards his new undertaking, threw a party to celebrate his first operational mission. Such gatherings, given the chancy, risky activities carried out by SOE agents, took on the feel of both a celebration and a wake.

Meanwhile, the organizational machine laboured on, albeit accompanied by some quite mystifying communications. A message dated 18 December from Cairo inferred that *Pallinode* might begin shortly, with the arrival of the relevant agent in Yugoslav territory, his meeting up with the Chetniks (at that time still supported by the British) and his departure for Trieste (with snowfall possibly extending the duration of the transfer even by a matter of weeks). This message continued to refer to the departed agent Kelly.

While on 26 December it was announced in Bern that the start of the operation was scheduled for mid-January, on 30 December Cairo confirmed the Kelly–Mallaby swap, stating that agent D/E 42 (Kelly) 'showed signs of nervousness' and agent D/H 449 (Mallaby) 'who has looked after him for the last three months is very eager to take his place. He offers a better, higher value element.'

This careful manipulation of the actual events was aimed at making a poor situation more attractive to London and seeking approval for a solution that had already been implemented. It is clear that the various local stations did not always guarantee SOE's leadership a full and detailed knowledge of relevant events. Even in its own internal communications, SOE's leadership casually and brilliantly indulged in misdirection.

On 3 January 1943, London messaged its firm approval regarding the prospective swap, asking whether Kelly might be comforted with a trip home (which might have been a sinister coded message). This is the last known message in which the original agent Kelly is referred to; in the days that followed, the name was used to refer to Mallaby, prior to his being assigned a different codename.[12]

SOE's leadership replied in a message dated 5 January 1943, acknowledging that the original agent Kelly's behaviour was predictable 'when a man is kept too long'. The message took some comfort from the fact that this had happened before and not during the mission and also confirmed that SOE's alleged Italian collaborators never heard of the swap, as the agent had not yet been identified to them.

Five days later, in response to the 18 December message from Cairo, at the same time as expressing high expectations of the new *Pallinode* incumbent, it was stated that agent 900 had given 'ample proof of his good faith and his skill. He is eager to allow us to let some of his men out for training and subsequent return.' Evidently Italian counterespionage personnel had decided to increase the degree of infiltration by seeking permission to send agents from Italy abroad to train with the British, and then for them to return home replete with invaluable information.

The Italian deception activities had been both excellent and comprehensive: the confidence expressed by SOE's leadership was almost complete, and if SIM's work had not been interrupted by the September 1943 Italian capitulation, in all probability its infiltration would have reached extraordinary levels without being uncovered.

Having decided that the agent would be parachuted into the area of operations, a further condition was also applied to the *Pallinode* mission, one that applied only every four weeks: a full moon. Usually, except in emergencies, SOE was given priority for parachute delivery of both *matériel* and agents when the moon was full. Weighing up the risks and benefits between active and passive visibility, it was decided that the needs of pilots, who often had to recognize light signals marking out drop zones, and those of parachuting agents, who preferred the best visibility possible even if this made them more visible and easier to intercept, should prevail.

On 14 January, a message was sent to Bern, the apparently banal contents of which help contextualize the situation at the time and, in particular, the lasting confidence that SOE's leadership placed in agent 900. When Cairo station proposed giving the special agent arriving in Trieste 130,000 lire in notes and diamonds (a very large sum), the Swiss station was asked for its opinion, given that, on the one hand, this benefitted

Bern as its available funds for both agent 900 and its other activities would thus not be depleted, while on the other it might look as if the organization had granted agent 900 too much financial freedom and control.

With the wisdom of Solomon, a proposal was made to provide the agent with a hidden reserve of 30,000 lire, while at the same time making it appear that he continued to depend on agent 900 for his maintenance. A message dated 15 February reveals the matter was concluded by giving the agent a further 100,000 lire destined for 900's group.

Bern assented, but warned Cairo on 18 February that the possession of currency would considerably increase risk if the agent was captured or investigated. This was one of the Swiss station's few commendable acts of foresight.

In the meantime, 'agent Olaf' had come into existence. The first time this codename was assigned to Mallaby for the mission comes in a 'double message' dated 17 January.[13] Even by British standards, Mallaby was evidently northern-European looking.

A further double message the following day from Bern stated that his arrival in Trieste could not take place before 7 February.[14] News from Trieste stated that the occupants of the apartment at No. 14 Via Diaz had decided to move away because of the Allied bombing, and so a new address was given, care of Mrs Paoletti, No. 65 Via dei Porta.

The original pass phrase had changed little: agent Olaf would present himself saying that he had been sent by Remo Dussi, to meet Mr Marco.

Mallaby continued his training in Cairo, whilst still acting as a radio-telegraphy instructor. Two further lunar phases passed by, but still the mission did not begin. In all the uncertainty, Dick Mallaby threw another party.[15]

The Italians, meanwhile, were not sitting twiddling their thumbs: Dick Mallaby continued, randomly or otherwise, to be a subject of attention for the Italian intelligence services.

A confidential memo from the Ministry of the Interior, dated 11 February 1943, indicated that he was to be found in Addis Ababa with the Intelligence Service 'attending special training courses, together with some Italian subjects resident there, for eventual acts of sabotage on Italian territory'. The information was mostly correct, apart from the geographical location, and showed that, beyond Italy and Switzerland, gaps in SOE's veil of secrecy had appeared in Africa too.

In the same memo it was reported that Dick's father Cecil Mallaby had made a conspicuous gift of 1,000 lire to the Fascist Federation of Siena in the last weeks of 1935, with an accompanying letter in which he expressed his 'disdain for the unjust and disloyal behaviour of Great Britain towards Italy and his solidarity with Mussolini's Italy'. Over the following years, however, his attitude towards the Fascist regime had changed radically, so much so that, in 1940, the Centro CS (Counterespionage Centre) in Florence had him filed as follows: 'diehard Anglophile, openly opposed to Axis policy, holds hostile feelings towards the Regime, which he makes no attempt to hide'.

The memo concluded by stating that 'at the outbreak of hostilities between Italy and Great Britain, Mallaby and his wife, although not subject to internment restrictions, were however required not to leave Poggio Pinci [their residence in Asciano] without permission. Their property was seized and handed to the Monte dei Paschi di Siena bank'.[16]

On 4 February, Cairo sent word that the operation would begin around 14 February, with the destination firstly Split and then Trieste. But once again the mission start date was postponed, due partly to the unavailability of transport, but also to doubts concerning the validity, security and functionality of the Maraschino and Maraschino Orange cryptographic codes (which used decryption keys taken from Giovanni Papini's 1939 work *Italia mia – My Italy*).[17]

At Cairo station, having relayed the postponement with a certain degree of resignation, all that remained to keep the mission on the boil was to confirm agent D/E 42's return to barracks, stating that his successor, D/H 449, was proving to be 'far more satisfactory' for the 'new way ahead' identified. Given the lingering uncertainty, coupled with the new agent's perceived value, the possibility of assigning him to another operation was mooted, and from the message it can be understood that this 'new way ahead' consisted of a secret overseas mission and the delivery of *matériel*, in particular radios, into enemy territory.

The unknown author of this top-secret memo was forced to admit that the lack of aircraft caused considerable problems, hence the need for alternative solutions.

Thus the idea of using Mallaby in an operation connected to the Tigrotti group (the Tiger Cubs – another fictitious Italian resistance group that had infiltrated SOE, run by Italian secret agent Luca Osteria and managed by OVRA) took shape, for which he would travel by sea and provide operational support to agent Galea. The agent, whose real name was Giacomino Sarfatti, had been personally recruited by McCaffery in 1940 and his installation in Italy (arranged with the help of agent 900) was considered one of SOE's greatest successes on the Italian peninsula.

Once again McCaffery and his team had not the faintest idea how things really stood.

Agent Galea was in fact another example of model counterespionage. Sarfatti was Jewish just like Klein, but in contrast to agent 900, he was also a genuine anti-fascist at a time when they were few and widely dispersed; however, his actions were similarly controlled and managed by SIM, whose personnel sought to achieve even greater results.[18]

On 19 February 1943, agent D/H 449's personnel card was formalized. The key identification data was as follows:

Sergeant Cecil Richard Mallaby, unmarried, not interested in politics, able to speak perfect English and Italian, very good French and also good German; completed schooling in Italy and England.

REAL AGE: 23

APPARENT AGE: 21

HEIGHT: 1.79m

WEIGHT: 70kg

FACE: Long. Fresh, clear complexion.

FRONT PROFILE: Oblique and irregular.

EYES: Sky blue and deep set.

NOSE: Straight. Nostrils visible.

MOUTH: Full.

CHIN: With a light dimple, well defined and clean-shaven.

HAIR: Straight, combed back, blond but credibly brown for operational purposes.

DISTINCTIVE MARKS: Scars on the right cheek, right elbow and both shins. Heart-shaped tattoo on the left forearm, red spot on the right thigh. Walks in a very upright manner.

This card failed to foresee Mallaby's future operational roles, given that (whether due to secrecy, a lack of updating or pure carelessness) it stated he could have made a useful employee, or at best an electrician!

The card specified, among the relevant notes, his familiarity with the area around Modena (and almost all of Tuscany), his marked Tuscan accent and his Nordic appearance.

In his application form for his training course, which was probably written for formal reasons on 23 March 1943, Mallaby declared himself to be a Catholic, and listed his order of preference for service duties: in special assault troops; in the secret services; or the infantry. He also highlighted having attended parachute, sabotage and assault courses. In the section completed by his commanding officer, all this was confirmed, as was his excellent skill in radio transmissions and sabotage, as well as his sound military attitude and good discipline.

In the weeks that followed, exchanges between Cairo and London reveal that Mallaby's first mission was still the subject of confused and wavering proposals and significant operational difficulties. These did not only come from transport and radio communications issues, but also the political and military situation in Italy, which was deemed unfavourable. Mallaby, eager to enter the fray, asked if he could take part in other operations, provided they were in a more advanced state of execution.

A new plan was drawn up that envisaged arrival by submarine in the area between Pescara and Bari, before probably heading for Naples. On 24 February, a message from Cairo objected that the submarine option would be even dicier than the parachute one, and pointed out that:

1 while agent Olaf might be in agreement, it
   should be considered as to whether the proposed
   change of destination introduces further risks,
   given his decidedly Nordic appearance;

2 the new cryptographic keys would be given to the agent only when the operational agreements with the Tigrotti and the details relating to transport had been finalized;

3 on the basis of previous experience, changes to missions tended to disturb agents, especially when the alternative plan was not yet confirmed;

4 given the apparent difficulty in getting in touch with the Tigrotti group, all decisions should be left to London;

5 for sake of his morale and trust, it was important to assign agent Olaf to some form of mission.

A message dated 4 March from Cairo, which announced yet another postponement of the operation until April's full moon due to a lack of transport, stated that agent Olaf was not showing signs of exhaustion.

Time continued to pass, but little certainty ensued.

Further messages in May 1943 reveal how erratic the situation was: on the 5th, SOE's Bern station suggested that Mallaby could reach Italy via the same route used by agent Galea, pointing out that entry into Switzerland from France would become more difficult after 17 May. A parachute entry was thus proposed.

The following day's reply revealed total confusion, signalling the preference for a drop over France 'in consideration of its non-hostile population' and asking for agent 900's help in organizing a reception team. Massingham, however, on 7 May noted that the drop over France might be dangerous if the agent did not speak good French. On 10 May, Cairo, more lucidly, stated that Mallaby's false identity needed to be that of an Alsatian, considering the fact that Mallaby did not speak excellent French (and had an accent) and his appearance was decidedly Nordic.

Although this might suggest that a new mission was being planned on French soil (which consistently absorbed a significant part of SOE's European activities), it was in fact merely exploring different ways of getting the agent to Italy.

Indecision continued to reign supreme, as further messages of this period mention Monte Nevoso – the highest point in the Karst region, which marked the border between Italy and Yugoslavia between 1920 and 1947 – as an alternative drop zone.

Mallaby's deep desire to 'enter the fray' would have been wiped out by his instinct for self-preservation if he knew of the lack of certainty hanging over his first mission. Things remained vague and unclear, and agent Olaf was even at risk of being replaced and sent on another operation (Operation *Cockney*).[19]

The messages sent between Algiers, Cairo and London on 13 May 1943 confirm again the operational difficulties; the only new aspect was the mention of a mysterious agent 1400, who was attempting to organize Mallaby's arrival in Italy in the Lake Garda zone.[20]

At last, after a few more days, the fundamental elements of the mission began to come together, when the RAF announced that finally a plane in North Africa was ready to transport agent Olaf to the objective.

What was still missing, however, was *the objective itself*.

There was still little certainty regarding the so-called 'reception committee' (those on the ground who were supposed to help Mallaby facilitate his mission); thus, the pragmatic – yet even riskier – proposal to send Mallaby in blind (i.e. without a reception committee) began to form, provided he could be guaranteed a safe house.[21]

All the delays and indecision did have some positive side effects. Had Mallaby entered action as planned in the first part of 1943 and up to 25 July, he would have automatically become one of the many agents caught – and most likely shot, if counterespionage attempts to interrogate and/or turn him had not succeeded. Alternatively, he might have been exchanged for Italian prisoners, should there be a desire to do so on the Italian side.

In the meantime, a further mission detail was finalized, with the creation of Mallaby's fictitious identity, which was as follows: Aldo Guazzini, son of Giuseppe and Maria Winter (whose foreign surname would explain his Nordic features, blond hair and blue eyes); born 28 April 1923 in Sinalunga; resident at No. 27 Via Pisana, Florence; occupation – student.

Sinalunga is in Siena Province, a few kilometres from where Mallaby had spent his childhood and adolescence. Guazzini is a fairly common Tuscan surname and two Guazzinis – Aldo and Alfio, coincidentally from Sinalunga – had been friends and schoolmates of

Mallaby's at the Convitto Nazionale Celso Tolomei in Siena a few years earlier, as the young Mallaby's diary testifies. Guazzino is also a district of Sinalunga town, about 20km from where the Mallaby family continued to live.

It is therefore clear that Mallaby not only participated in the construction of this false identity, but that he also – given that his mind would be bristling with cryptographic codes, information and various cover stories – made use of familiar references from his past, which could be simply recalled using mnemonic hooks.

This constructed reality, based on true and false elements, remained a constant in his missions and in the explanations he gave in moments of difficulty.

On 29 May, a further piece of the puzzle fell into place. Mallaby received an order to go to Algiers – officially for further specific training, but actually for the launch of his mission.[22] Once again, Mallaby had to request an advance on his salary to pay for a farewell party for his comrades.

At long last, in the first days of June 1943, Dick Mallaby reached the base officially known as Inter-Services Signals Unit 6, but universally known by the few who were aware of this secret institution by its codename Massingham.

Massingham was established in November 1942 in Africa and located, from February 1943, near a secluded pine grove in Guyotville, 24km west of Algiers, at a former bathing establishment, the 'Club des Pins'.

Massingham was both an operations and a training base, a rare occurrence, and served both SOE and American OSS personnel; it also hosted agents from all the European nations in which SOE operated, including, after September 1943, Italy. Logistically, the base was well located, in that not only was it close to Blida airport and Allied Force HQ in Algiers, but the beach and the surrounding dunes made for excellent training sites for parachute jumps and water landings.

In the words of Douglas Dodds-Parker, who was commander of the base from January 1943 and became a senior Conservative MP and junior minister after the war, Massingham was primarily a 'playboy's paradise' and was established 'for wide-ranging, but undefined tasks; it was to serve as a base for subsequent operations to the north, in France and Corsica and possibly in Italy, whose secret police, OVRA, were the most efficient in Europe'.[23]

Mallaby's mission was top secret – so much so that, exercising extreme caution, all technical equipment was to travel separately from the agent. Officially, even in the eyes of his Massingham colleagues, Mallaby was a regular member of the Cairo broadcasting section, sent to the base for a cypher refresher course, at the end of which he would return to Egypt.

Yet the plan for Mallaby was altogether different – as was his destination. Dick Mallaby was heading for Italy and would never return to Cairo.[24]

Up to that moment, SOE had achieved little of significance in terms of special operations within the

Kingdom of Italy's European territory. In general terms, between 1940 and 1943, things had not gone the way the British had expected – indeed quite the opposite, as demonstrated by the disastrous outcome of Operation *Colossus*, the British attempt in February 1941 to destroy the Apulian Aqueduct and deprive the ports of Bari, Brindisi and Taranto of fresh water.[25]

The next document concerning Mallaby is dated 8 June 1943 and indicates that the operation was scheduled for the night of 16/17 June.

It seemed like the time was finally right, as on 10 June 1943, a highly detailed report was circulated among the few relevant departments regarding agent Olaf, his training and the *matériel* with which he would parachute into Italy. Mallaby was to travel with a toilet bag containing a quartz crystal oscillator hidden in a shaving brush and seven more inside a box, and three sets of cryptographic codes – Maraschino Orange (for communications with Massingham), Maraschino (for those with London) and Pallinode (for Cairo) – as well as a very large amount of money.[26]

In addition to the identity card in the name of Aldo Guazzini issued by Florence Comune (the city's municipality), Mallaby carried the following: a blank identity card; a blank driving licence issued by Florence Comune and another issued by Trieste Comune; a temporary unlimited leave document; various photo cards; a letter of presentation addressed to Francesco Parisi (a warehouse owner, whose role will soon be revealed); and various small items.

The person who drafted the inventory, noting that Mallaby had become a high-level radio operator, recommended a careful check before his departure, especially regarding his clothing, as agent Olaf was not a fan of some of the items and was suspected of wanting to get rid of them. On the document, which pointed out that Mallaby 'was almost ready to make a few disappear', a handwritten note exclaims, 'The follies of youth!'[27]

Any further preparatory training for Mallaby, who had completed as many as seven courses and taught many others, was now redundant, and his equipment was ready – but still the mission was not launched. June 1943 passed by in vain, with Dick Mallaby still on tenterhooks in Africa.

Contemporary documents suggest that all the details of the operation had not yet been finalized and everything was very fluid. This was because, for the Allies, on the one hand important military actions were taking place, and on the other the political situation in Italy was rapidly changing.[28]

The plan that seemed to have gained the upper hand in this period was as follows: Olaf would arrive in Trieste with the help of the Yugoslav Partisans, only using the Aldo Guazzini identity card if absolutely necessary. En route, he would be given an address to head to. Following the suggestions of his Italian accomplices, he would fill in the second identity card, driving licence and the leave document, destroying anything that was not used. If questioned, Mallaby would state that he was in the area for a job interview with Francesco Parisi, a friend of his uncle.[29]

Clearly, agent 1400 (who, according to a message dated 13 May, was in charge of Mallaby's welcome committee around Lake Garda) had not yet been able to finalize the details.

For Dick Mallaby it was still early days for Lake Garda – he would visit this only later, in 1945, as part of his second operational masterpiece. For now, on his first mission, it was Lake Como that awaited him.

How much was the life of a young man worth, according to those who were throwing him in at the deep end? A document dated 29 June 1943 informs us that Dick Mallaby was paid the lowest daily rate of 9 shillings and 6 pence, including a 'parachute indemnity' allowance, and also revealed that he had obtained substantial advances on his wages.

As Benito Mussolini, 'Il Duce', was spending his final days after a 20-year tenure as Head of the King's Government in Italy, Mallaby's mission was still subject to upheaval and reversal.

On 30 June, a note from London stated that a final decision had been taken to have another agent, Finucci, accompany Mallaby on his mission.

At the same time, questions were asked about whether the radio in Trieste could be moved in advance, as agent Olaf's movements would be much less onerous if he did not have to carry this delicate and compromising object around with him.

On 2 July, a Most Secret message officially cancelled the original mission to Trieste. Everything had been reset to zero.

In spite of the frustration caused by the drip-feed approach to operational planning over several months, the indecision and delays to the mission's start did help ensure that its preparation was both adequate and well thought through. This is nicely demonstrated by a further important piece of information contained in the message of 2 July. A concern was expressed by some bright spark that the false identity card given to Mallaby indicated his date of birth as 1923 – as according to the information available at the time, this age band had been called up for military service. Mallaby had also been given a false document of unlimited leave for study reasons – but nobody could guarantee for sure that such a key detail was coherent, or whether in Italy it was possible to gain such a dispensation in time of war. If questioned, things could have gone badly wrong for Mallaby, whose documents would immediately have been revealed as false, or at least would have aroused the suspicion of the person examining them.[30]

Another Most Secret message of the same date notes that the boots given to Mallaby were military ones, which when 'worn by a civilian, would be the object of comment even in our country'. It was added that Mallaby would be given a more appropriate, normal-looking pair of waterproof shoes.[31]

At the start of the pivotal month of July 1943, Dick Mallaby's first special mission, although unfinalized, had at last been given a codename: *Neck*. It was a sign that the mission would shortly be underway.

The turbulent events of the following days – the Allied invasion of southern Italy, Mussolini's defenestration and the increasingly frequent and open Italian attempts to enter surrender negotiations – saw further updates to the mission's priorities, aims and ambitions, and once again delayed its execution.

A message from London dated 7 July, layering confusion on top of confusion, proposed landing Mallaby around Bari in southern Italy by submarine, or parachuting him in.[32] Mallaby was now being used as a guinea pig.

SOE was not exclusively responsible for all the indecision: it also resulted from SIM's manipulations in the light of the prospects facing Italy.

A cross-analysis of the various documentary sources reveals that the projected outcomes of Mallaby's mission were mainly the result of the frenzied work of the Italian counterespionage services.

Agent 900 had requested that he be kept informed of every detail and had indeed communicated that a wireless operator and a demolitions expert could be guaranteed welcome and shelter in Bari; that the best option was arrival by submarine in the Adriatic; and that the radio was no longer in Trieste and could be transported anywhere.

The Bari option began to take shape (despite the previous well-founded reservations regarding Mallaby's Nordic appearance), so much so that the name of the Bari contact was also transmitted – Mr. Dositeo Carli care of the Cima company at No. 131 Via Vittorio Veneto – as well as the pass phrase: 'I've been sent by Mr Gino Cuzzi from Milan, who needs some overcoats.'[33]

This reckless plan, however, never got off the ground. For one thing there was no time to contact the Royal Navy about transportation. Furthermore, London pointed out that it would be impossible to arrange the ground reception committee for a possible nighttime parachute drop to coincide with the full moon, and that the risk of operating in this area was unjustifiably high given the intense military activity, as well as Mallaby's northern appearance and Tuscan accent.

Previously, London had reprimanded Cairo station for the ease with which it tended to throw special agents into the fray without adequately considering their chances of survival. Recently released documents from both the Anglo-American and Italian archives demonstrate the level of hidden danger to which SOE agents were exposed in Italy. It is clear that SOE's leadership had little confidence that Mallaby would escape capture, and feared both the loss of their agent and the exposure of their (bogus) Italian network.[34]

In an effort to provide Mallaby with the best chance of success he received the highest level of personal training. In the period 12–17 July 1943, agent Olaf's schedule was intense: every day, from 9.00am to 12.30pm, he attended 'courses in demolition, sabotage and weapons used by the Axis forces'; from 2.30pm to 4.00pm, a motorbike course; and from 5.30pm to 7.00pm, a lesson in radio transmission.[35]

The option of dropping Mallaby over Lake Como finally won out. This time it was the real deal, even if the description of how Mallaby would arrive in Italy ('dropping in blind') was a little discouraging. The mission was about to begin. The coordination of transport was finally achieved, and in a message dated 14 July, Massingham announced that the RAF had confirmed the availability of an aircraft for Mallaby's drop.

On the same date, Bern confirmed that agent 900 had arranged a safe house in Como, so that the mission to parachute in the wireless operator and expert in demolitions, as well as a supply of *matériel* for the organization, could be actioned.[36]

An encrypted message from London dated 31 July, although still a little vague, clearly lays out the leadership's increasingly certain plan to drop Mallaby 'blind' into the area around Como, or over Lake Como itself, and leave him to reach the address provided to him; alternatively, if this option was deemed too risky, it should be insisted that agent 900 organize a reception committee. This message ends with an ambiguous, but significant, statement: 'the current reduction in checks should increase possibilities'. Although events would go on to prove this wrong, this analysis may have been a result of indications from the Italian front, or, once more, of misinformation activities by Italian counterespionage.

Thus, after further discussions and disagreements between Cairo and Massingham over minor operational details and Mallaby's false documents, August 1943 arrived.[37]

Meanwhile, in Italy a momentous event had transpired: on 25 July, Benito Mussolini had been uprooted from his position as head of government, arrested and locked up, to be replaced by Pietro Badoglio. The era of Fascism which began in 1922 had formally been brought to a close.

However positive this historic event may have been for the Allies, its consequences were less clear cut, in part because – both for the Allies and for the Italian king Vittorio Emanuele III – Pietro Badoglio's positioning and his intentions were unclear and ambiguous.

An encrypted message transmitted by London on 1 August 1943 confirms that, having arrived in Italy, agent Olaf was to act as an instructor for members of the resistance in the use of weapons and, in particular, wireless transmissions, linking this to developments in events. Moreover, Mallaby 'must stay in the north or head south', when '(perhaps before he departs) we will be able to understand if the Italian government wants peace'. The message ends by stating that, if there were need of a weapons instructor, the radio-telegraphist could be trained for this role, and thus, in the light of the Italian political situation, there were three options: send only a radio-telegraphist; send both a radio-telegraphist and a weapons instructor; or send two radio-telegraphists. In the end it was decided to dispatch 'all-round agent' Olaf alone, to destination unknown.

On 5 August, Massingham spelt out three possible alternative destinations, adding that 'Olaf has waited six months for this opportunity. I have to give him a definitive answer.'[38]

In this period, events were following one another in rapid succession, which provided further impetus and modifications to Mallaby's mission.

After Mussolini's fall from power, three semi-official Italian diplomatic approaches had been made in Lisbon, Tangier and Barcelona, in an effort to reach an agreed cessation of hostilities.

SOE had also been informed of this, which had heightened fears at the Foreign Office of what might result should Mallaby be captured.

The fact that agent Olaf had volunteered for a top-secret – and in many respects experimental – mission allowed him a familiarity and confidence with those in senior positions (who, evidently, also meant to keep a close eye on him, given the secrecy surrounding his task). Such familiarity was rarely granted to a humble sergeant.

During an evening spent in the company of some officers, Dick Mallaby (although oblivious to this at the time) met someone who would play a fundamental role in his life: his lifelong partner, future wife and mother of his children, Christine Northcote-Marks. The 18-year-old Christine was one of a group of young FANY (First Aid Nursing Yeomanry) personnel serving at Massingham, and was mainly responsible for the encoding and decryption of messages from agents serving in the various theatres of operation.

As often happens between people whom destiny subsequently unites for the rest of their lives, Christine's first impression of her future husband was not entirely positive: Dick seemed a rather haughty type, who liked to act the typical 'man with a mission'.

The evening they met, Christine's future husband's mind was anything but uncluttered or sunny: marriage, or the idea that his future wife was standing before him, were the last things he was thinking about – being understandably more worried about surviving long enough to marry anyone. He had just learned the final, confirmed details of Operation *Neck*.

The following was planned: a nighttime drop into Lake Como; making contact with Italian resistance members operating in the area; training them in sabotage techniques; and establishing a permanent link through the ether with Algiers using the wireless set sent by McCaffery, in order to provide instructions for future drops of *matériel* and subsequent missions. For Mallaby, all this meant having to learn names, codes and references and cover stories that matched his false documents off by heart, in case of capture. It should also be noted that Mallaby was also one of the first paratroopers in history to drop into water and at night; it remains uncertain as to whether he was the first ever to do so. [39]

Besides parachuting into Italy, which remained enemy territory, and not wearing a uniform, which meant he could be legitimately executed, there were other aspects of his mission of which he was unaware that were anything but reassuring for agent Olaf.

Firstly, the radio that had already been sent to Italy several months previously might not be serviceable. To overcome this, a plan was made to drop a new apparatus (complete with antennae disguised as clothes threads), which could be used by Olaf himself, or kept available for others.[40]

Secondly, the timing of the operation was governed by the lunar phase: it had to begin shortly before, or shortly after, 15 August, the date when the moon was full.

With only a few days to go, Mallaby's presence at and departure from Massingham was conveniently explained, so as not to reveal his actual role and the top-secret mission.[41]

On 6 August 1943, the point of no return was reached: the definitive outline of the mission was drawn up, and Dick Mallaby and his equipment were transferred to Tunis.

However, looking at the messages between the various offices around this time, what still emerges is a disconcerting and reckless state of disorganization. This was a result of the extreme secrecy surrounding Operation *Neck* and worsened by the absence of a direct telegraphic link between Massigham and Bern.

The mission was supposed to start on the night of 12/13 August, but it was postponed by 24 hours – a change that proved to be not without consequences.

According to the plan, agent Olaf, after parachuting into the middle of the lake, would need to reach the address of E. M. Avadini. This name was provided in a message from Bern dated 27 July, yet this same message pointed out that the name might be Cavadini, thus asking for verification using a telephone directory.

In addition, a list of farms in Como Province was sent to Massingham in order to provide agent Olaf with a false reference letter. Mallaby had in fact suggested that he should pretend to be an agricultural student, given that he had gained a familiarity with this subject from his father's business.

Arrangements were also made for agent 900 to move the radio to a secure location (preferably in a non-concrete building, in order to improve modulation efficiency) from which Olaf could operate, recommending that the site should preferably be in northern Italy, given Mallaby's appearance.[42]

Massingham had also been made aware that agent 900's group would take care of Mallaby's reception in Como and send him (alone, or in the company of another agent) even as far as Naples, thanks to the availability of appropriate permits.[43]

Agent Olaf was also provided with a false document that granted temporary exemption from military service due to his student status. In fact it was only a crude facsimile that needed adapting to match his other false documents. This draft was accompanied by two false stamps: the first was inscribed with 'Principal' (as requested), and the other 'Rector'. Someone should have first confirmed that Italian heads of universities were known by the title 'rector' and not 'principal'. The accompanying instructions politely suggested that 'in an emergency', the second stamp should be added to the document, while highlighting a further factor to be considered: if dated before 25 July 1943, the document should bear the words 'Fascist Year' accompanied by the appropriate Roman numerals, if after this date (i.e after the Fascist regime had fallen), then this should not be added.[44]

From 12 August 1943, all the departments involved in the operation received the necessary encryption and decryption details for agent Olaf's messages: the code key, transmission frequencies and verifications, and alternative frequencies – precautions for avoiding interception or to check if the agent was transmitting under duress.

In the wake of the extraordinary and unpredictable events that unfolded in the days that followed, such details would also be subject to the unexpected turns of fate.

Finally, on 13 August 1943, after months of waiting, Operation *Neck* began. The relevant personnel in the listening stations were informed that their activities were to begin on Saturday the 15th at 3.00pm.[45]

The official details of the mission were communicated to the few in the know in a Most Secret message dated 15 August – the point at which the intended mission had already catastrophically concluded, and the impromptu one had not yet taken shape.

Dick Mallaby was to be dropped at a distance of around 8km from his initial destination, and, having landed on water, was to row his inflatable dinghy to the eastern shore of the south-western branch of Lake Como. Once there, he would ditch his dinghy, jumpsuit and 'Mae West' lifejacket in the water, sinking them. Then, having hidden his waterproof bag containing his vital documents and quartz crystals (and drawn himself a map to remember how to find the place), agent Olaf would hide and await dawn.

At 7.00am, Mallaby needed to be on the third floor of No. 1 Via Borgovico in Como, and he was to ask for E. M. Cavadini (whose surname had finally been confirmed just before the mission's start), introducing himself as 'a friend of Pietro and Tommaso'. Cavadini probably was the mysterious agent 1400. The response phrase would be: 'How is Giulia?'

In case of capture, agent Olaf was to claim he was an aviator recently shot down over northern Italy, who had been captured and then had escaped immediately (a detail shrewdly added to avoid difficult questions about any prison camp).

Mr Cavadini would then recover Mallaby's waterproof bag and deliver its contents to the British agent to allow him to reach his destination. If it proved impossible or too dangerous for Mallaby to make it to Como, he was given two alternative addresses that he should head for, preferably without using public transport.

The first was in Milan, at No. 5 Via Calvi. Here, in the courtyard-facing apartment on the second floor, the agent, calling himself Olaf, was to seek out either Mr Bologna or Almerigotti, asking to meet Giacomo, who was none other than Giacomino Sarfatti (agent Galea).

The second safe house was in Genoa (inaccurately given as Geneva in some mission reconstructions) at No. 57 Via Granello. Here, the agent was to contact Mr Ricciuto, saying he was Mr Rossi of the Mirafiore company and had need of the accommodation reserved for him.[46]

The fact that the safe houses and contacts were controlled by SIM demonstrates the level of infiltration it had achieved into SOE's network. It is also clear that Mallaby was well and truly thrown in at the deep end, given that reaching Milan from Como without using public transport was a challenge in itself, while getting to Genoa (hundreds of kilometres away) under the same restrictions and while northern Italy was being battered by air raids and its roads were being ripped to shreds was almost asking the impossible.

These expectations did not seem extreme to London, Bern or Massingham.[47]

The icing on this poisoned cake was that the first contact arranged for Mallaby in Como, the Swiss Enrico Cavadini, head of the secret so-called Lupi (Wolves) group, was also an Italian intelligence services collaborator.

If he was forced to flee, Mallaby was to reach Switzerland, declare himself an escaped prisoner and request an interview with the British military attaché so that the War Office might be notified.

The person in charge of Operation *Neck* at Massingham was Richard Hewitt. He was in continuous contact with SOE's Bern station.

Even the bureaucratic and accounting aspects of the operation added elements of uncertainty. On 14 August, it was reported that agent Olaf had arrived from Cairo with 160,000 lire, but part of this amount was in notes that had been withdrawn from circulation; so Mallaby was quickly provided with 117,350 lire, and a simultaneous request for a receipt (Mallaby's handwritten one is preserved in the British National Archives).[48]

Despite the overall uncertainty and disorganization that characterized and undermined the mission, a report dated 15 August ended with the following statement: 'with just the right amount of luck, I think a first-class job will be done'.

The coded messages sent between Africa and Europe in the hours that followed contain various pertinent details. Some of these are significant, such as the fact that Mallaby was to communicate initially with Massingham, then with London and Cairo, in case of need; while others are less so, such as the reprimand given to Mallaby for having asked for a package to be sent to Christine Granville.[49]

Dick Mallaby set out on Operation *Neck* dressed as an Italian labourer. The only weapon he was carrying was a knife.

On Friday 13 August 1943, at his Tuscan residence, Cecil Mallaby wrote in his personal diary his impressions of the atrocious heat and the unlucky date.

At the same time, Cecil's son, the first British agent to begin a mission in Italy, was preparing to lay any superstition to rest and experiencing the tension of the final moments prior to the launch of Operation *Neck* in similarly hot weather. Mallaby junior had to make his departure dressed as an Italian labourer, on top of which he was also wearing a parachute smock, a jumpsuit and a wetsuit. It took two people (one of whom was Teddy De Haan) to help Mallaby get on board the plane, and even that was a struggle.

At 10.02pm on 13 August, agent Olaf took off from Blida on board a Halifax heading for Italy, piloted by the Canadian Alfred Ruttledge and accompanied by six other crew members. Mallaby was the only passenger on board.

As planned, it was a full moon night.

Despite the tension, Mallaby managed to catch some sleep on the flight to Italy. The aircraft flew over Minorca, south-eastern France and Lodi in Lombardy, and he was woken as it approached Lake Como from the south-west.

The flight was a turbulent one. Due to radar tracking around Nice, as a precaution the pilot dropped chaff; in Italian territory, there was flak in the Savona area and searchlights around Pavia.

The sky was clear and the full moon lit up the landscape described by famous writers such as Byron and Wordsworth. But agent Olaf had no time for poetic musings, and after the customary tap on the shoulder and a 'Good luck, mate' from the dispatcher, one Sergeant Wilson, Mallaby launched himself into the black void around 600m above the great Lombard lake.

It was 2.48am, 14 August 1943.

The plan was for him to splash down near the town of Torno, about 8km from Como itself, his subsequent destination. Mallaby's first challenge was to target the central part of the body of water – no easy task, given the narrowness of the lake at this point, and the air currents and micro vortices caused by the surrounding high mountains. Hitting dry land would have been very dangerous.

Dick Mallaby's parachute opened without problems. According to a subsequent report dated 28 September, 'The site pre-chosen for the drop was a place where it was highly unlikely anyone would be present after 10.00 p.m.'[50]

As the waters of the lake approached, Mallaby noticed that the banks were not as dark as they should be, and he could see flashes of light to the south.

The report submitted by the pilot who had flown Mallaby to Lake Como was not reassuring, and predicted the forthcoming disaster. It stated that agent Olaf had exited the plane flying at about 200km/h, and that the planned drop point was unsuitable due to the height of the surrounding mountains. Furthermore, it noted the unexpected presence of lights on the ground below and on the surrounding mountainsides. The report ended by reiterating, with fatal foreboding, that despite it being night, the villages around the lake were all lit up.[51]

To the south of Lake Como, a sinister light was spreading from the direction of Milan, which had been heavily bombed the previous night and was still burning. In the hours preceding Mallaby's jump, thousands of people had also fled to Lake Como: the surrounding area, despite it being night, was busy and brightly lit. Furthermore, the Italian anti-aircraft defences had been placed on alert.[52]

Thus the British agent was spotted while still flying about 1km from the southern shore and 3km to the east of the intended drop point.

Dick Mallaby hit the water safely.

After a brief, dangerous struggle to rid himself of his parachute, his next step was to activate the self-inflating mechanism on his rubber dinghy. Having clambered on board, Mallaby tried to orient himself, moving slowly on the lake using a pair of small paddles worn like gloves.

But the noise made by the British plane had raised the alarm. Mallaby, heading towards the western shore of the lake in the direction of Carate Urio, had no idea that he had already been spotted from there.

Using official documents and several eyewitness accounts, it is possible to reconstruct in detail what took place in the hours that followed, and correct several key misconceptions.

Mallaby was first spotted by Domenica Aquilini. From the balcony of her home in Carate Urio, she watched the British agent descend from the sky, and immediately raised the alarm.[53] Also in Carate Urio, Fulvio Borghi and the municipal rural guard Giovanni Abate saw agent Olaf enter the water between Faggeto and Pognana, off the eastern shore of the south-western branch of the lake. Seeking help, they met local policeman Emilio Rusconi and Amleto Morandotti, a convalescing soldier from the 42nd Genoa Infantry Regiment, and decided to take a rowing boat out to the mysterious parachutist. Another local, Domenico Taroni, also joined the group.

Given the method of transport used, it took some time to make contact with the target, but they were aided by the full moon. Tension grew on both sides. Mallaby heard the sound of hostile voices and saw the flash of torchlights; gunshots followed. Several minutes later, the British agent was intercepted in the middle of the lake around Pognana. From the rowing boat came a shout to halt.

From his dinghy Mallaby replied, 'Friends!' Cunningly trying to reverse roles, the best form of defence being attack, he asked with increasing insistence bordering on arrogance if those cautiously approaching him were fishermen.

The rowing boat came nearer, and when he was ordered to put his hands up, Mallaby dawdled, managing to drop the knife he had tied to his wrist into the water. He was soon surrounded by other boats and captured. As he was hoisted on board, Mallaby claimed that he was injured, and was offered a cigarette. Agent Olaf had been captured before his mission had begun.

There are two possible reasons why Mallaby's drop into Italy and the massive bombing raids in the area conspired to produce this negative result. The first is that there was a clear lack of coordination between SOE and the RAF, either deliberate, for reasons of mutual secrecy, or accidental, through having failed to identify a need for it. The second is that it was thought that both the plane and Mallaby were less likely to be spotted and intercepted in the confusion resulting from a period of devastating air raids in the vicinity.

The source materials from this period lean towards the former explanation: the area planned for the water landing was (and remains to this day) sparsely populated.[54]

Brought to shore, Mallaby immediately began to improvise, diverging from his instructions. He initially claimed to be an Italian aviator who had jumped out of a Caproni plane on its way from Taliedo airport, located a few dozen kilometres from Como.

This explanation was plausible but could only be short lived given the relative ease with which it could be disproved. It indicates that Mallaby was working out a definitive strategy, evaluating the situation and perhaps hoping to be able to escape in some way.

However, Mallaby's inflatable dinghy, with its highly visible English writing, immediately destroyed this explanation. The atmosphere changed abruptly, and the Italians began to use menacing sarcasm.

By now it was almost dawn, and when the group reached the shore the captured agent was immediately surrounded by steadily increasing crowds of people.

Anna Maria Rusconi, daughter of the policeman Emilio, clearly remembers seeing Mallaby at the small dock next to the current Fioroni hotel-restaurant, still wearing his camouflage floatation suit and with a small box tied to his leg.[55]

The captured and his captors were escorted to the Comune (town hall), under the surveillance of soldiers and Guardia di Finanza. The commander of the Como Carabinieri arrived and Mallaby's interrogation began. Although agent Olaf's fake Italian identity had already been discounted, Mallaby continued to claim to be a Caproni test pilot who had crashed into the lake.

In the course of the interrogation, a dark comedic moment ensued when Mallaby was asked to empty his pockets, and an innocuous tin of rations was mistaken for a bomb.

An examination of everything else Olaf was carrying proved to be highly compromising. The following items were found immediately: the quartz oscillators inside the small box tied to Mallaby's leg; 113,000 lire (less than the inventoried amount); the false documents; spare parts for the radio; and the negatives of the cryptographic codes, carefully hidden inside the book *Italia mia* by Giovanni Papini.

It was immediately understood that the captured parachutist was a precious find, and the deployment of forces increased. Faced with this situation, agent Olaf adhered to the number one rule of a captured special agent whose life is on the line: buy time.

His first interrogation did not last long, and Mallaby was quickly placed in a cell, before being interrogated again shortly afterwards by an officer from a Bersaglieri regiment who acted with greater incisiveness, and physicality. When the first blows started to land, Mallaby confessed his British identity.

Mallaby immediately understood that his capture had been a random event, and, consequently, that his interlocutors had no idea of the aims of his mission, nor of his destination, contacts and reference points on Italian soil. In order to avoid bringing down Italian checks and raids in the area, he improvised his story with his interrogators, changing only his surname and claiming to be Richard Norris, a second lieutenant in the British Army serving with 2nd Battalion, the Parachute Regiment. He claimed he was part of a special unit, on a solo mission aimed at informing the Italians that they would be treated well by the Allies when they completed their conquest of the whole of Italian national territory.

Malcom Tudor, author of *SOE in Italy: The Real Story*, asserts that Mallaby's immediate capture was the consequence of a mission 'compromised from the outset due to the Fascist infiltration of SOE's Bern branch'. This theory is a commonly held one and unfortunately has been carelessly taken up by other authors with a summary, tangential interest in Operation *Neck*.[56] The situation at the time of Mallaby's capture, however, was quite different.

For the sake of context, it should be recalled that the widespread infiltration of SOE's structures overseeing Italian matters was implemented and managed in Switzerland and Italy by the skilled, official systems of SIM, which was not in itself a Fascist institution. Furthermore, in August 1943, fascists had dissolved away in the wake of the fall of the regime on 25 July.

Mallaby began his mission in the midst of the famous '45 days' between Mussolini's defenestration and the disclosure of the Italian surrender. During this period, despite the proclamation of the new prime minister, Pietro Badoglio, that 'The war continues', the attitude that prevailed among the Italian political–military leadership was the will to end the war against the Allies, and the desire to avoid starting one with the Germans.[57]

Despite Italian counterespionage's almost total infiltration, and the supporting role played in Operation *Neck* by agent 900 and those around him, Dick Mallaby's capture was not a direct consequence of this.[58]

The involvement of agent 900 in the mission (as a contact for Mallaby, and keeper of the radio) does not constitute proof that SIM itself was aware of SOE's operational details. The fact that, in its Italian activities, SOE made use of a false anti-fascist network run by Italian counterespionage assets does not necessarily mean the Italians were able to intercept all the communications of the most secretive, well-protected element of the British armed forces.

Indeed, there is no evidence from any source to indicate that the Italians had even the most superficial knowledge of the fine details of Operation *Neck*.

The documents confirm that the Italian knowledge regarding the mission was far from complete. The official SOE report on Operation *Neck* states that Mallaby was to make himself available to agent 900 'who had been advised to wait for him' – *only* 'advised to wait for him'.

Even the unwary McCaffery, as the relevant papers make clear, had only alerted agents 900 and Galea that 'One of our colleagues – a reliable and technically competent friend – could visit you on Saturday 14th or the following days. His name is Tito [Mallaby's codename for the Italians, of course also known by SOE] ... Do all you can to look after him ... Give him the green suitcase we sent a few months ago.'

The above clearly does not contain any specific details.

In fact the secret messages sent between the various SOE offices in the first days of August reveal the constant worry (shared by Dick Mallaby himself) about guaranteeing safe addresses and back-up ones, without revealing the exact place of arrival to agents 1400 and 900.[59]

Considering, moreover, that agent 1400 was waiting for Olaf in Como and agent 900 in Milan (thanks to instructions given them by McCaffery), it is easy to infer (and Italian documents confirm this issue) that in both these areas vigilance was heightened.

Even the events both during and after Mallaby's capture in Carate Urio show that there was no detailed awareness, and allow us to conclude that what took place did so purely by chance. If the Italians had been aware of all the relevant details of Operation *Neck*, agent Olaf would certainly not have been captured by a local policeman, a convalescing soldier, a member of the rural guard and two passers-by.

Moreover, if Mallaby's capture had been the result of a counterespionage operation, the confidential reports drafted in the immediacy of his seizure (thankfully preserved) would see those responsible for the operation claiming the success as their own, and perhaps even informing the Germans. On the contrary, the relevant documents inform us that Mallaby was captured through a fortuitous sequence of events. In fact, in many ways it would have been more profitable for Italian counterespionage to follow Mallaby discreetly, rather than catch him immediately.

For the Italians, it was thus just a matter of (apparent) good fortune.

The improvised intervention of citizens and local police forces clearly ruined the potential for a complex strategy that could have made the brilliant infiltration operation carried out by the Italians even more effective and sensational.

An official SOE report, written some time after the events, partly explains the reasons why Lake Como was anything but deserted that night. It highlights, in an exaggerated manner, that after the air-raid sirens had gone off, 'thousands of frightened citizens fleeing from Milan' were camped on the shores of the lake, ironically concluding: 'never had an SOE agent been received by such a large and unfortunate reception committee'.[60] It makes no mention of SIM or its agents.

Mallaby's private memoirs clear up this matter definitively:

> In point of fact, the Italian espionage and counterespionage organization SIM had previously managed to plant an agent inside our organization in Switzerland. This agent was in fact almost entirely responsible for the development of the Italian 'resistance movement' and for passing information on to the Allies, naturally false. I learned all this later and also that I had been expcted by SIM, who hoped to use me, without my knowing, to pass further information of dubious nature back to our HQ. However as things stood, they were not sure as to whether I was the expected wireless operator and hence the continued gruelling [sic].

A final demonstration comes from the fact that it took a few days for the highly efficient SIM men – who had benefitted from reading the direct communications to agents 900 and Galea – to conclude that Tito was the paratrooper captured in Carate Urio (i.e. Mallaby).

To sum up: Mallaby's capture in Carate Urio had not been planned, but his arrival in Italy was known and SIM's plans were to control and manipulate him, not capture him.

Thus, his capture had ruined the plans made by both SIM (definitively) and SOE (temporarily).

In all this, despite Mallaby's capture, the Italian organization that had infiltrated Bern continued to enjoy the full and enduring trust, and even the concerns of SOE's personnel.

Despite the disastrous start to *Neck*, agent 900 allowed himself to indicate that he had arranged safe houses between Como, Genoa and Bari. This did not cause suspicion, only thoughtful interest.

On 21 August, Bern asked in an apparently cynical way, but actually naive:

> did agent 1400 not realize implications of Olaf's arrest for him, and is he not perturbed for his own safety?
>
> We have done anything to alter this and I think it may be as well better not to communicate anything further to 900 beyond what we are ourselves telling him today, namely that the friend he was expecting has had a grave misfortune and will not now arrive.[61]

Mallaby was handed over to the Italian counterespionage service, and on the morning of 14 August 1943 he was transferred to its Milan office together with all his equipment. There, during the course of a further interrogation, something unexpected happened. Agent Olaf was shown two pieces of US Army parachute equipment. Given the simultaneous discovery of this equipment, the Italians assumed that Mallaby had not parachuted in alone.[62]

Instead of remaining in the custody of Italian counterespionage, Mallaby was transferred to San Vittore Prison – most likely in an effort to extract confidential information from him using a SIM employee posing as a cellmate.

Whilst at San Vittore, further interrogations took place. Mallaby maintained the latest version of his story, and, above all, tried to sustain his captors' interest in him, in order to keep the firing squad at bay.

The official version of what happened to agent Olaf after his capture is in a British report, compiled almost a year after the events, on 1 August 1944, entitled 'The Mallaby Case'.[63]

This document is particularly important, being based on copies and translations of the secret reports drawn up a year earlier by the Italian officials. Clearly, this material had become available to the British as a consequence of the contacts established with the Italian Supreme Command and SIM following the September 1943 surrender and the declaration of war by the Italian 'Kingdom of the South' against Germany on 13 October 1943.[64]

Reading these Italian reports a year after the events, SOE's leadership was pleased with the way Mallaby handled his interrogations ('It seems that he thought the best version was the easiest') and with the very fortuitous and unforseen role he took on.[65]

With regard to the Italian side of things, the documents reveal not only efficiency and good organization, but also determination, in contrast to common perceptions of the morale of the Italian forces and population in the summer of 1943. Without delay, the Ufficio Protezione Impianti e Difesa Antiparacadutisti (UPIDA – Office for the Protection of Infrastucture and Anti-Parachute Defence) of the General Staff of the Italian Royal Army dispatched a recording on 14 August 1943, and subsequently, on 16 August, a memorandum and detailed reports to the Chief of Staff of the Army and to SIM. Besides documenting the step-by-step process of, and those involved in, Mallaby's capture, the message notes the engagement of 'all anti-parachute assets recently activated in the area'. In contrast to what had been assumed by the British, the Italians had intensified their vigilance, notably in Mallaby's landing area.

The inventory of objects found on Mallaby drawn up by the Italian investigators, accompanied by the customary mugshot, is much more detailed than all the reports compiled in the previous months by SOE. In addition to the ('perfectly falsified') documents, we learn of the discovery of a sweater that 'could be used as a chemical reagent if placed in acid', Giovanni Papini's *Italia mia* book (which, between pages 185 and 188, held the negatives containing the cryptographic codes), and a newspaper dated 29 June.

The Italians also listed a water purification compound, a small pot of boric vaseline (with a camera film inside) and an antenna (disguised as a clothes line). They also tried, unsuccessfully, to iron the other pages in the Papini book to see if any further codes could be revealed, but concluded that this would only be possible using a specific chemical reagent.

The report also stated that the 'fake' tube of 'Ideal' toothpaste and the toothbrush could contain small pieces of paper with codes written on them. Mallaby himself (with an ulterior motive, one assumes) had indicated that inside the tube of toothpaste there were other negatives containing codes and inside the shaving brush a quartz crystal. The person compiling the inventory pointed out that there was no razor in the razor box.

The first report, signed by Major-General Ruggero of the Comando Difesa Territoriale di Milano (Milan Territorial Defence Command), concluded by highlighting the voluntary civilian participation in Mallaby's capture and proposed that the five key figures involved be awarded a 'large cash prize' (with Borghi and Abate receiving the lion's share). No prize money was paid, however.

A further Italian report, dated 26 August 1943, provided the results of a thorough investigation, reporting that the captured parachutist was not called Richard Norris, but Richard Mallaby; that he was born to an Italian mother (confusing Mallaby's birth mother with his stepmother); that he jumped alone from a Halifax flown by six crew; and that his mission was to carry out radio-telegraphy activities, having replaced an Italian who had refused to take part in the mission at the last minute – the last element a clear and clever attempt by Mallaby to explain his lack of knowledge of the mission's details.

The most important part of the report relates to his telegraphic activities. Pointing out that Mallaby was carrying cryptographic codes, the report indicated that he was to have used a radio based in Milan and, according to the author of the report's view, the radio was the one that had been found (along with two pieces of paper containing the necessary codes, disguised as poetry) some time before in the Giussago area.

According to this document, Mallaby claimed that he had refused to be parachuted into Italy to carry out sabotage activities and was consequently transferred to North Africa to carry out propaganda work. He was then assigned a new mission of landing in Italy to carry out wireless work in unison with other agents, whom he would meet once in situ, after having recovered a previously delivered radio.

Italian documents held in the British archives hold a further secret report dated 5 September 1943. In this, it is explained that Richard Mallaby was the 'son of Cecil and of the deceased Mary Schofield', demonstrating that in a short space of time the Italian intelligence system had carried out effective investigative work, arriving at a precise identification (which included the place and date of his birth) and correcting his mother's particulars.[66]

The unveiling of Mallaby's true identity was certainly not the result of a breach of SOE's communication systems, nor of spying (as is sometimes inaccurately stated in certain published works), but was due to the diligent work of the Italians. In addition to monitoring the movements of British citizens resident in Italy, the Italian security services gathered names, photographs and personal data of British, British-Italian, and Italo-British citizens. By exploiting this precautionary work, they were quickly able to determine Mallaby's real identity and more.

The report summarized Mallaby's statements and the investigators' deductions, and ended by stating that further investigative activities would be undertaken 'by the Rome CS [counterespionage], to whom Mallaby was handed over together with the objects seized on his person'. Also, further investigations aimed at capturing the other elements present in Italy – especially those responsible for the ground light signals – had not met with success despite mobile checkpoints being set up in the border area between Varese and Como, partly as a result of the large number of displaced people present.

Two critical points emerge from the study of all these documents. Firstly, Mallaby revealed numerous details about his equipment; and secondly, his Italian inquisitors were able to quickly confirm his true identity and his family details despite the limited technology of the time.

In his interrogation Mallaby mixed together both true and false elements; thus employing an impromptu tactic (by instinct, or by training), he dripped confessional details that could appear important, but actually weren't and did not compromise either himself or SOE's activities, mainly in order to nurture the idea that he would be more useful alive than dead, avoiding the potential brutality of his captors.

It was thus a collaboration in appearance only, which conversely also allowed him the opportunity to carry out some useful disinformation work; it is possible that he was also seeking to ingratiate himself with his Italians captors, so that he might be allowed to transmit a wireless message.

Despite the flurry of reports, SIM's secret daily bulletins did not mention Dick Mallaby's capture, and what was omitted from the Italian intelligence services' confidential bulletins was instead splashed all over the front pages.

This was not fortuitous of course, but a conscious decision to involve the media.

We can only assume that this was not done for propaganda reasons, but for some subtle, hidden diplomatic/espionage purpose, which was certainly not connected to the tumultuous events that soon followed.

The front page of the Milanese daily *La Sera–Il Secolo*, published on Wednesday 18 August 1943, heralded the capture of the British agent with the headline: 'The Man who Fell from the Skies was Betrayed by Moonlight'.

Despite its imaginative style, the article reveals numerous significant details. It relates the disastrous beginning of Operation *Neck* and confirms that a fairly precise identification of Mallaby had been achieved in a short period of time.

This article could not have been published without the consent of the relevant authorities, for at this time, as far as freedom of the press and public order were concerned, Badoglio's first government had issued even more draconian diktats than those established in the previous 21 years under Mussolini.

However, publicizing Mallaby's capture made a further contribution to preserving his life: the article in the Italian newspaper helped spread the news more widely and more quickly. The article also alleged that Mallaby had adopted a surly tone with his captors, despite his desperate circumstances. This is something which McCaffery commented on in his unpublished memoirs ('No Pipes or Drums'), surprisingly stating that it appeared 'absolutely incredible that in such a desperate situation anyone could afford the luxury of arrogance, but an enemy newspaper could hardly have invented such a detail'.[67]

For the time being, Dick Mallaby had managed to avoid the customary fate of a captured, non-uniformed agent – namely the death sentence. This was chiefly because the Italian security services were extremely interested in him and his equipment, and hoped to extract further useful information, or use him to continue to spin their web of disinformation.

What did the British know about the immediate failure of *Neck* and the fate of its protagonist? In the days immediately following, some communications were sent (not always in a coordinated manner) which only briefly dealt with the negative outcome.

On 14 August 1943, Massingham had announced the beginning of the operation, noting that agent Olaf had departed in a keyed-up and confident state. The following day, SOE's Italian Department in London had summarized all the details of Operation *Neck*, with the umpteenth listing of Mallaby's equipment (which partly differed from previous ones).

On the 17th, a double message was sent from Bern to Massingham stating that agent 1400 had arranged everything in Como and should have escorted Mallaby from agent 900's care to Milan, although there was still no news of any developments.[68]

The bad news, however, began to spread that very day.

An encrypted message from London pointed out that various sources had stated that several parachutists had been detained near Como. According to the author of the message, the greatest concern for SOE's leadership was the technical equipment that Mallaby was carrying.

This generated panic in Bern. The Swiss office pointed out that the local press had learned from Italian sources of several important arrests, with a few fanciful details added, including the presence of women and Italians among the captured. It was feared that, under torture, Mallaby had revealed details known to him of the organization in Italy.

In the following days, London, with quite mystifying arguments, made it known to Bern that the news did not trouble the heads of SOE, in part because what was communicated did not fit with agent Olaf, who in any case was not carrying any documents that could compromise others. Their subsequent recommendation was: 'do nothing which may embroil anybody'. In a separate message, it was pointed out that the pilot of the plane from which Mallaby had jumped reported that the villages around Lake Como were not in blackout conditions, which evidently had contributed to the anxiety felt by those in charge of the mission.

On 19 August, Massingham also reassured all those involved, asserting that precautionary measures had been put in place, and that until their point of meeting, the British agent and the Italian ones operated in watertight compartments. The conclusion was that agent Olaf would not be able to 'compromise our groups'.[69]

The greatest concern related to the fear of such compromise and not the fate of Dick Mallaby himself.

On 20 August, in a message sent at 11.17pm and based on information received from Bern, Dick Mallaby's capture was divulged.[70]

A series of messages sent the following day from London to Massingham laid out the official sequence of events. Firstly they expressed satisfaction for the beginning of the mission, secondly best wishes for a successful outcome, but finally came the official news about the capture of the mission's central player. Of course this news had been made public in the *La Sera–Il Secolo* article three days earlier, but the message gave further details.

Agent 1400 had reported that, on account of the full moon, Mallaby had been spotted as soon as he exited the plane, was captured immediately and was awaiting trial in a military court; secondly, he also reported that he had already made significant attempts 'via the Major' to contact Mallaby and to make plans for his escape; thirdly, this pivotal agent stated that two other parachutists had been arrested, too.

According to a coded message sent on the 21st, agent 1400 had:

1 asked for confirmation about the arrival in Como of 23 General Staff officers, to attack them;
2 praised the accuracy of the bombing of Milan (adding it was a pity that they had ceased and allowed the Italians to catch their breath), and recommended continuous actions against smaller, specific objectives rather than large-scale raids;
3 with his group, claimed to have sabotaged telephone lines in Verona, Bolzano and Brenner

and slashed a large number of military vehicle tyres in Dongo.

A subsequent message dated 23 August adds a further, subtle, one-worded detail: that '1400 is working through the *Carabinieri* Major'.[71]

Having ascertained that Mallaby was indeed alive and in captivity, frantic efforts were initiated (chiefly via secret diplomatic channels) to save his life and obtain his release. Yet even before this, SOE attempted to make contact with their precious agent Olaf.

Cecil Roseberry, head of Department J, reported that he was able to obtain confidential information about the fate of agent Olaf and his place of detention and even let him know that there were plans to get him out of prison. Such information, however, like all that flowing from Italy, was obviously manipulated, and originated from the group of Italian agents who had infiltrated SOE Bern's network.

Mallaby's unpublished memoirs confirm the above events, stating that, after a few days in prison in Milan, another prisoner had informed him in a typically sibylline prisoner-to-prisoner way that, at the earliest possible opportunity, he would receive some help 'from his friends'. Having received this comforting reassurance, Mallaby faced further danger when, following another air raid on Milan, an unexploded bomb landed near his cell. Mallaby was then transferred, together with several petty criminals, to Como's San Donnino Prison. According to Mallaby's secret diary, 'there followed daily interrogations and each day I had to find some different sort of story to tell'. British declassified documents reveal the doubts and hesitations over how to end Mallaby's imprisonment, in part due to the need to avoid revealing too many details about the mission, even to other British service organizations.

A dispatch from Massingham dated 22 August suggested a few altentaive actions: activating agent Partito (who would need to be accompanied by a radio operator); or 'intervening' during Mallaby's trial (which according to the information available would be a rapid process) to get an acquittal, or a prisoner exchange, negotiated via the Vatican.[72]

Meanwhile, communications between the parties involved in Operation *Neck* were attempting to pinpoint the reasons for its immediate failure.[73] A lengthy Most Secret dispatch dated 25 August 1943, while acknowledging that not all the details were available, noted that the aviation side to the operation went without a hitch, recalling that four previous *matériel* drops had been made around the Italian lakes without any Italians noticing, while the single parachute to which Mallaby was attached had apparently been spotted immediately.[74]

A message dated 27 August gave news of the capture of two other parachutists (a radio operator and a 'guide') who had jumped on the night of 12/13 August. It also noted that the increased Italian vigilance might have been due to the extensive parachute activity that had taken place during the previous two full moons. According to an official SOE memorandum dated 24 August, the reasons for the presence of so many people on the shores of Lake Como in the middle of the night 'could not be explained'. It even considered a leak within SOE as a cause, or the improved reaction capabilities of the Italians (due to the fact that the noises British aircraft made were clearly distinguishable and, therefore, could trigger a state of alert when recognized).

Such conclusions attest to SOE's poor analytical skills, which mirrors the lack of wisdom of those who had failed to ask the RAF about any missions planned in the area before deciding Neck's launch date – or who even thought that such missions might actually be of benefit to Mallaby's. Moreover, it should not be forgotten that such statements, which would be seen by the upper levels of Allied military and political leadership, were aimed at reducing both the rightful apportioning of blame and internal responsibility for what happened.

The memorandum's author concluded by suggesting the following: firstly, avoid drops during full moons (in contrast to current practice); secondly, change aircraft trajectory and altitude before, during and after drops.[75]

While those frantic messages between London, Bern and Algiers were summarizing the details of *Neck* and its immediate failure, two dispatches, sent on 25 and 27 August 1943, reported that an OSS agent had been made aware of Mallaby's capture (presumably via McCaffery's office). Although the affair had not created excessive problems, reading between the lines the annoyance generated by the circulation of this embarrassing episode is clear. It was ordered to investigate, so as to prevent such things from happening again, 'as future cases of this kind may cause serious breach of security'.[76]

For Dick Mallaby it was time for a radical change. His salvation and the radical transformation of his status were not far off. Any doubts, or secret plans, harboured by the Italian security services were soon to combine with the achievements of a separate group of Italians, hundreds of kilometres away in Portugal, involved in another top-secret mission, led by Brigadier-General Giuseppe Castellano.

4

From Disaster to Triumph

Mallaby, the Armistice and the Allied
Invasion, August–September 1943

(Or: how Mallaby is rescued from capture to become the
person in charge of communications regarding the Italian
surrender to the Allies, and takes part in the flight of
King Vittorio Emanuele II and Marshal Pietro Badoglio
from Rome.)

> Wars can be won or lost. What matters most,
> when things go wrong, is to lose with dignity.
> However, I fear that our country will not
> be able to overcome the storm and face defeat
> with dignity.
>
> Giuseppe Cordero Lanza di Montezemolo
> (1901–44)

Since Italy's entry into the war, Italians anti-fascist
and even fascist had made a range of somewhat
fanciful, unstrategic approaches towards Great Britain
in an effort to reach a separate peace. The Italian
will to negotiate a final agreement became clearer

and was more intensely felt after the defenestration of Mussolini.[1]

Brigadier-General Giuseppe Castellano was tasked with conducting secret peace negotiations with the Allies – without Italy's allies knowing anything about this. The sole aim of Italy's new government was to dissolve their alliance with the Germans in the simplest and least harmful way, without getting into a fight with them.

Castellano spoke no English, and so he was supported in this mission by an Italian Ministry of Foreign Affairs civil servant, Franco Montanari, a half-American Harvard graduate who was distantly related to Marshal Badoglio.[2]

Castellano was supposed to gather information on the Allies' intentions and the military situation, and to seek Allied guarantees of military help in withdrawing Italy from the Axis. But even he lacked the appropriate credentials for negotiating with the Allied Command because of the fear that he might be intercepted by the Germans.[3]

Thus, Montanari and Castellano's Iberian mission was kept hidden not only from most of the Italian ruling executive, but also from the vast majority of Italy's military leadership (as well as the secret services). It was also flawed in other basic ways: the instructions given were vague and the presumed significant bargaining power was in truth non-existent.

Using a false identity ('Commendator Raimondi'), Castellano left Rome by train with Montanari on the evening of 12 August, and reached Madrid three days later, where he presented himself to the British Ambassador Sir Samuel Hoare. Castellano presented himself just with a note written by Francis D'Arcy Godolphin Osborne, Britain's Minister to the Vatican, and declared the aims of his secret mission to Hoare, who immediately informed London.

The Italian duo then travelled on to Lisbon, arriving on the evening of the 16th.

There Castellano and Montanari held a preliminary meeting on 17 August with the British ambassador to Portugal, Ronald Campbell. Two days later, at 10.30pm, Castellano began talks with several top Allied envoys: the American General Walter Bedell Smith (Chief of Staff at Allied Force HQ), George Kennan (US chargé d'affaires in Lisbon) and Kenneth Strong (Assistant Chief of Staff for Intelligence at Allied Force HQ). The Allied envoys were dressed in civilian clothes to maintain absolute secrecy.

The secret meeting ended at 7am on 20 August.[4]

Whether out of a desire to play a leading role, or through projecting his own opinions onto the entire Italian armed forces and people, or just as part of a hasty, ill-conceived tactic, Castellano overstepped his mission boundaries and the vague instructions given to him by wrongly informing the Allies that the Italians wanted to fight the Germans.[5]

In the end, Castellano failed in the difficult undertaking of securing an honourable exit from the war for the Kingdom of Italy. But not through his fault alone: in point 10 of Ambassador Campbell's report on the meeting sent to the Foreign Office, it was recorded that 'General Smith's handling of the shrewd Sicilian general was masterful' – perhaps aided by the minor historical detail of the usually abstemious Castellano partaking of several rounds of whiskey-based drinks.

Confusingly, another Italian general became involved. The leadership in Rome had become alarmed by the lack of contact from Castellano and so dispatched Brigadier-General Giacomo Zanussi, accompanied by an interpreter, Lieutenant Mario Lanza, and the British General Carton De Wiart – a prisoner of war in Italy – to vouch for him.

On 25 August, British ambassador Sir Ronald Campbell handed Zanussi the terms of what was known as the 'Long Armistice' in error. This document featured many more clauses, which were significantly harsher and outlined the political and economic conditions of surrender, of which Castellano (consignee of the 'Short Armistice') was totally ignorant.

Zanussi was supposed to come back to Italy. But when Eisenhower was informed that the Italian general had been given the Long Armistice, he angrily ordered Zanussi's flight to be diverted to Algiers in order to prevent the Italian leadership from discovering its terms, for fear of the Italians baulking at the drastic clauses and withdrawing entirely from the armistice negotiations. Zanussi was effectively imprisoned, albeit comfortably, for a few days at Massingham, which was enough time for the Italian leadership to confirm acceptance of the surrender.

Zanussi finally returned to Rome on 31 August. He was in the company of Castellano, who told him that he knew what was in the document containing the additional clauses of the Long Armistice given to Zanussi. At this point, Zanussi became convinced that the document was not particularly important, and once in Rome delivered it without indicating its priority.

To add to this, the Allies made inaccurate assumptions regarding the will and the intentions of the Italian people and those of the German Army.

To both sides, it seemed that the odds were stacked against a positive outcome. And it turned out that way. Italy firstly unconditionally surrendered and then split into two parts: one part fighting with the Allies against the Germans, and the other part fighting with the Germans against the Allies.

That led to a civil war, the effects of which linger into the 21st century.

In the short term it meant that the Allies conquered the Italian peninsula very slowly, and if this distracted the Germans from their other fronts, it also led to a series of bellicose managerial, operational and political complications that stretched beyond April 1945.

However, the meeting between Giuseppe Castellano and Eisenhower's staff led to unexpected developments for Mallaby's Operation *Neck*, his salvation, and his personal involvement in the major events that followed.

A message from the 23 August records the decisive turning point in the negotiations for the Italian capitulation and also in Mallaby's destiny, acknowledging a previous dispatch sent on the 'Lisbon' question.[6]

———

The handling of communications between Rome and Allied HQ in Algiers provided a considerable challenge, and in fact was the first operational problem that the Allies, in coordination with the Italians, were required to face up to.

Efforts had been made in the previous weeks to establish a secret radio link with the Italian leadership, but only during the Combined Chiefs First Quebec Conference (codenamed 'Quadrant': 17–24 August 1943) was it decided that the matter was a top priority.

So Eisenhower was ordered on the morning of 18 August to send two officers to Lisbon for the meeting with Castellano (there were actually three: Bedell Smith, Kennan and Kenneth Strong) and to establish a wireless link with Italy. He passed this task to Harold MacMillan, who actioned Douglas Dodds-Parker at Massingham. It was decided that a brand new, double transposed code plan would be used. Roseberry rushed after hours and without permission from the relevant office to obtain the necessary code plan.

When the clerk asked if authorization had been given and what name had been assigned to the plan, Roseberry, bluffing and perhaps with tongue in cheek, reported that the name was 'Monkey'. This also generated the historic codename of the radio station that Mallaby would use in a few days' time.

Roseberry was unable to board the plane for Lisbon on the 18th, and on the 19th the flight was cancelled. Finally, on the night of the 20th, he managed to make it to the Portuguese capital, arriving there early the following morning.

The official account of the meeting in Lisbon that began on the evening of 19 August noted that Castellano was to be given a radio, a cypher and full instructions for their use, and, on his return to Italy, 'he would take steps to recruit Italian operators who could use the appliance'.[7] Communicating quickly and in secret was essential, firstly because, on the basis of the agreements reached between Castellano and the Allied representatives, by midnight on 30 August 1943 the Italians had to communicate a response to the surrender proposals and their intention to continue talks.

So, just a few hours before Roseberry's arrival in Lisbon, the need of an effective and secure transmission system from Italy had become top priority for the Allies *alongside* the urgent necessity of a skilled operator fully able and English-Italian speaking. And just a few hours before, Roseberry received the official confirmation that Mallaby had been captured, but was still alive. Roseberry realized that Dick Mallaby's chances of survival were increasing, but also that his agent could become the top player in the crucial business that had arisen in Lisbon.

The importance of the solution that Mallaby offered can also be inferred from the fact that, in the light of the events that ensued, many in the Allied camp attempted to claim credit for it.

Kenneth Strong, who was personally present at the meetings with Castellano in Lisbon, recalled:

We gave a radio set to the Italians and reminded Castellano that Dick Mallaby, a member of Special Operations Executive recently captured by the Italians, was in prison in Milan … We suggested they should free him and make use of his expert signal knowledge.[8]

Had Roseberry been unable to reach Lisbon in time, the following alternative options were foreseen: parachute drop or infiltration of wireless operator and equipment; arrival in Rome of an SOE wireless operator; use of couriers; instructions to Castellano himself regarding the use of codes and radio; and having the wireless operators Carlo Montelli and Vincenzo Bruzzoni (two Italian SOE collaborators) shadow Castellano, with due guarantees given.

Bedell Smith, Strong and Kennan had by now left, and Roseberry found himself in Lisbon in blissful solitude to manage the situation.

Castellano, even after the meeting, was unaware of the exact details relating to communications, and knew only that he would receive a radio and a cypher before his departure.

Roseberry finally met with Montanari on the evening of the 21st, before the departure of the Italian duo.[9] The Italian version of events is provided in the memoirs of Brigadier-General Castellano:

All communications will be made in Italian ... Montanari, sent by me to the British Embassy, had received the radio, in an elegant leather suitcase, the cypher and the instructions ... The cypher key had to be deduced from a phrase that was known to radio station operators. It was agreed that this sentence was to be taken from an Italian book, one copy of which was sent to Algiers, one to London and a third to Rome. In Lisbon, Montanari found three copies of the book *L'omnibus del corso*, by Sanminiatelli. At the British Embassy he was approached by a gentleman who said he was a major in the British Army, who asked him to bring about, as soon as he reached Italy, the release of the parachutist Lieutenant Malloby [sic] who had been captured by us few days before. The latter knew perfectly how to use the radio apparatus we took to Italy.[10]

Apart from the spelling error in Mallaby's surname, Castellano confirmed that Roseberry met only Montanari at the British Embassy. He also stated that Roseberry's intervention was both unofficial and at the last minute, perfect SOE style.[11]

According to British reports, Roseberry met Montanari *and* Castellano, showing them the portable radio, codes and other required items, and emphasized that the preference was not to use Italian equipment, for obvious reasons of uniformity between the transmitting and receiving stations, and security. Roseberry stressed the need to follow the correct anti-interception procedures and to adhere to the prescribed transmission schedules with maximum precision too.

At this point the two Italians, who 'were daunted by these difficulties', asked how they might be resolved, admitting that they had no radio operator available who could perform these tasks in the manner required.

Roseberry evidently enjoyed pointing out the existence of an English agent who had parachuted into Italy for this kind of mission, telling Montanari and Castellano that although Mallaby was an English national, he had been born in Italy, a nation he loved and for which he was ready to risk his life in the struggle against Fascism. He also stressed that there should be no delays, given the agent's predicament.

The Italians raised the issue of how to convince the British agent to collaborate with them. In order to persuade Mallaby that he was not about to fall into a trap, information was provided that only agent Olaf and Massingham personnel could know, and some sentences containing elements that only Roseberry could have added and which Mallaby had also been trained to use if forced to communicate under duress.

The next question was: 'Where is he now?'

The answer was: 'In prison, in Como.'

Roseberry had achieved all of his aims: the Italians and Allies got not only the desired mean of communication, but also the right man to operate it.

Agent Olaf's status changed in an instant, immediately and dramatically, even if the implementation of this radical change was dangerously complicated.

Castellano and Montanari boarded their train to Italy on 23 August 1943, bearing the red-hot surrender documents, the B2 radio in its 'elegant leather suitcase', and the cypher based on Bino Sanminiatelli's book *L'omnibus del corso*, 'the only one which Montanari had managed to find three copies of, after a laborious search through all of Lisbon's bookstores'.[12]

The transposition of the Monkey code would have been based only on this book, so the other two copies were personally taken back to London by Roseberry. The copy intended for Algiers was then entrusted to the chosen courier, Major Harold Meakin, who left London on 24 August: he arrived at his destination at 6.00pm on 28 August. It was just in time, because the following day, messages started coming from a new station in Rome.

According to what had been agreed, as soon as Castellano arrived in Italy, he was to order Mallaby's transfer to Rome.

Phase one of the operation may have passed off successfully, but the subsequent phases were even more complicated and far more risky.

Castellano's mission probably saved Dick Mallaby's life, but most of all, if Mallaby had been unavailable, the difficulties in communications and in the negotiations between the Italians and the Allies would have been very marked indeed.

Then there were the security problems concerning communications, which worried SOE greatly.

The British feared that Mallaby had been tortured, or had revealed details in good faith, believing that he no longer needed his codes and, therefore, this could do no harm, given that the enemy did not know the verification and security codes.

In practical terms, this impasse was not unimportant, as it was impossible to be sure that Mallaby could operate using a complete and secure code system, in spite of what he would be provided by Castellano.

In Cairo, a code system based on Papini's book (which was found on Mallaby at the time of his capture) had been drawn up; from this, phrases could be extracted for his cross-coding operations. In Massingham Mallaby had been made to memorize a poem, to be used if, for any reason, the codes extracted from the novel were unusable. In Massingham fear was that the codes

extracted from the novel had ended up in Lake Como
– which, on the one hand, was good news (compared
with their discovery by the Italians), but, on the other,
represented an operational problem. In this promising,
but very complicated, situation began one of SOE's
most important operations, which, beyond its clear and
positive outcomes, the Baker Street Irregulars would
have enjoyed for the priority and exclusivity it was
granted over its British and US service competitors.
While the exclusion of the Italian intelligence services
(driven by Castellano) brought only unnecessary
complications and delays, excluding the British and
American secret services ensured maximum satisfaction
and boosted the confidence of SOE's personnel at a
critical moment for the executive.[13]

Operationally, despite the happy coincidence of
Mallaby's presence in Italy, there were significant
security issues regarding the planned transmissions
between Rome and Algiers.

Even if they were sure that their train would not
be bombed (thanks to specific instructions given to
the Anglo-American Air Forces), would Castellano
and Montanari make it to Italy with their dramatic
consignment without being intercepted by the
Germans? Such fears were well founded and there
were numerous complications involved. For example,
the *Daily Telegraph* had published an article containing
revelations about the arrival in Lisbon of an Italian
mission to negotiate an armistice, thus putting the

Germans in a state of maximum alert – one of the drawbacks of a free press.

The surrender documents were prudently entrusted to the unknowing Italian ambassador to Chile until the train reached Menton. The ambassador was travelling alongside Castellano and Montanari, who kept the radio and the cryptographic materials themselves.[14]

In this atmosphere of exaltation and tension, there was considerable trust in Dick Mallaby's training and 'highly retentive' memory, but, given the importance of the mission and the need for complete confidentiality, it was decided that new codes would be subtly transmitted to him, using the old ones. In order to reassure Olaf that they were not fake, it was decided that the transmissions should contain multiple specific references to his personal life that only he would recognize. Thus Mallaby's personal file was forensically analysed, and all those who knew him in Cairo and Massingham were interrogated without explanation, leading to the acquisition of highly personal information.

In this way, even if the transmission were intercepted, the transcript would only reveal that the new code's keywords corresponded (among other things) to: his mother's maiden name; his father's name; his favourite beer and his first car; his favourite movie, and the actress with whom he would most like to spend a (sleepless) night (for the record, *Metropolis* and Jean Harlow, respectively); and his (rather early) age at the time of his first sexual relationship. Only Dick Mallaby would be able to understand all of these data.

The two radio stations were named Monkey (at Mallaby's end) and Drizzle (at Massingham). The style to be adopted for the messages was to be 'informal and not stereotypical'.[15]

The plan of action was summarised in a message dated 25 August, sent to Massingham by Roseberry, highlighting the following points:

(A) 1400 is doing everything to delay a trial;

(B) if he senses the probability of failure through his major, he will try to carry out a rescue;

(C) General C [Castellano], as soon as he has crossed the border, will telephone Rome signalling that no action should be taken against Olaf until his arrival;

(D) General C will immediately request that Olaf be transferred into his custody, and will use him as an operator;

(E) we have provided General C with various messages that Olaf must recognize as coming only, repeat, only from us, so that he will have no hesitation in accepting them;

(F) one of these messages tells him to use Maraschino Orange.

General C has been told Olaf's real name and rank as well as his links to Italy, but that his loyalty to us is beyond any doubt. He has expressed his admiration for Olaf's courage and also considers that having available a fully reliable operator practising our procedures is the best solution.

From this message, and the others sent during this period, important historical details emerge, relating to the intentions and the evaluations of the two sides following the Lisbon meetings.

The Allies clarified that their operational plans would not be delayed as a result of the meetings in Lisbon. At the same time, the confident belief that the negotiations could continue in Rome was expressed.

According to Roseberry, '[The Italians] left with the fear that any delay on the path ahead or in the decision-making process could make it impossible for them to respond before our main attack was launched. The mission has formed a strong opinion that acceptance [of surrender] is inevitable.'[16]

Thus, Roseberry firstly sent a message hinting at the 'possibility' that transmissions using the Maraschino series codes could be sent the next day, and on 26 August informed Bern in message 3788 that:

1 Steps have been taken for Vatican intervention for exchange of Olaf.

2 Apart from this Olaf may be approached and asked to work a 'B' set. Contact will have with him certain messages which Olaf must recognize could only originate from us but he may despite this be suspicious that he is being asked to act treacherously.

3 If any means can be found of getting a message to Olaf he should be told that this is a genuine approach arranged for him by his friends.

4 We can demand that contact should say who authorized him (Olaf) to act. Contact may only be a cut-out and unable to reply and this should not make Olaf suspicious. If, however, reply is given the answer should be Mr. Roseberry (who fixed this up).[17]

But despite, or perhaps because of, his dramatic coup, Roseberry was the subject of criticism and complaints.

Massingham's leaders protested over the lack and delay of reporting, and Roseberry sent a message from Lisbon dated 23 August, triumphantly declaring that he had managed to get the Olaf option accepted, having described himself to Castellano and Montanari as a friend of Italy. Three days later he signalled Massingham again that, 'for your information, "C" [the British SIS] is furious that we got there before them and might try to sneak in'.[18]

Analysis of the plentiful British documents relating to this key moment reveals further relevant and unprecedented details of the event narrative as it unfolded contortedly in the closing days of August 1943. As a whole, the messages from this period allow us to understand the risks posed by the high level of secrecy, minimal operational coordination, and disjointed timings, the latter resulting from the technical impossibility of communicating in real time between the various offices involved.

Following the meetings with Castellano, it was decided to halt any plans to obtain Mallaby's release, as it was feared that the efforts of SOE's agents in Italy to free agent Olaf could interfere with what had been established in Lisbon.

The danger that the agreements between Castellano and the Allies might be affected was anything but hypothetical, even considering that in reality SOE's so-called network of collaborators in Italy had hidden objectives quite at odds with those of the British, something which was unknown – at least initially – even to Castellano and the Supreme Command.

On 28 August, Bern announced that: a 'trusted Como friend of 1400' named Luciano (agent 1401) had managed to meet Mallaby inside San Donnino Prison, bringing him 'greetings from Pietro', which left agent Olaf 'much impressed'; the escape of the prisoner (disguised as a soldier) could be planned for the following week, and Mallaby would be hidden in the countryside, to await further instructions.

Roseberry's answer, labelled 'most immediate to be marked personal', was lightning fast and skillful: 'Splendid work. Lay everything on *but do not carry into effect until Thursday September 2nd....* For explanation refer to our telegram 3788 para 2' (my emphasis; the telegram referred to is shown on pages 144–45).

The message for Bern was unequivocal: the operation to free Mallaby had to be postponed, since his liberty might be achieved in another way.

Roseberry informed Massingham the following day, tactically altering the details slightly, reporting that:

1 1400 has visited Olaf who is in prison at Como and says he can arrange in a few days to rescue him disguised in uniform and keep him hidden.

2 1400 has been instructed to lay everything on but not to put into effect until Thursday 2nd September.

3 This may jeopardize Olaf's chances but we must take this risk rather than deprive General. C of his services if he decides to use him.

4 Important that we should know without delay any developments so that we can instruct 1400 either to go ahead without waiting or to lay off altogether.[19]

SOE's chiefs found themselves in the tricky position of weighing up opposing risks and benefits in an operational context that further complicated their assessments, leaving aside the fact that they ignored the significant infiltration suffered.

SOE's Italian 'collaborators', SIM and other Italian investigative bodies, Massingham and Bern stations, the Allied leadership and Castellano were all acting at the time not only in different locations, but also with differing, imperfect knowledge and understanding of the events in progress. Moreover, all of them were united (for different reasons) by restrictions in communications. Castellano moreover did not have the slightest idea of SIM infiltration in SOE, and SIM was unaware of Castellano's mission.

If the option set up in Lisbon had concluded within the agreed terms, agent Olaf would be safe and sound and SOE would have notched up a notable success. On the other hand, if, for some reason, this did not happen (should Castellano fail to keep his word, or be ordered to renege), what Roseberry had revealed would have nailed Mallaby to the cross once and for all. The feelings of remorse would have been overwhelming, given that his release seemed to be well underway. Not forgetting the top-secret information revealed to the Italians, who also had a precious radio and cryptographic codes in their hands.

The dilemma was quickly set aside and the riskier, but potentially more profitable, option was chosen. This involved putting Mallaby's neck on the line for the potential of a successful outcome of negotiations for the Italian surrender.

As emphasized by Roseberry's above-cited message of 26 August, SOE was in fierce competition with other British and American intelligence services and secret bodies, both for prestige and the allocation of funds and resources. SOE's leadership, seizing the opportunity presented, was thus forced to choose between saving its agent's life or the exclusive management of an unexpected mission that was potentially both pivotal and of historic importance. And so it was, even if various discrepancies threatened to upset the apple cart.

In message number 460, dated 29 August, Massingham communicated the instructions through which Mallaby should be given reassurance that he was 'doing the right thing'. The Maraschino and Monkey group codes should be interweaved with messages that were 'entirely personal and featuring unequivocal elements of authenticity'. The instructions for the new codes were transmitted to the head of the radio-telegraphic department at Massingham, Bill Corbett, with orders to: decode the messages personally; keep everything in a safe; not allow more than two operators to know the codes; deliver incoming messages only to Dodds-Parker himself; and keep the outgoing messages himself, without further disclosure.[20]

SOE Bern dispatched a coded message on the evening of 30 August that regretted, with reference to the order to halt the plan to liberate Mallaby, that it had not been possible to stop Luciano, the trusted friend of agent 1400.

That same day, in a message sent at 11.59pm from London, Bern was informed that Olaf had been released – and not through Luciano's intervention.[21]

Despite this fact, there were still no concerns at SOE about the credibility of Luciano and the other Italian collaborators.

Agent Olaf had avoided the firing squad and was about to begin his new role. He was helped by the particular phase of war, in which the new Italian executive, whilst clearly hesitant in its decision making, had more to gain by keeping such a unique, important prisoner at its disposal, as opposed to dispatching him. Furthermore, the area where his capture took place was far from the war's front line in southern Italy.

Mallaby's capture had already generated significant controversial diplomatic activity between Italy and

Great Britain and this had greatly reduced the risks to him. Agent Olaf had become a key pawn for the two opposing sides, and the importance of those involved in the diplomatic discussions suggested that the prisoner was more than a mere paratrooper.

Previously, in a Most Secret message dated 26 August 1943, the Foreign Office had informed the Holy See that an Englishman with an ID card in the name of Aldo Guazzini, who had parachuted in civilian clothes into the area around Como on the night of 13/14 August, had been captured by the Italian authorities. The message sought confirmation that he had not been shot immediately.

On 26 August, in order to address the issue, the Envoy Extraordinary and Minister Plenipotentiary to the Holy See Sir D'Arcy Godolphin Osborne, 12th Duke of Leeds,[22] was asked to check with due urgency whether Mallaby had already been shot, and, if not, to intervene – unofficially, it was recommended – to prevent his execution in the following manner: 'Unless there are strong objections, by any means that is useful, making it clear that we are considering the offer of suitable Italian prisoners in exchange.'[23]

The author of the message expressed his conviction that any sort of approach would save Mallaby's life at this stage of the war. The message ended with an appeal to act with the utmost urgency.[24]

As a demonstration of the extreme secrecy and general disorder surrounding the affair, an urgent and confidential message was sent from London at 8.30am on 24 August 1943 (i.e. when the turning point for

Mallaby had already been decided, but not actioned). It stated that all possibilities of obtaining the release of agent Olaf should be explored, without the need to seek constant authorization, and even avoiding the involvement of Massingham.[25]

This message also noted that Vatican channels would probably be opened up and hinted that the treatment of a British officer might have been different to that previously reserved for captured Italian traitors (more or less immediate execution).

Mallaby was not an officer, but, with strategic timing, on 24 August 1943 he was unofficially promoted to second lieutenant. This would help Mallaby in his prison questioning by the Italians, increase his standing in the eyes of those with whom he would be dealing and raise concern over his status as a prisoner. The appointment was communicated to those who needed to know by order of Allied Forces HQ.[26]

So, following complaints from other departments about the resources allocated to saving Mallaby, SOE's leadership clarified on 28 August that the agent it was trying to safeguard was a British Army officer and full English national, effortlessly making use of his promotion to increase his chances of survival.[27]

At this stage, Dick Mallaby's fate remained the same. Despite the fact that he had become a key figure in the new scenario established in Portugal, nobody in Rome or Italy knew about it on account of Castellano's lack of communications, and it was thought that his execution was still a possibility.

SOE's leadership, in the meantime, had not been knocked back by the initial failure of Operation *Neck*, but it finally began to have some doubts about the Italian structure managed by McCaffery.

A series of messages over the following days reveals the high level at which negotiations were being conducted, including the direct involvement of the Italian Minister of Foreign Affairs, Raffaele Guariglia, as requested by the Secretary of State for the Vatican, Cardinal Luigi Maglione. This produced the first tangible results: news was received that Mallaby was alive and well and would probably be transferred to Rome soon.

On 27 August, it was revealed to Massingham that in addition to diplomatic efforts via the Vatican, the Castellano option also existed as a means of securing Mallaby's freedom, though surely it was impossible that Massingham did not already know about this!

These communications as a whole reveal the secretive nature of SOE. On occasion, this led to strange malfunctions and operational wastefulness.

On 30 August, Roseberry informed Massingham that agent Olaf would by now have arrived in Rome, and that this ruled out the possibility of any escape attempt that would jeopardize both his exchange and his employment by Castellano. On the same day, as already mentioned, Bern regretted having been unable to stop Luciano in time.[28]

Obviously unaware of the developments, on 20 September Massingham was asked by the Foreign

Office if agent Olaf was safe, to cancel the request to the Vatican; on the 22nd, Massingham confirmed that there was no longer any need.

By this date Mallaby was working almost officially alongside and for (some of) the Italians.[29] SOE's gamble had paid off.

———

Castellano had left Lisbon on 23 August with a copy of the Short Armistice, and finally arrived in Rome on the 27th, where he relayed the Allied conditions to Marshal Badoglio and the Italian Foreign Minister Raffaele Guariglia. First of all he issued urgent orders to have Mallaby brought to the Supreme Command and taken into his personal custody. Prior to this, as soon as he crossed the border into Italy, he had ordered that the English prisoner should not be executed, as promised to Roseberry.

And so it was that Mallaby was rapidly transferred from San Donnino Prison in Como to Regina Coeli Prison in Rome, where he arrived on 29 August.

He did not stay there long, as what was agreed in Lisbon quickly began to take shape. Having left Regina Coeli Prison, the young Englishman, while being driven by car through the centre of Rome and unaware of the positive outcomes that had been achieved in his favour, was afraid that his brief journey, through streets and past monuments and palaces, was only taking him to a firing squad. The comfortable method of transport used, however, allowed for a glimmer of hope.[30]

At the end of his short journey, the British agent was astonished. He had been driven to a majestic old building with obvious military importance – in fact the most militarily and strategically important location in Italy: Palazzo Vidoni, home to the Supreme Command of the Italian Army. It was the last place where an enemy soldier should have been.

Mallaby was brought before Brigadier-General Giuseppe Castellano and Franco Montanari, neither of whom he had ever met before. Castellano informed Mallaby, in a rather peremptory manner, that he was in possession of a British radio transmitter with which the agent was to immediately contact Allied Force HQ in Algiers.

Mallaby, speaking in Italian, objected that, as a British soldier, he could not obey Castellano's orders. He was then shown the letter from Roseberry.[31]

Mallaby carefully read the note authorizing him to cooperate with Castellano and, for his safety and confirmation, details were given about the training camps in Algiers he had attended in the previous weeks, which no Italian could have known about.

Nevertheless, the British agent was far from ready and willing to provide the requested collaboration, as he feared a complex trap. He then thought up a plan that would allow a definitive verification.

Having convinced himself that it was OK to proceed, Mallaby was taken to another room where the radio, which indeed turned out to be one of SOE's, was located.

So, proving that truth is often stranger than fiction, from a room on the top floor in the most strategically important and restricted place in Italy, a few metres from offices that still witnessed the daily presence of top-level German commanders, Dick Mallaby, a member of the most secret unit of Italy's and Germany's enemy, began to transmit.

Mallaby started with a conventional tuning message for about a minute, using the codes given to the Italians in Lisbon. Then, for verification purposes, he used the Maraschino Orange series codes to confirm his identity and signal that he was not under duress.[32]

Then, using the new double-transposed Monkey code, Dick Mallaby sent his first historic message around 4.00pm on 29 August 1943. It contained no confidential information, but when it was decrypted at Massingham (which had been listening out from 26 August) it was greeted with enthusiasm and relief: 'Sergeant C. R. Mallaby, to Allied Forces HQ North Africa: I have been instructed by General Castellano to establish radio contact between the Italian Government and Allied Headquarters. I request instructions.'

The personal verification message that followed was more particular but gave further confirmation that the finger-tapping on the telegraph key belonged to Dick Mallaby: 'Christine, I love you.'[33]

The answer from Massingham (only to the official part of the message, obviously) was: 'Proceed. Continue transmissions.' However, Mallaby was not informed that he was no longer a sergeant, having been promoted to second lieutenant.

Moreover, the Allies did not lower their guard, remaining still unconvinced of the good faith of the Italians. A message from Roseberry to Massingham dated 29 August, sent almost exactly at the same time that the transmissions from Rome began, advised checking carefully to see if the style of communications corresponded to that of Mallaby's. The following day, Massingham signalled that, having listened to the first five Monkey messages, there had been at least two radio-telegraphists at work (one of which had been recognized as an Italian, by some details in his use of numbers and letters and his operating procedure).[34]

With the beginning of the Monkey–Drizzle transmissions of full messages on the morning of 30 August, specific steps were taken. Roseberry's presence was requested at Massingham as a leading expert on Italian matters, and extra staff were brought in, notably Italian and French translators.

The only other account from this early stage of Mallaby's new mission is that from Luigi Marchesi of the Supreme Command:

> The general said that the responsibility for connecting to the r.t. [radio transmissions] office of the Allied HQ was entrusted to Lieutenant-Colonel De Francesco. I was to watch over the English officer, who was not to have contact with anyone outside our office.

To monitor him and help him in his transmissions, he was shadowed by Radio Marshal Baldanza. Mallaby was extremely suspicious and worried. Although Castellano had told him and proved that he was to act on the orders of the Allied HQ and his direct superiors in the Intelligence Service, he failed to understand. His position was very tricky ... He was arrested in civil clothes and with a radio on... his position regarding all the war laws was unequivocal. Now suddenly his position was reversed.[35]

After the ice had been broken, the members of the Italian General Staff decided that, as a precaution, given that the Supreme Command HQ was frequented daily by Italian and German VIPs, Dick Mallaby should assume a new, Italian identity. As recalled in Castellano's memoirs, those in charge of Mallaby's custody and management decided on the name 'Squarzina', inspired by the large supply of quartz crystals found on him at the time of capture.

According to certain British published sources, Mallaby and his radio were even hosted for a few days inside the Palazzo Reale del Quirinale (the king's official residence). However, this is highly unlikely, as confirmed by Mrs Christine Mallaby.[36] The misunderstanding probably originated from the fact that in the autumn of 1943, there was a successful attempt made from Brindisi to establish a first radio contact with the Roman resistance, which was achieved using a radio left in Rome and kept at the Quirinale. Mallaby himself managed this series of transmissions, which were known with the code Rudder.[37]

Over the following few days, Dick Mallaby tirelessly transmitted messages from the Italian Supreme Command and the head of government to Allied Force HQ, and received the latter's responses.

On the basis of the Lisbon agreements, the Allies were awaiting communications from the Italians by 30 August 1943 regarding acceptance or not of the unconditional surrender proposed to Brigadier-General Castellano and possibly arranging the next steps. This first achievement was easily communicated in time thanks to Dick Mallaby.

The communications transmitted by Mallaby (Monkey) and those destined for him (Drizzle) followed one another with increasing intensity.[38]

Mallaby's tasks were not only top priority and top secret, but also very demanding, just considering the need of exchanging messages mainly in Italian, but in English too.

At Massingham, Douglas Dodds-Parker had assigned his four most trustworthy FANY personnel to the Monkey–Drizzle communications. They worked in pairs in eight-hour shifts. Among them was one of the most famous Yeomanry personnel, Paddy Sproule. Their working space comprised a bathroom, in which they were locked (from the outside) for security reasons.

The messages were transmitted in Morse code, in groups of five letters, using pre-established models, which included opening sequences and agreed textual errors to allow further verification of authenticity. The Monkey–Drizzle radio-telegraphic traffic was normally encoded and decoded, in double transposition, using the key taken from the aforementioned Bino Sanminiatelli's *L'Omnibus del corso* (sent to Massingham from Lisbon, via London, just in time). The other codes (Maraschino/Maraschino Orange, Pallinode and Sleet) were available for service and personal communications, and for messages to and from London.

The Allies had also placed the station in Malta on alert to retransmit to Algiers any messages sent by Rome which had not been received by the North African office.

According to Mallaby's memoirs, his activity in Rome began on 29 August 1943, which establishes not only the precise date of his liberation, but also that of the beginning of the historic secret transmissions between the Italian and Allied leaders.

Besides Baldanza, a small team of Italians had been installed alongside Mallaby, made up of the most trusted collaborators of Major Luigi Marchesi: Otello Griffoni, Luciano Del Col and Mario Della Corte. The mediator between this team and the leaders of the Supreme Command was Lieutenant-Colonel Renato De Francesco.[39]

Mallaby carried out the task for which he had been freed, and in those days worked continuously night and day. Thanks to the relationship established with Griffoni and the others, he was able to take a few hours' rest, having instructed the Italians in how to use the radio, something which Massingham immediately detected, via analysis of the style of transmission and syntax, as already noted).

After a few days of transmitting, Squarzina began to fear that the Germans, by means of radiolocation, might be able to locate the source of transmission. This was not groundless, given that the Germans had installed a powerful interception station in Monte Vetta, south of the Italian capital. Consequently, Mallaby and his caretakers were moved to an unspecified apartment on the outskirts of the city, which was located opposite the staff of the German Red Cross office.

The Monkey–Drizzle messages constituted the sole means through which the Italian and Allied leaders communicated, at a distance of thousands of kilometres from each other. The historical relevance of these messages is unique, immense and unquestionable.

There is no complete collection of all the messages sent. Copies of most of them are available, in order of quantitative importance, at the Dwight D. Eisenhower Presidential Library in Abilene, Kansas, the National Archives in London and the Archivio dell'Ufficio Storico dello Stato Maggiore dell'Esercito in Rome.

Some messages in the series were lost, or rather, destroyed.[40]

All the seemingly unresolved debates and enigmas about the Italian unconditional surrender and the resulting catastrophe are clarified by the messages that Mallaby typed and received in those days. They are contemporary documents and are hard to manipulate, something which has preserved their integrity and veracity.

After decades of research in the Italian, British and US archives, and analysis of hundreds of publications relating to the events of September 1943, I believe I have compiled the most complete collection of messages between Monkey and Drizzle, although I continue to hope that I will be proved wrong by the emergence of unpublished papers from some corner of the world.

Those messages constitute the detailed chronicle of the days that were crucial to the fate of World War II.

A technical point should be clarified here, to provide the right context: from the moment the messages were authorized for transmission, to the time of their reading, hours sometimes passed. The text had to be encoded, transmitted and, upon receipt, decoded. This added confusion to confusion, as messages crossed with each other and often what was requested in one message had been dealt with in a previous message yet to be decoded.[41]

My gathering and collation of the messages indicates that the first *official* message documented between Rome and Algiers was that of 30 August 1943. It was received by Massingham in the late afternoon, and announced the imminent arrival at Termini Imerese, Sicily, of Brigadier-General Castellano, which logically implied the Italian acceptance of the terms of surrender, and their readiness to sign it and act accordingly.[42]

However, the ideas of the Italian leadership were unclear, mystifying and somewhat ambiguous, pointing towards disaster.

Vittorio Ambrosio, Chief of the General Staff, asked Castellano whether it was possible to give the Allies an answer which was neither an acceptance nor a refusal, and Castellano recorded their conversation in his report dated 15 December 1943:

On the morning of the 30th, I was summoned by the Head of the Government to a meeting with His Excellency [Chief of the General Staff Vittorio] Ambrosio, Minister [of Foreign Affairs Raffaele] Guariglia and Minister [of the Royal Household Duke Pietro d'] Acquarone. I was ordered to leave the following morning for Termini Imerese (as agreed with General Smith, should we accede) to inform the Allies that, if Italy had been free to act, it would have accepted the conditions offered, but that it was not possible to implement them since Italy's military forces were vastly inferior to Germany's, which could overwhelm them. The whole country, and Rome in particular, would have been subjected to German reprisals.

Italy could seek an armistice if, following Allied landings in sufficient numbers and in appropriate locations, the current conditions changed. These directives were given to me in writing: the Head of the Government added verbally that it would be necessary to land at least 15 divisions.

The rest of Castellano's report testifies that the Allied leadership obviously communicated 'that it could not budge an inch from what had been communicated to me in Lisbon, and that only two options were open to the Italian Government: fully accept the armistice conditions and required procedures, or not accept them'.[43]

Badoglio's request for 15 divisions was ludicrous, lying beyond both the operational capabilities of the Allies and what was effectively needed. Walter Bedell Smith's comment on this was emphatic, but helps give an understanding of the underlying 'mutual incomprehension': 'if we had so many divisions available, we would certainly have done without the contribution of Italian forces'.

On the evening of 30 August, a Drizzle dispatch was sent by the Allies in reply to the Italian message:

For General Castellano from General Smith. Generals Strong and Smith and the other representatives of the Allied High Command are definitely awaiting General Castellano at Termini Imerese airport around 9am on

Tuesday 31 August. There are many points to discuss. General Castellano's plane should fly at an altitude of 5,000ft during its journey. General Frattini [none other than Brigadier-General Giacomo Zanussi], who is here, will also be present.[44]

Castellano reached Sicily secretly on the morning of the 31st, without being intercepted by the Germans, and in a military tent met with the Allies in company of Zanussi and Montanari. Edward 'Teddy' de Haan, one of SOE's central figures in the Mediterranean during the period, attended the meeting, officially as a translator.

Massingham informed Rome that it would continue to listen without interruption.[45]

The meeting was inconclusive; the Italians asked for some military help in order to defend Rome while the mutual incomprehension kept on going.

On 1 September, Monkey received message No. 11 from Drizzle – a promising one, which read as follows:

With reference to your conversations yesterday with General Smith, the Supreme Allied Commander has agreed to commit a large airborne force in the vicinity of Rome at an opportune time, provided the necessary conditions presented to you by General Smith at the conference are guaranteed by the Italians.

The most important part of these conditions is that the Italians seize and maintain possession of the necessary aerodromes and cease all anti-aircraft fire, that the Italian divisions in the area around Rome take active and effective military action against the Germans and that the armistice is announced at the moment required by the Allied Forces.[46]

In response to this, Mallaby transmitted message No. 7 of that day, in which the Italian Supreme Command stated that Centocelle, Urbe and Guidonia airports could be used for landing the airborne troops.[47]

It seemed that some kind of fair cooperation was starting.

Thus, after a heated meeting, the Italians decided to go on.

Mallaby transmitted news of the acceptance: 'The answer is affirmative, I repeat, affirmative … In consequence known person [Castellano] will arrive on the morning of Thursday 2 September hour and place fixed'.[48]

But just to layer further complications and ambiguities into the negotiations, the Allies requested that Castellano (codenamed 'Ferrari') be legitimized in signing as a declared representative; the Italians took almost a whole day to reply only to confirm that the previous message contained an 'implicit acceptance of the armistice conditions'.[49]

The events proceeded as follows.

In a three-part Drizzle message dated 2 September, from Sicily, the Italian general announced:

The Supreme Allied Commander will in no way discuss military matters unless a document of acceptance of the armistice conditions is first signed.

As military landing operations on the Italian Peninsula will begin soon, such a signature is extremely urgent.

The Supreme Allied Commander will accept the signature of Ferrari [Castellano] if this is authorized by the Italian Government.

Please send this authorization within a day by these means, and provide an urgent confirmation to Minister [Sir D'Arcy Godolphin] Osborne that I have been so authorized.

The Supreme Allied Commander will operate in accordance with the agreements already explained by me and with sufficient strength to ensure the degree of security we desire.

I am personally convinced that the operational intentions of the Allies are such as to ensure the satisfaction of the needs that we discussed at the conference on the morning of the 2nd of this month.[50]

Castellano found himself in an increasingly unpleasant position in Sicily, something which he made clear to Rome, surrounded as he was by various leading Allied commanders, who were openly condescending towards him.

On 3 September Badoglio firstly informed with message No. 8 the 'implicit acceptance of the armistice conditions', but message No. 9 of 3 September actually contradicted that by announcing: 'Our number 8 is cancelled. General Castellano is authorized by the Italian Government to sign the acceptance of the armistice conditions.'[51]

The transcript of this decisive message was delivered to Castellano by Edward 'Teddy' de Haan of SOE, demonstrating that the Baker Street Irregulars continued to be deeply involved in the delicate and secretive negotiations.

Thus, the Italian delegate signed the historic unconditional surrender in Cassibile that same day, 3 September, a fact communicated in message No. 22 received by Dick Mallaby: 'At 1700 hours today by proxy as authorized by Marshal Badoglio, in the presence of General Eisenhower I signed the armistice conditions corresponding to the agreed text. Castellano.'[52]

The Short Armistice was signed. But the Italians hadn't realized that in signing the first one they also accepted the Long Armistice, which didn't get attention, despite the fact that it was in their possession. Also, the Allies had decided not to attempt to coerce the Italians into signing the more punitive Long Armistice at this key moment.[53]

However, the additional clauses of the Long Armistice were nonchalantly handed to Castellano immediately after the signing. The Italian brigadier-general was furious, but Article 12 of the Short Armistice should have at least aroused his curiosity, and that of the others involved in the decision, given that it stated: 'Other conditions of a political, economic and financial nature with which Italy will be bound to comply will be transmitted at a later date.'

Although fundamental and monumental, the entire armistice negotiation was personally referred to by

Eisenhower as a 'gigantic bluff' and 'a dirty business', the details of which would not be made public 'until ten years after the end of the war'; so, although present, Eisenhower refused to sign the document, though he was pictured in official photos shaking hands with Castellano.

———

Although the armistice was signed on 3 September, it was agreed to keep it secret until such a time as the Allied leadership was ready to implement it in line with their planned operations on the Italian peninsula. The original discussions had suggested that it would not be implemented until 12 September.

On 3 September, Marshal Badoglio met with Italy's military leaders in Rome, but did not mention the signing of the armistice.

The Allies' forthcoming plans for the peninsula envisaged that the Italian surrender would be announced simultaneously with a massive landing around Salerno and a parachute drop by the American 82nd Airborne Division north-west of Rome (Operation *Giant II*), something which had formed part of the agreement to support the Italian defence of Rome from the Germans.

The Allied invasion of the Italian mainland began on 3 September. The Allied XIII Corps crossed the Straits of Messina from Sicily to Reggio di Calabria, and gained a first foothold on the toe of Italy. The landings were lightly opposed, with German forces electing to withdraw northwards. The Italian forces in the area for the most part also offered little resistance.

On 5 September, in message No. 29, the Allies informed the Italian Supreme Command that Brigadier-General Maxwell Taylor would arrive in the early hours of the 8th to agree all the details of the planned *Giant II* airborne landings near Rome, with 'full powers from the Supreme Allied Commander regarding the paratrooper operations'. The transcript of this message in the Archivio dell'Ufficio Storico dello Stato Maggiore dell'Esercito contains the following postscript: 'It is not clear if and when it was received.'[54] In reality, the message had probably been ignored.

On 6 September, Algiers sent a message to Rome expressing some of General Castellano's personal needs: 'Please send me another pair of boots with my military aide, another bottle of "citross" from "NAI", my glasses and the cigarettes in my office.' This was clearly a coded message, given that the photos of Castellano in the act of signing the Italian surrender show him wearing a pair of glasses.

Messages Nos. 34, 35, 36 and 37 sent by Drizzle on 6 September bear witness to the rapidly and dramatically evolving situation, and make clear how everything that was happening at the time, in both Italy and the wider Mediterranean, revolved around the communications between Mallaby and the SOE base at Massingham. The four messages are transcribed as follows:

Please confirm receipt of the following message contained in this number (34) and number (35): please maintain constant vigilance every day for a very important message that will be sent between 9 and 10 GMT [Greenwich Mean Time], I repeat 9 and 10 GMT, on the 7th or after the 7th September, I repeat 7th September. Once you have received this important message, you will need to immediately respond that it has been received and understood.

Besides all the other agreements for the announcement of the great (G) day, the Italian radio broadcast by the BBC will present two brief news items on the Nazi German activity in Argentina between 1130 hours Greenwich time and 1245. I repeat between 1130 and 1245 Greenwich time.

This transmission will indicate the great (G) day.

Telegram No. 36. There will be no, I repeat, there will be no special music program as requested, please acknowledge receipt.

It is very important, I repeat very important, that you should be ready to receive my messages every three hours or less, I repeat every three hours or less, until otherwise notified.

This is No. 37. I will have numerous important messages for you during the next few days which must not, I repeat must not be delayed. I tried to send you three messages after 1900 hours the other night.[55]

The information communicated was unequivocal: the day of the announcement of the Italian armistice was very close and the agreed forms of communication were being renotified. The news came from the person who had predicted, and convinced all those who had to know, that these events were scheduled for 12 September: Brigadier-General Giuseppe Castellano.

Nevertheless, on 7 September, Italy's political–military leaders were apparently taken by surprise when they officially learned that the announcement of the Italian surrender, the principal landing at Salerno and the *Giant II* landing near Rome would actually take place, in rapid succession, beginning on the 8th.

Those responsible for the catastrophe that engulfed Italy in September 1943 have always maintained in their defence that they assumed (basing their supposition on the conjecture reported by Castellano) that the surrender would be disclosed on 12 September, and, therefore, that they were taken by surprise to discover the actual date was the 8th.

But what could have changed in those four extra days, regarding the actual proposals and the existing political–military situation? The Germans, whether their armed forces were strong or weak, were nonetheless present in Rome, and only through a planned anticipation of the Salerno landings before the announcement could Field Marshal Albert Kesselring's forces have been drawn from their Roman barracks and sucked towards Salerno. Secondly, would the Italian leadership, within the space of a couple of days or so, have discovered a lucidity and willingness to take firm action, instead of cunningly waiting for events to happen before trying to shape them to their advantage? Many factors lead us to doubt that this would have happened. Conversely, what clearly emerges too is the Allies' strategic myopia in this period in their handling of events, and, above all, their inability to amend their planning, at least at the tactical level.

On the other side, the Germans' behaviour was becoming more hostile by the day.

The pressure on the Italian leadership at this point was very intense.[56]

The Allied High Command was by now having doubts about the Italian desire to engage the Germans around Rome following the proclamation of the armistice, and so Brigadier-General Maxwell D. Taylor of the 82nd Airborne Division undertook the daring reconnaissance mission (announced on 5 September, in message No. 29) to assess the prospects of *Giant II*'s success. Accompanied by USAAF Colonel William T. Gardiner, Taylor arrived in the Italian capital late on 7 September, following a secret disembarkation at Gaeta in Lazio. After spending the night at Villa Badoglio, located between Via Bruxelles and Via di Villa Grazioli, in Rome, they learned from a recently awoken Marshal Badoglio that the Kingdom of Italy did not intend to proclaim the surrender duly signed, nor guarantee the security of the airports needed for Operation *Giant II*. Badoglio also requested a deferral of a few days for the armistice.

At 2.55am on 8 September 1943, the two American officers took advantage of Monkey's availability and attempted to officially communicate news of the Italian volte-face via the following urgent message:

> To the Commander-in-Chief of 15th Army Group. Given Marshal Badoglio's statement about the impossibility of proclaiming the armistice and of guaranteeing the airports, *Giant II* is impossible. Reasons given for change are irredeemable lack of fuel and ammunition and new German measures. Badoglio asks Taylor to come back to report government opinions. Taylor and Gardiner await instructions. Acknowledge receipt. Taylor.

Unfortunately, this very message was unable to be deciphered in its first transmission and was only correctly transcribed more than three hours later, at the dawn of 8 September, X-Day.[57]

The following messages (15 and 16) from Italy's leaders, transmitted by Dick Mallaby early on 8 September, left no doubt about Italian intentions in the hours leading up to the expected proclamation of Italian surrender. The first read:

> Given changes and precipitous situation and presence of German armed forces in the vicinity of Rome, it is no longer possible to accept the immediate armistice since this will lead to the capital being occupied and the

Government overthrown by the Germans. Operation *Giant II* is no longer possible given the lack of sufficient forces to secure the airports.

The second message stated:

General Taylor is ready to return to Sicily to report the government's views and awaits orders. Badoglio.

In a growing atmosphere of dismay and tension, Brigadier-General Taylor, having received the shock news and fearing a disaster, focused on cancelling his men's departure for the Rome mission, take-off for which was scheduled for 6.30pm.

As the disturbing news reported through Mallaby reached Allied Forces HQ in Algiers on the morning of the 8th, the members of Eisenhower's entourage were thrown into consternation (Eisenhower being in Bizerte at the time). After formally communicating, on their own initiative, the cancellation of *Giant II*, they asked the General Staff whether the Italian surrender should be announced anyway.

Further confusion on this key day was caused by an absence of immediate replies to the Italian messages from Allied HQ, as well as the failure to transmit by radio in English at the pre-established time the agreed coded announcement indicating the date of the surrender proclamation. It is not clear why this happened. However, the air raid that took place on Frascati (a small town south of Rome, which housed the German General Headquarters for the Mediterranean) – which was a further, pre-agreed event that announced X-Day to the Italians on 8 September – put paid to any doubts about Allied intentions regarding the proclamation.

At this precise point, Reuters, even before Eisenhower could manage to do so, announced the Italian surrender to the world, following a peremptory and unequivocal telegram sent to Allied Force HQ from Washington DC, which stated:

> It is the opinion of the President and of the Prime Minister that, the agreement having been signed, you should give public announcement considering that this would facilitate your military operations ... For the personal attention of Eisenhower and Smith. You should have no consideration, I repeat no consideration for the difficulties that this could cause for the Italian government.[58]

A hopeless and embarrassed Castellano was subjected to the direct outbursts of the Allied leaders in Sicily. The Italian negotiator had learned of the imminent proclamation of surrender even after his colleagues in the Supreme Command. In his report sent to General Ambrosio on 15 September 1943, he stated that 'at about 12 p.m.' General Eisenhower had informed him that 'he had already telegraphed the Italian government'. Eisenhower showed him the telegram, 'which was actually very extreme. In turn, I sent a telegram to the head of the government highlighting the gravity of the situation.' However, according to the declarations of Luigi Marchesi, during his questioning on 17 December 1944 at the Commission of Inquiry for the failure to defend Rome, 'Around 5 p.m. on the 8th, through the secret radio we learned that the armistice would be announced in the evening.'[59]

At the Palazzo Reale del Quirinale in Rome, at 5.30pm, an emergency meeting known as the Council of the Crown (Consiglio della Corona) was held. This involved almost all of Italy's military leaders (excluding General Roatta, who was meeting with the Germans), the relevant government ministers and, of course, the king and Marshal Badoglio as head of government.

Simultaneously, Eisenhower and his staff, fearing that the whole negotiation instigated by Castellano could prove to be an elaborate trap and also, consequently, that the Salerno landings would be a scene of dreadful carnage, contacted Dodds-Parker to check if the Monkey–Drizzle transmissions were secure. Massingham's commander answered that they were secure, in so far as the Germans had not managed to crack the Monkey–Drizzle codes (their only direct knowledge of what was happening came from interceptions of the transoceanic phone calls between Roosevelt and Churchill).

Dick Mallaby with his father, Cecil. (Mallaby family)

The telegram delivered to Cecil Mallaby in 1921 that announced
his Italian inheritance. (Mallaby family)

MONKEY PLAN

CALL SIGNS

MONKEY .... Y H N

BASE .... X J K

FREQUENCIES

MONKEY .... 9050 A. Main Day
9630 B. Reserve Day
4525 C. Main Night
5820 D. Reserve Night

MONKEY may also use: 9350 R.
4675 L.
3979 M.
5777 P.

BASE ... 8436 E. Main Day
8630 F. Reserve Day
4645 G. Main Night
4540 H. Reserve Night

FREQUENCY CHANGE SIGNALS

X J ... "Change your transmitting frequency to ......"

H N ... "I am changing my transmitting frequency to ..."

SCHEDULES

At the following times G.M.T.
MONKEY

DAILY at 1300 hrs. Transmit on A. Listen on E.

0630 hrs. " " C. " " G.

TRANSPOSITION TABLE

1	2	3	4	5	6	7	8	9	0
G	T	S	A	E	Q	D	O	L	K
J	B	U	V	R	C	Z	P	M	I
H	W	Y					X	N	F

DAY INDICATING TABLE

Sun.	Mon.	Tues.	Wed.	Thur.	Fri.	Sat.
2	5	1	3	4	7	6

ADDITIONAL CONTACTS

You write down the time required, say 1900 hrs. Add the
day indicating figure for say Monday. Thus you have 19005.
Then transpose into letters from any line of Transposition
Table, thus: GMIKE or HNFKR or JLKFE &c.

Dick Mallaby's mugshot.
(Mallaby family)

A portrait of Marshal Pietro
Badoglio. (Photo by Popperfoto/
Getty Images)

(Above) The unconditional surrender of Italy to the Allied Forces was signed
in the headquarters tent at Cassible, Italy, on 3 September 1943. (Photo by
Mondadori Portfolio via Getty Images)

(Left) The Monkey plan used for Dick Mallaby's secret and historical
communications in August–September 1943. (Mallaby family)

COMANDO SUPREMO

Generale d'A.	AMBROSIO	Vittorio	— Capo di S.M.Gener.
Generale	ROSSI	Silvio	
Ten.Col. S.M.	MELLANO	Pietro	
" " " "	DE FRANCESCO	Remo	
" " R.A.	MARAVIGNA	Manlio (1)	
" "	JANNUZZI	Emanuele	
Maggiore di S.M.	MARCHESI	Luigi	
" " "	ADAM	Augusto	
" " "	ROSSETTI	Alfredo	
" " "	GALATERI DI GENOLA	Angelo	
" " "	CORDARO	Enrico	
" A.A.	VASSALLO		
" A.A.	MAGINI		
Capitano medico	CONTI	Enzo	
Maresciallo	BALDANZA		
Serg.Magg.	GUAZZINI (2)		
" "	ROBOTTI	Stefano	
Sergente	GRIFFONI	Otello	
"	DELLA CORTE	Mario	
Caporal magg.	FARINACCI	Arturo	

(1) — In volo per l'Egeo, ove doveva recapitare dei documenti, ha atterrato casualmente a Pescara per fare rifornimento. Ivi ha ricevuto ordine – data la situazione – di seguire il Comando.

(2) — Trattasi di un ufficiale inglese dell'I.S. (Ten. Mallaby).

The list of the Italian Supreme Command staff moved from Rome on 9 September 1943, including a 'Sgt Maj. Guazzini', who, the second footnote explains, is an 'English officer of the I. S. (Lt. Mallaby)'. (Professor Gregory Alegi Archive)

Dick Mallaby after his first mission.
(Mallaby family)

The unpleasant message to Cecil
Mallaby from local teacher Maria
Rispoli, beginning 'God strike the
English', Asciano, 1944.
(Mallaby family)

Dick Mallaby with some Italian soldiers in Monopoli in 1944.
(Mallaby family)

Dick Mallaby in Poggio Pinci, *c.* 1944–45. (Mallaby family)

Dick Mallaby in Italy in the final years of the war. (Mallaby family)

Obergruppenführer Karl Wolff, with whom Mallaby ended up negotiating during his second SOE mission in February 1945. (Photo by Keystone/ Getty Images)

Dick Mallaby and Christine Northcote-Marks, seen here after the war on their wedding day, 30 March 1946. (Mallaby family)

Dick Mallaby with his first three babies: Caroline Mary, Elisabeth Spray and Christopher John. (Mallaby family)

One of the last photographs of Dick Mallaby. (Mallaby family)

As the Italian Council of the Crown was fiercely debating a proposal to issue an official statement of denial and refusal of surrender, Major Marchesi, the lowest ranking among those present, intervened. He read out the third part of the lengthy Drizzle message No. 45, which had just been phoned through to him by Lieutenant-Colonel De Francesco.

The message contained Eisenhower's furious reply to the Italian vacillation. Its content was hard-hitting, direct and unequivocal:

From the Allied Commander-in-Chief to Marshal Badoglio.

I intend to transmit via the radio the acceptance of the armistice at the time already agreed. If you or any part of your armed forces fail to cooperate as previously agreed, I will have the details of this deal published throughout the world. Today is X-Day and I expect you to do your part.

I do not accept your message of this morning postponing the armistice. Your accredited representative has signed an agreement with me and Italy's only hope is linked to your adherence to this agreement. According to your urgent request, the airborne operations are temporarily suspended.

You have enough troops around Rome to ensure the momentary security of the city, but I request exhaustive information on the basis of which arrange as soon as possible for the airborne operation.

Immediately send General Taylor to Bizerte informing in advance of his arrival and the route of the airplane.

The plans have been made in the belief that you are acting in good faith and we have been prepared to carry out future military operations on this basis. Any failure now on your part to fulfill all the obligations of the signed agreement will have the most serious consequences for your country. No future action of yours could do more to give us back some confidence in your good faith, and [if refused] the dissolution of your government and your nation would consequently follow.

General Eisenhower.[60]

Drizzle message No. 49, sent by Castellano, doubled the dose:

Failure to announce the armistice by radio at 1830hrs this afternoon would be considered by the [Allied] commander-in-chief a failure to fulfill the solemn commitment already signed. If there is no announcement of the armistice at the appointed time, all the agreements will be null and void and the Allied commander-in-chief affirms that the non-announcement would prove disastrous for the future of Italy. Respond immediately.

The message that followed stated: 'Essential that the proclamation of the Chief of the General Staff contains explicit orders to the armed forces to collaborate with the Allies.'[61]

Thus, Italy's political and military leaders realized, having also listened to the king's decisive words on the matter, that their unrealistic demands had been emphatically bulldozed over. The decision was taken to announce the armistice immediately.

The Italian surrender was officially announced first by General Eisenhower in a broadcast on Radio Algiers at 6.30pm Rome time, 8 September. Shortly after this, Marshal Pietro Badoglio made his way to the studios of EIAR (Ente Italiano per le Audizioni Radiofoniche – the Italian public service broadcaster) in Via Asiago, Rome, where he then broadcast the following message to the nation at 7.42pm that evening:

The Italian government, recognizing the impossibility of continuing the unequal struggle against the overwhelming enemy power, in order to spare the nation from further and more serious disasters, has requested an armistice from General Eisenhower, commander in chief of the Anglo-American allied forces.

The request was accepted.

Consequently, every act of hostility against the Anglo-American forces must cease by Italian forces everywhere.

However, they will react to any attacks from any other source.

The final part of the proclamation was highly ambiguous, and doubt persisted as to what exactly had been agreed in the armistice among the Italian population and its forces. This was one of the main points of blame put on the Italian government.

But one of the Monkey–Drizzle messages, sent just prior to the announcement of the armistice while confirming what would be announced by Eisenhower and Badoglio, provides a vital piece of information regarding the origins of this costly ambiguity. Message No. 10 sent by Drizzle on 8 September stated:

> The [Allied] Commander-in-Chief, in order to prevent any possibility of misunderstanding by our troops who have not, I repeat, have not been informed of the facts, requests that the final paragraph of the Proclamation be changed to 'Consequently, all acts of hostility towards the Anglo-American forces must cease on the part of Italian forces in every location. However, they will react to any attacks from any other source.'[62]

This key message No. 10 attests that the decisive and controversial and ambiguous part of the proclamation was the work of the Allied leadership.

According to the prior agreements, the radio announcements made by Badoglio and Eisenhower should have been simultaneous. The Monkey message transmitted by Mallaby around the same time gave the Italian reply to Eisenhower's earlier ultimatum, and explained the lack of synchronicity. The message did not come from Marshal Badoglio, however, but from the Italian Supreme Command. The Italian Supreme Command justified themselves in the following terms:

> The failure to receive radio signal agreed and delayed arrival your No. 45 has not permitted diffusion agreed. Proclamation taken place as requested also without your message. It is sufficient for us engagements taken. Excessive hurry – found our preparations incomplete and has caused delay sailing fleet.

Finally, one way or another, the Italian surrender was officially public knowledge.

In his memoirs, Mallaby recalls that immediately after the announcement, like in a miracle he was embraced by the Italian soldiers. Wine was brought out to celebrate the *common* triumph over the Germans.[63]

'After all we were no longer enemies' pondered Mallaby in his secret diary.

Despite having first-hand knowledge of the whole situation, Dick Mallaby was unaware of the Italians' unprepared state. But, only a few hours after the announcement of the surrender and the celebratory refreshments, Mallaby realized that the situation was deteriorating.

As time passed, he understood that he was once again facing a dangerous, out of control situation, while at the same time still burdened with managing the incoming and outgoing messages, which were flowing frenetically during those dramatic hours.

In the early hours of the following day, 9 September, the main Allied invasion force landed near Salerno on Italy's western coast, in Operation *Avalanche*. It was led by General Mark W. Clark's US Fifth Army, which contained the British X Corps and the 82nd Airborne Division in reserve. *Avalanche* was supported by Royal Navy battleships and fleet carriers.

At the same time the Allies had begun (via the link with Rome) to issue military instructions to the Italian armed forces. The priorities were: the direction and management of the precious Italian naval fleet, which was to be handed over to the Allies; supporting Allied troops in gaining their foothold on the Italian peninsula; and protecting Italy's infrastructure from German destruction.[64] A rapid Italian military collapse was, however, about to take place .

On learning about the armistice, the Germans had immediately begun Operation *Achse*, attacking and disarming their former Italian allies on the peninsula, as well as in the Balkans and France, imprisoning thousands of them and taking military control of the part of Italy not yet occupied by the Allies. German forces, after initial confusion, began to seize key infrastructure facilities from the concentrations of Italian troops around Rome, sending waves of panic through the Italian political and military leadership based there. The panic was such that the head of government, Badoglio, and the Italian royal family fled Rome early on 9 September by car, heading for Pescara on the Adriatic. Luigi Marchesi later recalled:

On the morning of the 9th, around 5 a.m. while I was resting, I was woken because of an urgent call from His Excellency Ambrosio who was at the Ministry of War.

I went straight to him and found him putting some papers in order. He told me that the royal family had already left with Badoglio and that the Supreme Command and the Chiefs of Staff were to follow them.

I pointed out to His Excellency Ambrosio that it was not possible to leave Rome at such a serious time and I also reminded him that he had always declared that he would never abandon the capital, and that we had also prepared, of which he was aware, a secret location from which the Supreme Command could operate.

General Ambrosio told me that he had received orders from the King and that he lacked the courage to disobey the Sovereign.

My insistence was to no avail, because General Ambrosio replied that he would never discuss orders received from the King.

He ordered me to inform General Silvio Rossi and some other officers – myself included – of the order to leave for Pescara immediately, and to tell General [Vittorio] Palma to remain as the representative of the Supreme Command: he would then be given further orders by radio. I immediately hurried to get the secret radio with which I was in communication with the Anglo-Americans, and together with the General, accompanied by General Rossi and others, we took the plane to Pescara.[65]

Mallaby had now become even more important, not only for the Allies, but also for the Italians. When he was told to pack his belongings and the wireless set, Mallaby thought that meant a further change of location for security reasons.

But, to his surprise, Mallaby and his radio were hurriedly loaded onto a large military truck and driven to Centocelle airport, where several planes were lined up, ready for take-off. There, he and his escorts boarded a cargo plane, which was packed full of military commanders and staff fleeing from Rome. According to Mallaby's private memoirs, nobody seemed to know the destination and the plane needed almost the entire length of the runway to become airborne (just as Benito Mussolini's would do after he was sprung from his Gran Sasso prison a few days later, due to the extra weight of the accompanying SS commando Otto Skorzeny on board the light Storch aircraft).[66]

Mallaby thought they were heading southwards in the direction of Sicily or North Africa, but immediately after the take-off he realized that they were flying towards the east.

This same day, 9 September, in the afternoon, a third Allied landing on the Italian peninsula took place. Operation *Slapstick* saw the British 1st Airborne Division land on Italy's 'heel' by sea, due to a lack of air transport. The operation was in response to the Italian offer made during the armistice negotiations to open the ports of Taranto and Brindisi to the Allies. Opposition was once again mostly light, save for some resistance by the 1st Fallschirmjäger Division, and both ports were quickly captured with all facilities in working order. The capture of Brindisi in particular would be particularly important for Italy's fleeing leadership and Mallaby himself.

Meanwhile, the plane carrying Mallaby and his radio landed safely in Pescara and Mallaby immediately received the order to set up his radio in one of the airport rooms. The order was carried out by Mallaby, and to the amazement of the Italian soldiers present, it was revealed just how easy it was to contact Massingham using such a small device in contrast to what was reported, perhaps deliberately, by some Italian sources, and instrumentally by Roseberry in Lisbon.

Mallaby's private memoirs and the declassified documents from this time offer clear historical evidence that it was only via the Monkey–Drizzle transmissions that the Allies were able, despite the considerable confusion, to gain information about and have contact with Italy's political and military leaders. This information was also critical for passing on detailed instructions, notably regarding the movements of the Italian Royal Navy.

It is worth bearing in mind that, in contrast, this precious information, at such a crucial time, was to all intents and purposes almost unavailable to those who had remained in Rome and to the Italian military headquarters scattered across Europe.

The German reaction to the armistice began to be felt. On 9 September, the Italian fleet had been ordered to sail to Sardinia and then to Malta in order to surrender to the Allies. However, while in the area of the Strait of Bonifacio, its ships were attacked by Luftwaffe bombers. The battleship *Roma* was sunk with the loss of 1,393 lives, including Admiral Bergamini.

In a message dated the same day, the Allies considered it opportune to signal to the Italians that the attacks on the fleet had been carried out exclusively by the Germans. The message also guaranteed that when the convoys had reached an adequate distance from the coasts ('our coasts' in the original), they would be provided with air protection. In only a few hours, the Allies had come to consider the Italian peninsula as being a possession of theirs.

In Pescara, Italy's leaders did not issue any specific orders to the country's troops, and Mallaby was asked only to reiterate to Massingham the now out of date, generic and slightly surreal Italian requests for general support.[67]

Castellano remained faithful to his position, either for consistency or for some hidden reason, assuming that the Italians only wanted to fight the Germans (as he had maintained to the Allies ever since his first meeting with them). In the early afternoon, via Drizzle message No. 23, he asked for indications on targets to be bombed and invited the Allies to impede the movements of Italy's former ally, ignoring the fact that at that moment there was no way of confirming the request, nor of passing on orders for this to be done.[68]

Likewise, the Allies could not understand what had happened in Rome and what the Italian military leadership was doing, or more accurately was not doing; so much so that at 4.45pm, Drizzle had sent Monkey Eisenhower's request for even basic information about the situation in Rome.

At the end of the afternoon, General Francesco Rossi, who had flown in from Sicily with Taylor and Gardiner and was out of step with the events, informed General Ambrosio that he had insisted to the Allies the urgent need to execute air and sea actions near to and north of Rome, calling for 'the greatest information possible for the potential parachute division drop'.

The Italian insistence on the matter lasted for a few days, in spite of events. This is perhaps why Badoglio, at that time, announced that he would return to the capital imminently. The Italian position appeared to be based on a lack of realism, or may have been yet another demonstration of the persistent inability to view the events in progress and their dynamics with any form of accuracy.

The Allies, beginning to realize the seriousness of the situation, emphasized the importance of their sole remaining asset in message No. 53, which stressed to the Italians how it was 'absolutely vital for future projects to keep the Monkey communications going'. The message also anxiously provided reserve communication codes and recommended that the Italians make the most of the help Second Lieutenant Mallaby could offer.[69]

At this frantic and tense time, on the afternoon of 9 September an official but secret communication from London notified the resignation of Charles Hambro as head of SOE. His farewell message, after stating that 'it is a great pride to me to think that I leave you at the moment when the capitulation of Italy, in which SOE played such a vital part, marks the first phase of the conquest of Germany, and the beginning of the end', concluded with: 'Good luck to you all, good hunting and thanks.'[70]

After sunset, Mallaby and his radio, along with the other members of the group from Rome, were subject to a further transfer. Before being forced to interrupt his transmissions by the intervention of a senior officer, Mallaby was able to inform Massingham that there would be a further relocation with the following message: 'We transfer ourselves to to Taranto. We shall re-establish communications tomorrow, 10th September. Cordial salutations.'[71]

Mallaby and the rest of the convoy set off in the night heading southbound along the Abruzzo coast, crossing the paths of retreating German troops. They arrived at the port of Ortona, where a small crowd was waiting to board. Mallaby was told to stand by to board.

They were all waiting for the corvette *Baionetta*, a 728-ton warship that had sailed unharmed from Pola and was now approaching.

Baionetta stopped at 11.40pm in front of the port.

A short distance from him, to his amazement, Dick Mallaby recognized King Vittorio Emanuele III and his wife Queen Elena, Prince Umberto, the Chief of the General Staff heading the Supreme Command, General Vittorio Ambrosio, and a whole series of high-ranking officers from Rome. There were some 250 people in total. Marshal of Italy Pietro Badoglio had pre-boarded the ship in Pescara as a precaution, together with Admiral Raffaele de Courten, Chief of Staff and minister of the Italian Royal Navy.

In his private memoirs, Mallaby confirms – and this is backed up by the account of eyewitness Tommaso D'Antuono, recounted to me – that in order to leave Ortona port as soon as possible, *Baionetta*, which could not dock on account of the shallow water, did not even throw its anchor and boarding was carried out using small boats.

Although the pre-warned local Carabinieri had requested reinforcements and made everything ready for the ferry, confusion and great tension resulted even where it should not have done. Disorder soon broke out, with quarrels and heated discussions all around.[72]

In addition to the lateness of the hour, the absence of embarrassing witnesses was a result of Carabinieri Captain Migliorati, who as a precaution spread word around the vicinity of the imminent arrival at the port of a large contingent of German troops. This news also reached the ears of the departing boatload, greatly increasing the panic of many. Moreover, among those witnessing the boarding of the *Baionetta* were 'some perplexed Germans', who watched 'dumbfounded the King's embarkation from the harbour wall'.[73]

While the first elements of what Mallaby, in his private memoirs, sarcastically called 'a distinct company, almost like a society gathering' began to embark at 12.30am on the small boats that would ferry them to the *Baionetta*, the British agent was informed that their destination was probably Brindisi, chosen, he was told, because it was soon expected to be (and indeed would be) in Allied hands.[74]

Once he saw the boat close up, Mallaby realized that it would be impossible to get everyone on board, given the corvette's limited capacity. Otello Griffoni reassured him, reminding him that he possessed the most important virtual boarding card: without Mallaby, it would be impossible for the Italian VIPs to continue transmitting and to maintain contact with the Allies.

Admiral de Courten, who was in his element and committed to carrying out his duties, objected to the boarding of Marchesi and Mallaby's group, unaware of their crucial role. It required the personal intervention of Supreme Commander General Ambrosio to resolve the situation, ordering Mallaby's embarkation, since 'by now he was part of the Supreme Command's nucleus'.[75]

In fact, a very rare and unknown official document from the Supreme Command listing 20 of the personnel 'transferred to Pescara' includes 'Sgt. Maj. GUAZZINI'. An accompanying footnote states: 'This is an English officer of the I.S. (Lt. Mallaby).'

Finally, a few minutes after 1.00am on 10 September 1943, the *Baionetta* departed. This time, there was no full moon. On board, apart from the crew, there were exactly 57 passengers, just one of whom was a British national. Only a few days previously, Dick Mallaby had been ready to face the firing squad; now his role as a key player – maybe the most strategic, certainly the most active – had been emphatically confirmed.[76]

Otello Griffoni, like many others, was not given a place on the *Baionetta* and made his own way to his native region of Le Marche in central Italy, reaching Ancona that same evening. There, he went into hiding until late 1944, when he rejoined the Supreme Command. He never saw Dick Mallaby again.

In common with Griffoni, the others left behind on the harbour walls, fearing the arrival of the Germans, fled the port in all directions. They either had no knowledge of, or lacked the patience and courage to wait for the corvette *Scimitarra*, which was on its way to board them.

Mallaby was asked to contact Massingham immediately, but, on the point of collapse after days without adequate rest, refused – most likely not in obedience of instructions received, but by his own decision. His long-awaited rest was initially on deck towards the bow and then near the ship's funnel; the latter guaranteed a comfortable warmth and protection from damp sea air, which was particularly intense at night.

Mallaby slept for a long time, because in his private memoirs he noted that he was awoken by the cries of alarm caused by the sighting of a German plane that had started circling above the *Baionetta*. It was 1.10pm. He also noted that the order was given to take shelter below deck and that those manning the guns on the *Baionetta*, who were ready to fire, did not engage the plane, allowing it to fly off.[77]

The Italian historian Ruggero Zangrandi, who also referred to the appearance of a British submarine (which is confirmed by another historian, Agostino Degli Espinosa), draws evidence from this episode to support his theory (not backed up by the available evidence) of a specific agreement between the Italian and German political and military leaderships. According to this view, the undisturbed flight of Italy's political and military leaders from Rome was granted in exchange for Italy's lack of opposition to German forces in securing control of the capital.[78] However, this seems unlikely. Kesselring and his staff were occupied with events at Salerno and in Rome and probably understood that it was much more profitable to have a leaderless Italian army, rather than an army and a nation fired up by the capture and imprisonment of their king, queen, crown prince, head of government and other prominent figures. Thus, at most, it could have been a case of tacit agreement, but more likely it was a good example of fast and clever tactics by Kesselring.[79]

During the final stages of the *Baionetta*'s journey, Mallaby attempted to resume transmissions. He did not succeed, due to his less than optimal position.

At the time, Massingham was transmitting messages from Eisenhower, who had no idea what had happened and what was happening. His communications reiterated the request for updates 'at appropriate moments' regarding the situation in Rome.[80] But the only operational link between Eisenhower and the Italians was hundreds of kilometres away, and could offer little in terms of updates over what was happening in the capital.

Admiral de Courten had ordered 'a most rigorous wireless telegraphic silence, so that the presence at sea of the precious vessel, which lacked any form of escort, either naval or aerial, was not discovered'. Thus the communication blackout was total for many hours, also because there was fear that some of the transmissions received from Rome were false ones sent by the Germans. At 6.30am, the light cruiser *Scipione* had appeared near Vieste and began to escort the *Baionetta*, and this indirectly ended the radio silence, because the *Baionetta* began to use optical communications to link with the *Scipione*.

Finally, after completing the standard port checks, the *Baionetta*, preceded by the *Scipione*, entered

Brindisi harbor, cautiously and without notifying the port authorities of its precious cargo. Then it stopped.

It was 2.40pm on 10 September 1943.

The journey was over.

In the capital, a few hours earlier, the surrender of Italian troops to the Germans had been accepted and signed.

Italy had surrendered twice in the space of a few days: first to the enemy, then to its former ally.

It was a bit much for any nation.

———

Regarding the final destination of Brindisi, it should be noted, and is often ignored, that *Baionetta*'s arrival there was unplanned. The appearance of the German reconnaissance aircraft during the voyage led to the belief that it might result in air raids over the area. Thus, the corvette decided to head for land and the nearest port.[81]

According to some recent reconstructions of events, entry into the port of Brindisi was also the work of SOE and of Mallaby.

On the morning of 10 September 1943 – a fact overlooked in Italian commentaries – one of the British Army's least orthodox units had arrived in Brindisi, confirming that the city was free of both German and Allied forces. This was Popski's Private Army, officially entitled No. 1 Demolition Squadron, which consisted of fighting patrols in well-equipped jeeps with large-calibre machine guns mounted on them, led by Major Vladimir Peniakoff, known as Popski.

Popski and his men had landed in Apulia and were immediately tasked with a sensitive mission: the formal acceptance of the surrender of the Brindisi stronghold by its military commanders, and notification of this to the British HQ in Taranto. Once this had been obtained, the green light for the *Baionetta*'s entry to the port would have been communicated by radio from one of Popski's jeeps and then transmitted back to Mallaby.

Immediately after the landing, a brief German bombardment of Brindisi ensued, which was countered successfully by the guns of the ships at anchor. This took place just when Mallaby was setting up his equipment in a tower room in the Swabian castle in the city (which housed the Admiralty's headquarters) to give his transmissions a better chance of success.

Mallaby transmitted another historical piece of news: the king of Italy was now under the protection of the Allies. In his secret diary he states that:

> The Germans had by now left the town and there seemed to be little danger other than from the Italian ack ack which went into operation on the slightest excuse. Not that they had much ammunition left, for most of it had been shot away in the glorious firework display to celebrate the armistice. It was therefore something of a relief to operate under these conditions, but 24 hour watch was still mantained.

Mallaby's private memoirs also reveal that he was asked, in case of contact with German forces, to respond that he was Radio Marshal Guazzini of the Italian Army Transmissions Section. The request jarred glaringly with the workman's overalls that Mallaby had been wearing for almost a month. This small detail seems to further counter the hypothesis of an agreement between the Italian and German leaderships, while endorsing the considerable confusion surrounding, and lack of information available to, the Italian High Command at that point.

Meanwhile, Massingham sent anxious messages reiterating the urgent request for updates on the situation in all parts of the Italian peninsula and to do everything to guarantee complete control of the land, air and sea (including Sardinia). In the following hours, it also asked when the radio left in Rome would begin to transmit, demonstrating that the Italian catastrophe had not been fully understood by the Allies.[82]

On the morning of the 11th, Dick Mallaby continued his work; everybody desperately sought information on the situation in Rome and in other parts of Italy and Europe. Massingham sent an emphatic message from Castellano: 'The Germans are suffering...Above all Italy will arise like one man and we will take every German by the throat.'

According to Mallaby's memoirs, the first contact between the Allies and the core of Italian leaders now in Brindisi took place the same day with the arrival of a British submarine, but he could not meet the crew because 'my duties did not allow my leaving of the set'.

SOE had dispatched to Apulia Captain Teddy De Haan, Captain Freddie White, and two radio operators: Sergeant Ken Royle and Edward Archibald Case (the latter remembered for his incredible speed on the telegraph key). The group, during the journey to Brindisi, always kept their radio, code plans and cyphers wrapped in straw, with matches to hand, in case of contact with enemy forces.

De Haan had witnessed Mallaby's departure for Italy on 13 August and had been present at the historic signing of the Italian surrender at Cassibile on 3 September. He appears in some of the photos of the latter, demonstrating the critical role played by SOE in the armistice.

On 12 September, Dick Mallaby, having learned of his colleagues' arrival, set off to find them at the Hotel Internazionale, which had been requisitioned. This, however, was made more difficult by the poor state of his clothing, which he had worn for over a month.

An Italian officer generously gave him 10,000 lire to buy something decent, but Mallaby, eager to meet his colleagues, headed straight into the hotel's lobby, where he was immediately thrown out. Fortunately, he was recognized by Teddy de Haan, who, along with his other colleagues, besides reviving his spirits with some food and drink, also managed to sort him out with an urgently needed bath, his first in four weeks.

Thus De Haan, who was with Mallaby at the beginning of his mission, in fact marked the happy ending of it.

The British soldiers then found an almost complete officer's uniform for Mallaby (although the lack of cap incurred the wrath of a zealous superior) and arranged a room for him in the hotel, where he took the wireless link.

In the course of some modest celebrations, Mallaby received official news of his promotion to second lieutenant (officially effective from 24 February 1944!). The following day Mallaby caused considerable amazement among the Italian soldiers he had been spending time with, when they saw the person they thought was an Italian sergeant-major dressed as a British officer.

A few days later, De Haan, together with an exhausted Dick Mallaby, Major Marchesi and Major Maurice Page, set up, at the Hotel Impero, the first Anglo–Italian special wireless telegraphic communications group. It focused on special operations, chiefly at that time making secret contact with the clandestine organizations that had risen in Rome and elsewhere against the German occupation. This was an additional heavy job, because the staff continued working on the secret transmissions to and from North Africa and London.

Mallaby's diary reveals that there were heated discussions about just how far the cooperation with the Italians 'could or was to go', but also that after a few days' instruction he realized 'what excellent material' the first trainees were (coming from the Italian Navy and Genio Trasmissioni).

Over the following days, Mallaby carried out further valuable work using Monkey, coordinating the movements of the Allies in the Italian peninsula and acting as a bridge between the embryonic structures of what would be called the Kingdom of the South and the Allies themselves. He also acted as the link to the various branches of the Italian armed forces scattered across Europe, which were subject to different destinies, of differing tragic proportions.[83]

The transmission traffic managed by Mallaby was even more intense than in the previous days. The problem that immediately presented itself was how to adapt the cryptography of the transmissions to the much higher number of messages, as well as increasing and diversifying the groups of cyphers available.

By now, the Monkey–Drizzle system had its days numbered, but its swan song comprised a series of further important and historical communications. In message No. 38 dated 11 September 1943, Badoglio issued a sterile, incoherent attempt at a motivational message to the scattered and confused Italian armed forces.

Other messages that day had greater relevance and more precision. For example, Massingham pointed out the dangerous behaviour of some Italian aircraft in the combat zone, which, despite making friendly signals, were flying too close to those of the Allies, and risked being shot down.

On 12 September, Brigadier-General Castellano sent a message from Algiers to Brindisi for the attention of the Italian Foreign Minister (who was actually still in Rome). It stated that Allied intelligence had requested all Italian diplomatic representatives in neutral countries (in particular, the consul in Lourenço Marques, modern Maputo, in Mozambique) to forward to them any information of military interest in their possession, even information previously acquired by the German intelligence services.

The following day, Castellano, while requesting news and updates from the Italian Supreme Command, complained that he did not even know its new location, and asked where the departing Allied mission should head for, something which indicated the enduring chaos of the situation. The same problem was reported to Mallaby. And when Massingham's leaders had reported with friendly sarcasm that they had fallen asleep awaiting wireless telegraphic contact to resume, Mallaby checked the message, revealing that he was in Brindisi, adding, with equal sarcasm, 'therefore Italy'.

On the same day the Allied mission arrived in Apulia, preceded by an imperious message from Algiers to Badoglio forbidding any publicity about this. The mission was led by the British Lieutenant-General Sir Frank Mason-MacFarlane and the diplomats Robert D. Murphy (for the United States) and Harold Macmillan (for the United Kingdom) and its first act was the eviction of Italian Chief of Staff of the Army from the Hotel Internazionale.

An urgent message from Algiers asked that it be pointed out to the Italian population (which when subjected to nearby shellfire, as many often were, would wave white flags) that the Allies had no choice but to target the German lines of communication in order to hinder their movements.[84]

At this point, Mallaby's work mainly comprised the reception of messages, decoding the multiple requests from Italian commanders (fighting the Germans from Sardinia to the Aegean Sea) and messages from the Allied mission personnel arriving in Apulia (who needed information on the availability of airports, transport and infrastructure).

Confusion was endemic in this period, and the Monkey–Drizzle transmissions once again constituted the only form of communication between the Italian nucleus in Brindisi and the Allies. They also served as a link between the scattered groups of Italian soldiers who were attempting to control the overwhelming situation as best they could. On 13 September, for example, Algiers requested an update about General Giacomo Carboni, who was in charge of the defence of Rome, asking if he was in Brindisi. The following day, General Ambrosio ordered Brigadier-General Castellano to try to establish communications with the diplomatic missions 'since it is impossible for us to do so'.

Mallaby was tasked with receiving and transcribing another famous message from the Allies in this phase, the content of which was not particularly pleasant for Badoglio. In this message, the head of the Italian government was bluntly invited to take action to liberate Italy from German control.

Pietro Badoglio, with typical nonchalance and the detachment from reality that characterized his efforts in this period, communicated via Mallaby his great happiness at the arrival of the Allied mission in Brindisi and proposed a summit meeting to discuss 'further actions in the Italian theatre, which, naturally, we are experts in'. The debate will continue as to whether this message resulted from an unconscious detachment from reality, or was a deliberate attempt to evade his duties.

From Algiers, however, on the same day, 13 September, Castellano sent the following message in code: 'We are sorry that the cigarettes are so bad.' This confirms that coded sentences had been previously agreed between the Italians, in order to exchange information without being understood by the Allies. Probably, considering the aforementioned message on 6 September, cigarettes meant the 'situation of the Italian Supreme Command'.

The message sent by Monkey to Massingham on 14 September provides clear evidence of a further major strategic error on the part of the Allies, regarding their evaluation and management of events in the wake of the Italian capitulation. In this, the

Italian leadership in Brindisi asked Brigadier-General Castellano to point out to the Allies that, 'as we are unable to operate at sea, due to the armistice, vital strategic positions have already fallen and are likely to fall into German hands. These are the Ionian Islands, Valona, Corsica, Elba. There is an urgent need for naval forces, including Italian ones, to monitor the situation and hinder landings.'[85]

There was no response to this request and what had been predicted by the Italians actually happened.

From 18 September, London's SOE leadership finally started sharing some details of Dick Mallaby's daring adventure with Bern, stating for the future that: 'we consider that the spiritual side of resistance is of paramount importance if we are to forestall the risk of apathy in the German occupied region. We are therefore infiltrating leading members of the Giustizia e Libertà movement and wish you to support all the elements likely to keep the people keep fighting; funds particularly for support of workless become important' and conceding that 'our knowledge of resistance movements and figures deriving from your work in recent months has proved to be of great value'. A few weeks later, this assessment would be blatantly contradicted, when the true nature of the Italian resistance movement was revealed to SOE's astonished leaders in Apulia by the Italians.

On the 20th, Roseberry sent a conciliatory note to McCaffery explaining that at the outset of the matter, there was little certainty over the good faith of the Italians. He also stressed that distubring the discussions while events were ongoing would have had fatal consequences, given the extreme secrecy surrounding them.

But this message contains further important inform-ation, highlighting, while at the same time noting that it should not be repeated, another careless statement by Castellano. According to him, the inability to make rapid decisions after the overthrow of Mussolini, which resulted in the influx of large numbers of German troops, was the fault of the king and Badoglio, whom he described as 'older than their years'.[86]

On 21 September Roseberry sent another message to McCaffery, which is essential for any study of the events of the period. It read:

The armistice is a purely military instrument and only military consideration with the Italian military considerations have any weight at present.

Our view is that we must take full advantage of collaboration with the Italian military staff whilst independently supporting the liberal elements.... Our chief preoccupation has been and still is firstly to ensure complete withdrawal of Italian military resistance to allies and accordingly fullest possible measure of military collaboration. This could only be done with the de facto government.

Badoglio and company regard a military government as the only form which will work at present and this cannot be disputed as regards the area on our side of the line.

Badoglio undoubtedly expected to be able to hold Rome and south of Rome and present military situation was not envisaged in his plans.

But the most striking statement, one that is characteriscally ramshackle and groundless in nature, appears at the message's end:

> For your strictly private guidance. General Castellano gave J (Roseberry: e.n.). the inside story of the original coup and it is evident that they and Ambrosio merely regard Badoglio as a useful instrument to be discarded when no longer needed. Ambrosio is the real power at present.[87]

Ambrosio may have been the real power in that moment, but on 18 November 1943 he was replaced by Giovanni Messe: a decision endorsed and authorized by the Allies given their absolute domination of the weak government of King Vittorio Emanuele and Badoglio.

Castellano evidently thought he had carried out his mission in an irreproachable manner, and had no remorse for the armistice catastrophe. Being unable to contain himself, he did not even understand that such statements, regardless of their validity, always leave a bad impression, notably among the British. In their wake, and because of the way he behaved, he never managed to appear as if acting in good faith during the negotiations.[88]

Meanwhile, it was only on the 22 September that the Foreign Office was informed that the mediation of the Vatican was no longer required to save agent Olaf. This was further proof that the unexpected developments in Operation *Neck* had been kept secret. On the same day, Dick Mallaby, who clearly had not been allowed to do so up to that point, sent a message to Cairo for the attention of Christine Granville, informing her that he was safe and sound.

Over the following days, SOE's leadership in Massingham and London were forced to explain why they had enjoyed full exclusivity in managing the Italian capitulation. The need for these clarifications partly stemmed from the intense, unrestrained frustration felt by some members in competing offices, which had led them to speculate, in the absence of better suggestions, that the occupation of Rome by the Germans had been a consequence of this exclusivity.

On 28 September 1943, with ill-concealed pride after 'so many requests', Cecil Roseberry in his capacity as head of Department J of SOE circulated among the few authorized to know the previously mentioned memorandum relating to Dick Mallaby's first mission, entitled 'The Olaf Story'.[89]

The enormous importance of what Mallaby had accomplished was recorded and freely recognized by those in the know. But amnesia at all levels, in Britain and in Italy, followed.

Over three densely packed pages, Roseberry summarized the details of Mallaby's involvement in the negotiations for the Italian capitulation and his journey to Brindisi. He also revealed that the British agent was training Italian wireless telegraphists at that time, but was itching to begin a new mission in enemy or occupied territory.[90]

The reason for the underestimation and ignorance of Mallaby's achievements, which have endured for decades, is highlighted by Massingham's commander, Dodds-Parker. He remembers how, at the time, few were party to the contents of the Monkey–Drizzle messages, and above all, that Eisenhower in person had ordered that knowledge of the part SOE played in the Italian surrender 'should be kept to a minimum'.

In his 1984 memoirs, Dodds-Parker complained that even he had not had the slightest opportunity to check the details of the events that he was about to recount, because, despite the recommendation of a former prime minister, he had not been allowed to access the relevant documentation. Up until the extensive declassification of documents in the 1990s and later, complaints of this kind were routine among British academics. Even Michael R. D. Foot pointed out that, thanks to the documentation left by SOE in Denmark, academics there had been able to draw on an abundance of sources that were unavailable to those in Great Britain.

Eisenhower, on the other hand, recognized that the events in which Mallaby was a key player had changed the course of World War II, completing a series of 'negotiations, secret communications, clandestine journeys of secret agents and frequent meetings in hidden places', where 'plots of various kinds were hatched, only to be abandoned because of changing circumstances' that 'if encountered in the fictional world, would have been scorned as incredible melodrama'.[91]

According to Leo Marks, the unpredictable developments leading on from Operation *Neck* guaranteed SOE, for the first time, the express appreciation of Churchill and the British General Staff, an event that would be repeated only once again, when SOE agents in Denmark managed to pass on valuable information about the German missile site at Peenemünde. They also brought further pleasure to the Baker Street Irregulars, who had handled the matter in splendid isolation without interference from their rivals in SIS.

On 7 December 1943, Dick Mallaby was awarded the Military Cross (even though a DSO had been proposed). Apart from some customarily flowery language such as 'dropped alone into lake of Como by parachute'; finding himself 'in conditions of unexpected difficulty that tested his courage'; and being 'handcuffed and beaten', demonstrating 'exceptional coolness, perseverance and devotion to duty', his citation states that if it were not for his excellent Monkey radio work, 'the Allied landings on the Italian mainland may have been made with Italy still an enemy'. Cecil Roseberry sent Mallaby a personal letter on 11 December 1943, in which he emphasized that he was 'very proud' that this was the first honour for his section, while predicting that it would not be its last.

Although Operation *Neck* and its unexpected developments have, over time, been sporadically and summarily revealed, its details and the most remarkable implications have always been ignored and have remained hard to pin down. According to Foot, what happened 'has been in print for over thirty years, and generally ignored, as too improbable (like much of SOE's actual work) to be true'.[92]

The encoded Monkey–Drizzle transmissions officially went off air on 17 September; the last message from Monkey was No. 114.

The following farewell message was broadcasted from the Cumulus, the new radio station placed in Italy by the Allies: 'He has done a marvelous job many congratulations to him'.[93]

Dick Mallaby's first mission had come to an end and agent Olaf had ceased to exist.

A second special mission would begin for Mallaby more than a year later, and this one too, after several initial disasters, would have unexpected and remarkable results, and, moreover, would remain hidden even further in the shadows for decades.

The Second Mission

Mallaby and the German Surrender, February–March 1945

(Or: how, having been captured once again near Lake Como, Mallaby again manages to get away with it, convincing the surprisingly receptive Supreme Commander of all SS forces in Italy to begin secret negotiations for the local German surrender to the Allies.)

Decidedly individualistic, inconsistent in obedience, instinctively disrespectful of the law; easy to guide and misguide but difficult to control, impressionable in the presence of high rankers, prepared to imitate Machiavelli and convinced that everyone is equally inclined to do so, and more interested in form than content.

Description of the average Italian, according to the British Foreign Office handbook, dated 26 July 1943

More than servitude I fear liberty endowed by others.

Giuseppe Mazzini (1805–1872)

> The omnipotence of God, once the events are
> over, is not able to modify them subsequently,
> whereas historians can do so by changing the
> narration of the events that actually happened.
>
> Voltaire (1694–1778)

In the immediate wake of the Italian armistice in September 1943, the northern and central areas of Italy were occupied by the Germans. The Repubblica Sociale Italiana (RSI – Italian Social Republic, informally known as the Republic of Salò after its de facto capital) was established, under the command of Il Duce, Benito Mussolini. The south of the country, where the Italian civil and military forces loyal to the king of Italy were trying to reorganize, was in the hands of the Allies. Italian partisan forces, whilst of disparate political ideologies, began to fight against the Germans and Fascists with the support of the Allies. The beginning of the conquest of Italian territory from July 1943 caused inevitable disruption in the operational and organizational needs of the Allies and consequently SOE. The occupation of almost all of southern Italy had increased the ranges of Allied air sorties by hundreds of kilometres, and the airfields in Apulia, in particular, brought the Balkans much closer.

Following changes in the locations of various Allied organizations in the Mediterranean, SOE's leadership began to set up bases in the Italian peninsula.

Although the Allies' power to requisition was absolute, problems arose between the various armed forces in finding suitable locations for the different departments and branches. Given that no space was available in Brindisi, Monopoli (a little town 40km south of Bari) was chosen, and from the initial site there soon arose a whole series of offices, administration centres and training centres in the vicinity, all of which, in the words of Dick Mallaby, took place 'in great secrecy'.

The base at Monopoli, established on 18 September 1943, became fully operational in mid-October and was codenamed Maryland, after Mary, the wife of its commander, Gerald (or Gerry) T. Holdsworth, also a member of SOE and a leading expert in sabotage and explosives.

The SOE department operating in Italy, for mysterious reasons, was given the name No. 1 Special Force.

Maryland's value as an advanced logistics base continued to grow, given that all the missions targeted at the area of Italy governed by the RSI originated from Apulia, as well as many of those destined for the Balkans. As early as November 1943, all of SOE's transmission activities in Italy were moved from Brindisi to Monopoli.

As the front line pushed north, Holdsworth moved to Rome, leaving his deputy, Hewitt, to run Maryland.

Dick Mallaby was obviously one of the first to be based at Maryland.

Mallaby was keen to conduct another special mission, but despite his repeated requests, he would have to wait more than a year, even though he was kept busy. This considerable gap was not only the result of lengthy preparations, but was also because he had been captured, photographed and precisely identified during his first operation; as a result, SOE's leaders considered Mallaby better suited to the equally valuable, but less draining and risky, role of instructor and coordinator of direct missions to the areas of Italy under control of the RSI.

But there were further specific reasons for this decision. According to Dick Mallaby's private memoirs, his requests for immediate reassignment to operations were not accepted because 'I knew too much about the organization.'

To this must be added that Mallaby was the key player in and witness to the controversial armistice between the Italians and the Allies, an episode that was both well known and widely censored. Little of what Mallaby had seen, heard and transmitted coincided precisely with the official versions, while the desire to pin down the actual terms of the Italian unconditional surrender was not only of interest to journalists and academic historians, but also at the time to all the various parties – the Italians, Germans, Soviets, French, and not least the Allies themselves.

Mallaby's superiors, while relying on his abilities, always kept in mind that he needed careful handling.

Under no circumstances was he to fall into the hands of the Germans and RSI Italians, and, in any event, it was better that he had little contact with Allied personnel outside SOE.

Given that former agent Olaf was not to be used for missions into German-occupied territory, Mallaby was assigned to the wireless telegraphy section located about 15km south of Monopoli, in the Selva di Fasano area.

Mallaby's memories of Apulia were positive: despite the hard work, the setting of the base allowed for some fun to be had in his free time, and its proximity to the sea was particularly appreciated. A small group of FANYs was also ordered to leave Massingham and relocate to Apulia. Among them was Christine Marks.

The journey of the future Mrs Mallaby and three of her colleagues to the heel of Italy was somewhat long, arduous and perilous. From Algiers, after a truck transfer across hundreds of kilometres of desert, her group arrived in Bizerte. From there, according to the original plans, they would travel by plane to Italy; however, organizational problems arose, and they were forced to stay there for 14 days, during which they took care of wounded American soldiers. When they finally left for Italy, the four FANYs travelled instead on a small landing boat, in far from peaceful, hygienic or comfortable conditions.

Having arrived at Monopoli, the FANYs found it in a fairly chaotic state. There was a water shortage and little available space, so much so that in its early phases some sections were based out in the open. Eventually some space was found for them, with the FANYs' office based on the first floor of a building. The secret, precious communications that the girls had worked on were sorted on the ground and second floors, and were lowered and raised between the three, somewhat primitively, by means of a beach bucket attached to a rope. They worked 12-hour shifts, and every few days one member of the group would take a break, leaving the other three to carry on working.

Now that they were reunited, Dick Mallaby and Christine spent Christmas 1943 together in Apulia. Dick asked Christine to marry him once the war was over. Christine said yes, and both hoped that developments in the war would not interfere with their marriage and future plans.

The peculiar situation that had evolved in Italy meant that in the months following the September 1943 surrender, the Allied special and intelligence services were the only ones effectively supporting anti-fascist forces both in the Italy ruled by the king and Badoglio, and the Italy under Mussolini's control. In the opening months of 1944, Second Lieutenant Dick Mallaby (now officially seconded to SOE with the proviso 'not to be made public', according to his personnel file) continued his work begun in the previous months of coordinating and training agents in the Kingdom of the South and members of the resistance groups intending to operate as clandestine wireless operators in RSI territory. Mallaby was also one of the few recipients of the daily reports of the Italian interception service, demonstrating the importance of his role.

In the meantime Dick Mallaby's mysterious existence was constantly and carefully monitored by the enemies' intelligence agencies. A 1944 report stated the following: 'It is known that [Mallaby] in the second half of August 1943 dropped into Como Province, where he was identified and placed under arrest. It seems, however, that he later managed to escape and rejoin Allied troops fighting in southern Italy, and currently is in Bari with the rank of captain.'[1]

The opening war years had seen the confiscation of the Mallaby family's businesses, restrictions on travel and school attendance for the children, and isolation from the community in Asciano – few of whom even greeted them by now. In 1943 the dramatic news that Dick had been shot reached them: Mrs Mallaby did not want to tell her husband, but the pharmacist in Asciano came down one night to Poggio Pinci to break the news to him. Fortunately, it turned out not to be true, and was probably the result of local malice.

After September 1943, things became worse. Cecil Mallaby was warned not to leave his Asciano residence without permission. He would certainly have been interned, had it not been for the timely coded telegrams sent to him by friendly presences in the local Prefecture, who forewarned him of any likely attempts to detain him. Thus, Mallaby senior, like the partisans and the draft dodgers, took refuge in safe houses, where he spent a considerable amount of time. After September 1943 he established contact with a partisan known as Fulmine ('Lightning') from the Amiata group. If stopped by German troops, in order to mask his English accent he planned to gag himself and slur his words, pretending to have terrible toothache.

A typical event in wartime Asciano was the primary school march, organized by local teacher Maria Rispoli. She, together with her pupils, used to march to the Mallabys' house, where the children were ordered to shout: 'May God strike the English!' (a famous phrase with which the militant journalist Mario Appelius concluded his anti-British propaganda radio broadcasts). To mark Easter 1944, the same teacher left a handwritten note at the Mallaby residence with the following message: 'May God strike the English. May God strike the English. May God strike the English. May God strike the English. To the wishes of my students, I add mine a hundredfold. Maria Rispoli, Easter 1944'. Cecil Mallaby took the unpleasant note and inserted it into his private diary, where I found it almost 70 years later.

On 16 July 1944, a further key event, unrecorded in any other historical work, but relevant in this one, took place: a father saw his son reappear after almost five years of war.

The Allies had taken control of the province of Siena a few days previously, and in his private diary, Cecil Mallaby noted:

> At 9 o'clock a large military truck drove up to the house, and when I reached the hall I found at last my dear boy Dick, looking very thin and quite wornout looking. He bore the pips of a lieutenant and the ribbon of the M.C.! I had not seen him since I saw him off at Milan Station on 1 September 1939 (a boy of 20 is now he is a wornout old man of 25!) – A great pity that this is only a 'stolen' visit he had to punch off again early in the morning – We have so much to talk about and so many people wanted to see him and salute him – as it was we did not get to bed till past 11.30 in spite of the early start tomorrow – Thank God for his mercies.[2]

The news spread through Asciano and many people came to the Mallaby house to see 'Dìcche' again and admire his Military Cross.

Cecil Mallaby's private diary also reveals that his son left Poggio Pinci the following morning at 6.31am, heading for the town of Macerata in eastern central Italy. Archival documents confirm that Dick Mallaby accompanied Major John Henderson to the Macerata area for a brief fact-finding mission among the partisan groups in the area.[3]

For the remainder of 1944, Mallaby was also involved in the analysis of *matériel* provided by

SIM's interception service, and participated in some of the details in the planning of Operation *Rankin* – the secret activities designed to prevent, or curb, the conquest of Western European territories by the Soviet Union, in the event of a rapid and total collapse in Germany.

Finally, in the closing weeks of 1944, Mallaby was tasked with his long-desired, new special mission.

The way in which Mallaby's second mission developed borders again on the unlikely and, apart from the creative courage shown by SOE's young agent, the others involved – many of whom were well known – do not come out of it well.

SOE had been working with the Brigate Fiamme Verdi (Green Flame Brigade), a clandestine Catholic formation with branches all over northern Italy, the activities of which were being affected by its lack of adequate radio contact with the Allies. Mallaby volunteered to enter northern Italy covertly with some of its members to set up a transmission station in the mountainous area between the provinces of Bergamo and Brescia and instruct operators on site, in order to facilitate air-drops of *matériel*.

Initially, SOE's leadership opposed Mallaby's return to northern Italy, due to reservations resulting from his previous mission. A warm personal letter sent to Dick Mallaby by Cecil Roseberry on 3 January 1945 nicely summarized both Mallaby's deep desire to begin a new mission, and the risks that his return to action might pose:

Dear Dick,

I have never answered your letter of the 14th. Nov., but this is not to be taken as any lack of appreciation – I was delighted to hear from you again. As you know, I take an 'uncle's' interest in you and am always glad to hear of your doings. Your letter made me think that you would try to find some way of getting on to the dirt track again and now, you young devil, you seem to be half-way there. It's no use my preaching anything about the risk to yourself personally – I know that does not count and that you could argue that it is safer than the trenches or even a bombing area. I do feel, however, that your risk is bigger than the next bloke's as your appearance and your carriage are exceedingly individual, you are already 'on the books' and moreover, if they like to play cat-and-mouse they could give you a delightful little run until they had plotted all your contacts.

So it behoves you to act with more than ordinary circumspection. I feel sure you and JQ will have hit it off well and I hope you did not forget to thank him for the efforts he was making – not knowing the other line I was working – to get you out when you were in the bag.

Following his earlier capture, Mallaby's details had been put on file. If he were captured again, this would guarante the firing squad for him: in northern Italy the situation, atmosphere and mood were quite different to those of August 1943 and there were now two enemies instead of one.

But the operation was subsequently authorized, under the codename *Edenton Blue*. Following a covert entry into Italy from the Swiss border, the official aim of the mission was to provide operational and wireless transmission support to Lombard resistance groups, as well as further SOE missions, up until the German surrender. However, Mallaby had been confidentially informed that he was to remain in northern Italy, exercising full caution, and, following a cessation of war activities, was to be ready to move immediately to Milan, to take control of all British wireless communications in northern Italy.

In fact, Britain's political leaders, and consequently SOE's, were thinking ahead to winning the peace, after winning the war. The following outcomes were justifiably feared: the triggering of indiscriminate and bloody vendettas; attempts at insurrection; substitution in public office of elements politically oriented towards and controlled by the Soviet Union, without adequate representation of all anti-fascist forces; and Tito's expansionist ambitions into eastern Italy.

Before departing for his second mission, Mallaby learned that, following further advances in the front northwards, No. 1 Special Force would move to the Tolomei Institute in Siena – the school that Dick had attended only a few years previously.[4] The move took place in February 1945.[5]

Mallaby's new mission was soon underway. He reached Lyon in France on 15 December 1944 in good company, his travelling companions being Edgardo Sogno, Alfredo Pizzoni (president of the Comitato di Liberazione Nazionale Alta Italia – CLNAI, the Committee of National Liberation for Northern Italy), and Ferruccio Parri (deputy commander of the Corpo Volontari della Libertà – CVL, the Volunteer Freedom Corps), among the most important figures in the Italian resistance movement.[6]

Mallaby then continued on to Lausanne, and then to Bern – this tortuous route was imposed by the need to avoid the front line. He remained hidden in the British Embassy in Bern until 13 February (mirroring his unnerving wait prior to Operation *Neck*), when he moved to Lugano and met up with the other members of the mission which he was to head: the priest Don Giovanni Barbareschi; a radio operator (codenamed Anselmo – real name Everardo Galassini); and another priest, Don Mario Zanin (alias Byron), who was a member of the Brigate Fiamme Verdi.[7]

The first stage of their journey was to the Bergamo mountains, a quieter spot than Milan, which was to be their final destination. The radio equipment would travel separately for security reasons.

Unfortunately, despite the delays, which were due mainly to the arrests of Parri and other important members of the Italian resistance, the mission lacked adequate preparation, especially regarding their movements and false documents, both on account of the trust placed in the abilities of Don Giovanni Barbareschi, and the lack of involvement of the head of the SOE Lugano branch.

On the evening of 14 February 1945, Mallaby's group, led by two smugglers, secretly crossed the border between Switzerland and Italy through the Val Cavargna, a popular route for contraband traffic, soldiers on the run and spies; they had no radio sets and codes with them because they were already in Italy. Theirs was not an easy passage, because in order to avoid suspicion, it was decided that no one would wear mountain boots, even though the area was covered in snow.

The four rested for a couple of hours in a small mountain shelter near Carlaccio after their hard night march, in which the only kind of comfort was a bit of wine and two beds that were much sought after.

At dawn on the 15th, they came within sight of Lake Como. After a couple of hours of further walking, the group crossed Lake Como, from Menaggio to Varenna, aboard a rented boat. And there the problems began.

The plan was that at this point the group would travel by car to Bergamo, having found a safe way to get hold of one. This was not possible, and so the four (separately, so as not to arouse suspicion) reached

Lecco 'laughing and joking with the other hitch hikers' on board a big truck with a trailer.

Instead of pressing on towards the Bergamo mountains, Don Barbareschi persuaded Mallaby to head straight for Milan, where he had 'many friends who could help us'. A car was found in Lecco, but as it would take a few hours to get it ready, the four went to a tavern to refresh themselves. It was a decision that proved fatal.

Mallaby prudently decided not to sit with the two priests. This appeared to be a good decision because, after a while, he noticed that another client and the owner appeared to be taking a particular interest in the imprudent conversation of the two men, who 'rather forgot that they were still in danger and spoke too loudly and openly of matters which would have been better left unsaid'.

Following a tip-off by one of their travelling companions on the trucks, or by the client in the bar who had suddenly left the premises, a few minutes later two non-commissioned officers of the Brigate Nere (Black Brigade – more formally, the Corpo Ausiliario delle Squadre d'Azione di Camicie Nere) appeared. Although the documents of Mallaby, Barbareschi, Galassini and Zanin were in order, the somewhat agitated behaviour of the two priests led to personal searches.

Nothing compromising was found on Mallaby and Anselmo, but Giovanni Barbareschi was carrying a large amount of Swiss francs, while Don Zanin had Swiss cigarettes, powdered coffee and letters from Switzerland addressed to Italians, as well as a message from the former Senator Piero Puricelli in which he requested a significant sum of money for the priest to take abroad. This made the NCOs suspect that the four were smugglers, a positive result that appeared to offer them some hope.

The details of what happened next are recorded not only in Mallaby's memoirs, but also in British reports and in the RSI documents acquired by the Allies at the end of the war.[8]

On 15 February 1945, Dick Mallaby was facing the double risk of being unmasked and recognized. Reflecting on the fact that Lake Como did not bring him much luck, the SOE agent hoped that no one recognized him as the paratrooper who, not even two years previously, had been in the same area, and in the same situation; or, that this did not emerge from the files.

However, things soon got worse. With some hesitation, especially from the two priests (only Barbareschi was in a cassock, adding further confusion and suspicion), the four stated that they had met on board the truck that had brought them to Lecco.

Immediately after this, a decisive and frightening detail was revealed: three of their false identity documents (prepared by an Italian collaborator at SOE's Lugano branch) gave the same address in Milan

(No. 1 Via Sant'Agnese) and, to boot, the building corresponding to this address had been destroyed by a bombing raid two years earlier.[9]

Things went downhill rapidly, and the four were arrested. After a short trip to the nearby police station, they were taken to the Brigate Nere barracks in Lecco and detained in separate cells.

Shortly thereafter, an Allied air raid took place and in the confusion that followed, Don Zanin managed to escape.[10]

Mallaby, who had previously tried to escape through an open window, managed to leave his cell and reach the courtyard without being seen, but was immediately caught by a member of the Black Brigade, who fortunately did not shoot him.

And at this point, the nearly 26-year-old Mallaby began to act decisively. His first goal was, again, to abide by the first commandment of a prisoner of war facing execution: gain time, and, given that the original mission had failed, he believed that the only hope was to invent a very basic bluff, embellishing it with mentions of key figures at the highest levels.

As he noted in his private memoirs, 'I sat down on a bed and summoned the situation. I was after all the Senior person there and the welfare of the party depended on me. I thought over my previous experiences and decided that the only way of gaining time and, therefore, of being able to escape was for me to take the matter up to as high a level as possible'.

In all likelihood, this attempt grew out of the fertile bed of confidential information about the situation in northern Italy given to him before departure, in order to provide him with some context on the situation in the area and the enemy's status quo.

And so, with the air of someone who finally wishes to unburden themselves, Mallaby confidentially asked to speak with the station commander. He declared himself to be Captain Richard Tucker (creating a fictitious identity with a changed surname once again, to simplify things, and cleverly raising his military rank), on a special mission from Field Marshal Harold Alexander, tasked with passing on a highly confidential message for the exclusive attention of Marshal Rodolfo Graziani, Minister of War of the RSI.

The choice of Graziani was probably because he had been captured by the Italians.

Mallaby also had the foresight to specify immediately that his special mission did not involve spying, but was aimed exclusively at the direct transmission of a personal message to Graziani, and, given its highly secret nature, it could not be conveyed through the usual diplomatic channels.

Mallaby's statements left the Brigate Nere officers in a puzzled and incredulous state, especially in view of the fact that Mallaby had been arrested in the company of two priests. He clarified that their presence was necessary, as the best means of contacting Graziani was considered to be via the Archbishop of Milan, Cardinal

Alfredo Ildefonso Schuster: the two priests were to take Mallaby to the cardinal.

At this point the Brigate Nere officer decided to check this by cross-examining Don Giovanni Barbareschi. Unfortunately, according to Mallaby, the young priest continued to be of little help because – although certainly in good faith – he denied this version, accusing Mallaby of being an impostor, clearly fearful of having been betrayed by him.

Mallaby, with great skill and adapting his tactics to the circumstances, pointed out that the two priests were simply tasked with taking him to Schuster, and therefore did not know the details of his mission.

Thus, on the afternoon of the 15th, Mallaby was taken to the commander of the Como Brigate Nere, who immediately asked him for details of the message he had been instructed to deliver to Graziani.

Surprisingly, when he refused, Mallaby was not returned to a cell, but taken to the officers' mess for the night, having solemnly promised that he would not attempt to escape. The atmosphere had suddenly become cordial, and Mallaby was told he had assumed the status of a prisoner of war. Representatives of the RSI appeared interested in listening to the proposals brought by the so-called special messenger from the Allied leadership.

The next morning Mallaby was taken to Milan, where he met with Brigadier-General Edoardo Facdouelle, Chief of Staff of the Brigate Nere. Facdouelle welcomed him cordially, and expressed his conviction that Mallaby's 'special mission' would be carried out successfully. After a brief discussion, Mallaby had lunch with Facdouelle, the head of the Fascist Women's Auxiliary Forces and Facdouelle's equally cordial daughter. During the lunch, Mallaby was led to believe that he would without doubt be returned to central-southern Italy, and was even asked to send greetings to Facdouelle's brother, who lived in San Miniato in Tuscany.

On the morning of the 17th they left Milan, heading for Graziani's headquarters. Mallaby was left alone while Facdouelle went to meet Graziani. Despite his insistence, Mallaby did not manage to meet the Marshal of Italy: he was informed that Graziani did not consider it opportune to speak with him because of the danger that the Germans would find out about it.

Mallaby was then taken to Volta Mantovana to the headquarters of the Italian counterespionage organization to be interrogated by the head of SID, Colonel of the Carabinieri Candeloro De Leo, who had been summoned from Milan, and personally given this 'important mission' by Graziani.

Dick Mallaby was surprised at the fact that, despite the often pre-dawn timings and it being winter, all his transfers, even the longest, took place in open-topped cars. It did not take him long to realize, when an intense Allied air raid began, and without any need for further explanation, that travelling in an open-topped car made jumping into the nearest ditch a lot easier. He also realized that even the cars of the highest institutional offices of the RSI were open-topped.[11]

After being once again impeccably hosted – even enjoying a real coffee, his first in a long while – the first meeting between Mallaby and De Leo took place on the 18th.[12]

De Leo, who informed Mallaby that Graziani could not meet him 'for obvious reasons' and had delegated him to do so, turned out to be a skilful and observant inquisitor. He employed a verification strategy that consisted of asking Mallaby to sign the minutes of his statements and then making him repeat them several times, with new statements and signatures, allowing for comparison between the various minutes.

Since his insistence on a personal interview with Graziani had borne no fruit, Mallaby began to reveal the details of his phantom mission, which with the passing of the hours he had been able to improve and refine, to an ever less inquisitorial and ever more interested De Leo. The latter confessed – sincerely or for some ulterior motive – to Mallaby his concerns about what could happen in northern Italy after the cessation of hostilities, saying that the RSI's leadership strongly feared partisan reprisals, communist attempts to seize power through violence, and the resulting chaos. Mallaby enjoyed reassuring him, 'revealing' that the Allies had foreseen such a scenario, and had made specific plans to be able to oppose such reactions. With the consent of the RSI's leadership, even the resistance forces could be exploited to avoid unnecessary bloodshed and damage to the assets and productive resources of northern Italy. Finally, Mallaby reiterated that he had been instructed only to report Graziani's response to his superiors, having no power to negotiate.[13]

Mallaby pointed out that the Allies wanted to verify the possibility of agreeing a *modus operandi* with Mussolini's republic, in order to avoid destruction in northern Italy by the increasingly brutal retreating German forces following Hitler's scorched earth orders, together with the removal of industrial machinery and works of art.[14]

In order to avoid all this, a proposal was made to establish preliminary contact with the leaders of the RSI, with a view to setting up a permanent line of communication to make plans for the moment when the Germans began their foreseen retreat.

The detail of the proposal formulated by Mallaby to Graziani was as follows:

1 In the event of a German withdrawal from northern Italy, the Italian troops under Graziani's command should do everything possible to preserve Italian industrial installations and public services from destruction by the Germans;

2 In such circumstances they should also do what they could to maintain law and order in the face of any attempt at disturbance from whatever quarter;

3 Partisan formations, who would carry out similar tasks in the areas controlled by them, would be directed by Allied missions sent in at the appropriate time;

4 These measures were aimed at avoiding unnecessary bloodshed alike between Allied and Italian Republican forces and between the latter and Partisan formations;

5 In the event of Italian Republican forces being unable to keep order in difficult local situations, Alexander would send in adequate airborne forces for police duties.[15]

Dick Mallaby had laid out these five points on the basis of the information at his disposal and the concerns expressed to him by De Leo. Graziani, should he be willing to engage, could travel to Allied Force Headquarters on an RSI aircraft, or even an Allied one.

Finally Mallaby informed De Leo that because of his capture the plans were miscarried, so it would be necessary for him to collect the wireless equipment in Switzerland.

In his secret diary Mallaby reflected as follows: 'I was very lucky that I managed to tell a story that proved to be entirely watertight and was not broken down in later cross-examination'.

De Leo concluded the meeting by assuring Mallaby that he would report the contents to Graziani, expressing a curious regret over the fact that the operation had lost some of its secrecy.

De Leo kept his word and on 19 February sent Graziani the declaration signed by Captain Richard Tucker containing the proposed conditions.

But in the Italian camp, the matter caused some embarrassment, partly because, just regarding the loss of secrecy, some of the Brigate Nere had already informed Benito Mussolini in person as early as 16 February. But the turning point was close and would still have been surprising, even if seasoned by moments of panic.

Mallaby could not know that, due to loyalty and transparency – or rather, due to the impossibility of doing otherwise – the RSI's leadership did not intend to hide the matter from the Germans – and perhaps this was the subject of De Leo's aforementioned regret.

In any event, the Italians did precisely this, and Mallaby, after the confidential conversation with De Leo, firstly remained confined and then was interrogated again.

Afterwards, Mallaby was told to pack his things. In the hall of the beautiful villa there was an SS captain, who, after introducing himself, kindly asked the British agent to follow him.

Mallaby felt the same sequence of emotions in the moments that followed as those he had experienced in August 1943 in Rome, when he had been escorted from prison. The most logical assessment seemed to be that he had fallen out of a (not particularly hot) frying pan and into the fire.

In his words, 'My uneasiness increased further as looking over the shoulder of the officer who sat in the front seat, I noticed that he was reading a signed copy of my statement to Graziani. However, there was little to be done except carry on the bluff, for a slip at this stage would have meant the end of everything both for me and my friends in Como'.

Mallaby was shepherded into a German vehicle and driven to the headquarters of the Sicherheitsdienst (SD – the SS intelligence agency), at the Palazzo delle Assicurazioni, in Corso Vittorio Emanuele (now Corso Porta Nuova) in Verona.

Dick Mallaby would have felt reassured if he had known of the awareness that was spreading through part of the German military leadership regarding the inevitability of their defeat, and the consequent determination of most of them to achieve a viable exit from the war, avoiding as many of the foreseeable post-war consequences as possible.

Mallaby underwent a typical German interrogation: he began with the story of his life, from childhood to his capture. Everything was meticulously minuted and every answer gave rise to further questions. There was no chance to relax, given that the interrogators switched over after brief summarizing consultations.

What his interrogators did not know was that Dick Mallaby understood German, so that he was able to follow the content of the conversations that took place in his presence and process his responses with greater efficiency and with more time to think. Moreover, in order not to fall into contradictions, Mallaby, as usual, recounted and confirmed, as far as was possible and prudent, personal details about himself that were true. Tuscany was by now under Allied control, and, as far as his family and their safety was concerned, there was now no possibility of it feeding back, nor of retaliation. Naturally, Mallaby was less sincere with the Germans about the details of his activities and, in particular, about his first Italian mission in August 1943 and everything that flowed from it.

The problems came when his interrogators asked him what his credentials were for this special mission. Mallaby replied that, for obvious reasons, he did not have any documents with him, but, once again improvising on the spot, he went out on a limb, saying that Archbishop Schuster would have received information about his mission directly from the British headquarters.

When asked how he was supposed to contact his command, Mallaby repeated that a radio was available in Switzerland. It was a shrewd but credible answer.

The Germans, however, did not see it as such, and it was interpreted as a clever attempt to evade German custody, and not come back. As the situation began to become more problematic, Mallaby felt like an unprepared schoolboy saved by the bell, as the umpteenth Allied air raid sent everyone rushing to the shelters.

He was further grilled by the SS, who, as the hours and days passed, tried to get him to contradict himself. Mallaby held firm and he was not tortured or drugged.[16]

A female SS collaborator from Merano was in charge of accompanying Mallaby to the shelter and bringing him back during each air raid, while the captain joined them when they went to the mess, which was located in another building.

As reported in his secet diary, Mallaby optimistically thought 'that by now they trusted me fully, for no guards ever accompanied us or were placed over my room'. But at the end of his final interrogation, Mallaby was informed that he would be taken to a German general.

Once again, just when appearances suggested a terrifying, or at least very uncertain outcome, something unexpected happened.

On the evening of 26 February, Dick Mallaby was taken to a splendid villa in Fasano, near Lake Garda.

Left alone in one of its very luxuriously furnished rooms, Mallaby first saw a woman appear in evening dress, and then none other than Obergruppenführer Karl Wolff, head of the police and military plenipotentiary of the German armed forces in Italy. In practical terms, Wolff was in charge of all the areas not directly involved in the fighting (the latter being under Albert Kesselring's control) and thus headed the brutal anti-partisan war.

The surprises continued as Wolff, via the elegantly dressed lady, who was officially present as an interpreter, began to engage with Mallaby in an unexpected way.

In his sober uniform which bore only a single decoration, Wolff paternally and lightly pointed out to Mallaby how lucky he had been not to have been shot as a spy yet. Mallaby as usual pretended not to understand German.

After the cordialities were over, Wolff categorically told Mallaby that Marshal Graziani could not adhere to his request, as Italy's destiny in the war was inextricably linked with that of Germany, in accordance with the latter's principles of chivalry and honour.

What actually happened in the weeks that followed showed just how diverse German behaviour was in that decisive and difficult moment from what was pompously declared by Wolff.

Wolff, who also claimed that the stories relating to SS atrocities were 'quite untrue', continued to inform Mallaby rather erratically that he had provided ample guarantees to Cardinal Schuster that, in the case of a German surrender, it would be in accordance with the German tradition of chivalrous loyalty. He continued arguing about the military and political situation, boasting of his personal friendship with Hitler, Göring and all the German leaders.

After this general, conciliatory preamble, Wolff indicated that what Mallaby had said was considered false by the Germans. The Polizeiführer then contradicted himself, stating that the moment would come soon when the Wehrmacht's leadership would need to make contact with their British counterparts. Wolff put himself forward as official or unofficial liaison official, by virtue of his self-proclaimed ability to negotiate with ease. The following dialogue developed, recorded by Dick Mallaby in his private memoirs:

WOLFF: To considerably simplify the approach ... Tell me, Captain Tucker: are you in a position to send a message to your headquarters?

MALLABY: If I had my transmitter, yes.

WOLFF: And where is it?

MALLABY: In Switzerland.

WOLFF: There are no problems. We have agents in Switzerland and can bring it here.

MALLABY: I'm sorry, but that's practically impossible.

WOLFF: Why?

MALLABY: The apparatus is in the possession of my comrade in Bern and only I know how to find it.

WOLFF: You can give me a letter addressed to him. So he can hand over the transmitter to our agent.

MALLABY: I am sorry, sir, I cannot do that.

WOLFF: Your way of doing things is ruining your story, Captain Tucker.

MALLABY: But I certainly cannot give you the addresses of British secret agents in Switzerland! You can understand that. I suggest an alternative: I will go to Bern myself and bring the transmitter here. I give you my word. If I can go back, I will do it.

WOLFF: Hmm. I have to think about that.

Mallaby inferred from the tone of Wolff's statements and from the non-negative response to his bold proposal that Wolff was fully aware of imminent defeat and was attempting to curry favour, putting himself forward as an intermediary between the Germans and the Allies.

Encouraged by Wolff's increasingly persuasive and cordial tone, Mallaby also realized that if he managed to return to Switzerland, it would open up the possibility of him playing a decisive role in this matter, thanks to this unexpected opportunity. Thus he reiterated the proposed plane journey already presented to Colonel De Leo: either an Allied aircraft could take Wolff to a part of Allied-occupied Italy, or Wolff could travel there on board a German aircraft.

After their two-hour meeting, Wolff revealed that he was convinced of Mallaby's good faith and made a rather naive (or rather, naively sly) offer that was really uninviting: if Field Marshal Alexander agreed to interrupt the supplies of *matériel* to communist partisan groups in northern Italy, he would allow all the other Italian patriot formations who wanted to, to cross the front line and enter the south.

Mallaby, for his part, gave his word of honour as a British officer that he would return with a radio within a week to relay Alexander's reply. Furthermore, he promised not to reveal the locations of the various strategic sites which he had been escorted to.

Mallaby was in good spirits as he planned his trip to and back from Switzerland. While for the second time he had unexpectedly saved his skin, without endangering his two companions still in prison, and without having revealed any secrets, he understood that the opportunity presented to him was highly favourable for obtaining results that were both hard to imagine and very important.[17]

As Mallaby noted in his private memoirs: 'I realized that at this stage little or no harm could come to me or to my friends in prison. It was in fact the chance of a lifetime, and if it had been successful it might have meant a great shortening of the war in Europe and the saving of many lives… it was with great difficulty that I masked the emotion I felt at the success of my series of bluffs'.

The end of the meeting was accompanied by a significant change in the atmosphere: in fact, Wolff, appointing Mallaby as his go-between, told him that he would be allowed to return to Switzerland, and wished him luck.

Mallaby was then taken back to Verona.

The next morning, Mallaby learned that Obergruppenführer Wolff had indeed ordered his release, but his departure was delayed for several hours due to further air raids.

In his private memoirs, Dick Mallaby also recalled that, despite the obvious danger to his life, the sound of the bombs dropped by his fellow countrymen and the Americans always helped to keep him in high spirits, giving him the irrational feeling that 'our boys are coming'. This intimate detail alone suggests something of his emotional state and the tension under which he was forced to live, beyond any formal detachment that he maintained.

On 28 February, Mallaby, after another air-raid delay, left Verona and was first escorted by the Germans to a

villa in the western part of Lake Como. Having reached
Cernobbio, about a kilometre from the Swiss border, he
agreed with Wolff's men the precise location at which
he would return to Italy and the stock phrase that would
be sent via standard BBC transmission (used for those
who were not able to receive encrypted ones): 'Per
Giovanni' ('For Giovanni'), to advise the Germans of
his arrival and later to give indications of the date and
time of his return to Italy and any other necessary details.

Mallaby reiterated his promise to return with the
radio within a week. This commitment was not carried
through, however, and for the third time out of three in
Mallaby's military service, his mission did not develop
in the foreseen manner. On 1 March 1945, at 7.00am,
Mallaby, who ought to have been able to return to
Switzerland without issue, arrived confidently at the
Swiss border in Chiasso under the guise of Bernardo
Francini, a member of the Swiss secret intelligence
services – a false identity that had been previously
agreed with the Swiss services through Edgardo
Sogno's partisan group Organizzazione Franchi.

However, once again Mallaby discovered that those
who should have put him in a position to act without
hindrance had not been up to the task. The right hand
did not know what the left was doing on this occasion
either, and the Swiss border police had not been
informed of the arrival of Bernardo Francini. The
border officials got wind of the fact that this person was
not just a mere illicit presence, and diligently contacted

the relevant office, the head of which, Guido Bustelli, was unavailable, while the official specifically sent to Chiasso knew nothing about Bernardo Francini, and refused to identify him.

Mallaby had managed to escape any consequences of arrest by the Brigate Nere, and had managed to establish a dialogue with the leaders of the RSI and the SS, but had not taken into account the state apparatus of neutral Switzerland, and, above all, the slovenliness of those who had organized and run his mission.

There were no alternatives: faced with a return to Italy, Mallaby opted to be taken into custody by the Swiss, hoping that his presence would be reported or make someone curious to know more about him. He was immediately imprisoned along with a group of smugglers, after a stopover at the decontamination center, with no way of communicating with the outside world. Once again Mallaby found himself enduring a terribly frustrating wait, especially considering that time was of the essence.

Despite his protests, his imprisonment continued, and he was moved from one detention camp to another. Only on the 8th was Mallaby able to secretly send a message from Bellinzona Camp through Giorgio Casagrande, a member of the Red Cross. Casagrande's father was in contact with McCaffery, who had heard about the immediate failure of the mission, but had received no information on Mallaby's fate.

Despite the conciseness of his communication, Mallaby took care to summarize everything, and, above all, requested transmission of the message 'Per Giovanni: detained, continue to listening'; the message was broadcasted immediately in the evening.

Neither Mallaby nor McCaffery knew that, as a result of the tumultuous developments of previous days, Karl Wolff in that precise moment was secretly in Switzerland, busy in a meeting that led to crucial events. And above all they did not know that Dick Mallaby's instructions should not have been followed.

In early 1945, Christine Northcote-Marks and her group of FANYs had been transferred from Monopoli to Siena in Tuscany. In her office within the Istituto Tolomei, after a few days, she noticed the name and photo of Dick among the lists of former pupils, but after having waited days and days for the latest news on Dick's fate, she was unofficially informed that he had been captured once again.

Mallaby's fiancée could not bring herself to report the bad news to Mallaby senior (who, however, received it by other means). More than that, after a few days, she was forced to return to Britain for a period of convalescence, where she received official notification that Dick Mallaby had 'disappeared during active service'.[18]

Mallaby's ruse following his capture helped the positive conclusion of Operation *Sunrise* (or *Crossword*, as it was known to the British), a series of covert activities and secret negotiations between the Germans and the Allies which sought to arrange a local surrender of German forces in northern Italy and avoid further deaths and the destruction of Italy's infrastructure.

Thus in Lugano on 3 March, in a discreet room of Restaurant Biaggi, a meeting took place between Eugen Dollmann, Guido Zimmer (a leading figure in the German intelligence services) and the OSS agent Paul Blum. The American representative, while not making concessions or demonstrating willingness, asked the Germans, as a clear demonstration of the effectiveness of their intentions and of their good faith, to free the most important resistance member held in Italy, Ferruccio Parri, and another key Allied agent, Toni Usmiani. To their surprise, Allied intelligence learnt a few days later that Parri and Usmiani had been released and were in Switzerland.

The next key move in *Sunrise* saw Karl Wolff himself secretly, and perilously, leave Italy for Zurich, Switzerland, on 8 March 1945, without the official consent of Hitler or Himmler, and without the Italians knowing, meet Allen Dulles, head of OSS in Switzerland.[19]

Wolff began the meeting with a brief personal résumé, which included, rather incongruously, letters of recognition from an ecclesiastical source, and personal references from the Pope and the Führer's former deputy Rudolf Hess, who, in his words, was 'currently in Canada' (sic). The initial atmosphere of embarrassment and suspicion, with Dulles wondering whether or not to shake hands with Wolff, became more collaborative. Wolff, taking responsibility for the initiative and stressing that he was not seeking any personal post-war benefit, managed to prove, if not his own good faith, to be at least minimally trustworthy. He also repeated his insistence that he was determined to avoid ruining Italy and its artistic heritage.[20] Wolff, however, presumed a greater bargaining power than he actually possessed at that time.[21]

In return, Wolff sought the unmolested withdrawal of Army Group C's forces back into Germany as the Allied forces in southern Italy advanced northwards to take their place.[22]

Dulles appears to have made a secret agreement with Wolff which allowed the latter to avoid prosecutions in future war crimes trials, even though Wolff had been clearly implicated in various criminal acts.[23]

While Churchill and Roosevelt were kept closely informed of the *Sunrise/Crossword* negotiations between Wolff and Dulles, Stalin was merely informed on 12 March that discussions were taking place. Soviet negotiators were excluded from the meetings, which led to tensions between Roosevelt and Stalin that foreshadowed the Cold War.

Further *Sunrise/Crossword* meetings also took place with the American General Lyman Lemnitzer and

British General Terence Airey. The death of Franklin D. Roosevelt on 12 April 1945 brought an end to the *Sunrise / Crossword* negotiations: the new US President, Harry S. Truman, halted the talks in Switzerland, and Truman would ensure that a Soviet representative was involved in the final negotiations for the German surrender in Italy. But at that point things were nearly at an end.[24]

———

Mallaby was finally released from his detention and managed to return to Bern on 11 March. There, he learned on one hand that the stone he had rolled had turned into an avalanche, and on the other that the negotiations with Wolff were now in the hands of the Americans.

Despite his arrest, what Mallaby had helped start had begun to take concrete form, even if the events were shaped by complex, top-secret political and diplomatic decisions. His spur of the moment ruse led to the decisive development of events, or, at least, accelerated them.

Interestingly, Giovanni Barbareschi was also released quickly. He always believed Dick Mallaby was responsible for this, and remained grateful.

But why did Mallaby find such a receptive subject in Wolff? Mallaby's appearance on the scene occurred at the lowest point in Italian–German relations, based as it then was on continuous fictions and mutual suspicions, which served to clarify the Germans' general lack of loyalty. Karl Wolff, despite having been mildly disgraced in 1943 for having divorced his wife, was a prominent figure in Nazi Germany and, as such, had intimate knowledge of the internal mechanisms of the German leadership and the character nuances of all its leading figures. Wolff, above all, had a very relevant personal goal: currying favour to avoid the consequences of his involvement in criminal acts.

But the unexpected developments that spun out of Mallaby's mission generated concerns, leaving the very few who were able to know of them puzzled and even suspicious.

In his official recordings, Cecil Roseberry appeared very pleased with how his agent had behaved: 'Dick appears to have put up a good show. The last time he got free it was one chance in a million and this time it was one in a thousand. He will think these things are easy!'. In private, however, as will be shown, he expressed different opinions on Mallaby.

The secret documentation of the time, in fact, reveals far less enthusiastic evaluations. The British leadership immediately considered what Mallaby had done to be impracticable – and perhaps far from commendable – and did not want it disclosed even within SOE.

From the highly confidential reports of early March 1945, it transpires, in fact, that inside SOE, a 'Mallaby case' had arisen, so much so that in order to try to reassure the London leadership, an urgent communication was sent, stating that the agent had been carefully interrogated in Switzerland over his impromptu operational liaison with Wolff.

The attitude of the highest authorities involved had as its basic premise, at the political–military level, the disagreement between what was instigated by Mallaby and the British guidelines on the matter, and more generally, the institutional phobia of being double-crossed.

It is hard to believe that the unjust treatment suffered by Dick Mallaby could have been the result of a very critical report produced a few months earlier regarding his father. This report, which made use of confidential information gathered by the Italians over the previous years and now available to the Allies, was triggered by Cecil Mallaby's protests addressed directly in a long letter sent in December 1944 to Commodore Ellery Stone (Chief Commissioner of the Allied Control Commission), deriving from the enduring confiscation of the family's assets, and the political and economic situation around Siena after the front line had moved on.

Lieutenant-Colonel E. H. J. Nicholls, provincial commissioner of the Siena Allied Military Government for Occupied Territories (AMGOT), replied to these criticisms very aggressively, pointing out that Mallaby senior had not been interned during the war thanks to the contribution of 'all the political and Fascist authorities' and concluding that 'I understand he is a rich man who wants to take advantages of the times and become richer'. The acrimonious and personalized content of this document may have resulted from the aforementioned confidential reports, which underlined Mallaby senior's initial financial support to Fascism in the 1930s, but more than that to malicious local rumours.[25]

Dick Mallaby, in his interrogations, had diligently summarized the details of his mission and the events that took place. The subsequent SOE confidential reports relayed this in the following manner:

On 10 March 1945, London had received a message from Bern concerning the establishment of a very important contact with a man in the German military leadership, who had promised Parri's release to demonstrate his amenability; on the same day SOE Bern had also reported that an English agent named Mallaby was about to be freed to go to Switzerland on a special mission;

The following day Bern had made it known that the important German contact was none other than General Wolff;

Eventually, on 13 March, it was confirmed that Mallaby had returned to Switzerland and had been released following internment in an illegal immigrant camp and had provided a report on his contacts with De Leo and Wolff.

According to Mallaby's report, moreover, Wolff offered himself as an intermediary between the Allies and Kesselring, or any other German authority with which the Allies needed to get in touch, pointing out that:

- the Italians would defend the cities of northern Italy alongside the Germans;
- reassurances were also given to Cardinal Schuster that no destruction would be implemented;
- the devastation that would have been inevitable would not have required more than a year to return to its previous state;
- supplies to the Communist groups were to be suspended and, should this be the case, the other Partisan groups would have been allowed to freely cross the border to go to the south;
- there was awareness that Germany had lost the war and it was feared that the nation would fall under communist control.

Mallaby had emphasized that he had been released on his word of honour and that he needed to return to Italy, partly because the lives of the other two Italians who had been captured with him and held hostage depended on his return.[26]

For the purposes of adequately assessing this matter, it is important to highlight that the decisions taken concerning the handling of Wolff's contact initiated by Dick Mallaby determined not only the course of events at the time, but also the long-standing curtain of secrecy that was drawn across the British agent's contribution.

The secret documents of the time clearly indicate doubts, perplexities and fears, and confirm that the British leaders considered it inappropriate to develop the embarrassing contact with Wolff initiated by Mallaby. They chose to hand everything over to the Americans, suggesting that the OSS 'should have sole responsibility for these negotiations'.

Thus, Head of SOE Colin Gubbins advised the ill-informed McCaffery in a general sense to help Dulles only at his request.

The Americans, pragmatically, responded to Wolff's advances with consequences that were slightly different to those that the SS Obergruppenführer had envisaged, which were, in any case, highly profitable for both the Allies and Italy.

When Mallaby finally returned to the Swiss SOE base, he willingly volunteered to complete his masterpiece in a sort of remake of what happened in August–September 1943. The response was a categorical no. In fact, McCaffery practically shut him away, and he was told not to talk to anyone. Thus, to avoid embarrassment and tension, on 20 March, under the pretext of adherence to local regulations, Mallaby was handed over to the Swiss authorities to complete his period of quarantine, and was bundled into three different Swiss camps, the last of which even involved labouring.

On 28 March, Dick Mallaby returned to Bern, where he remained practically imprisoned until 19 April, before being sent back to Italy.

Following the seismic events unleashed after his meeting with Wolff, Mallaby's position had become extremely sensitive. The situation was such that in the final report dated 12 April 1945, his name was mentioned only at the beginning, with the preferred term for him being 'the subject' throughout.

The reasons for this fury are hard to fathom, even supposing that someone tried to make Dick Mallaby a scapegoat; in fact, scapegoats are more useful when things go wrong. In this case, essentially, some extraordinarily positive things had resulted, and the agent's behaviour had been both irreproachable and also the start of the fruitful negotiations that followed.

Considering the type of mission and the unforeseen events that Mallaby had to face and overcome, there was no room for dispute, even over his methods. Objectively, Mallaby should have been garlanded with compliments and praise.

It is clear that personal animosities between the various organizational structures, accentuated and fed by six years of elevated wartime tension, had reached levels of acute paranoia laced with an excess of aggressiveness.

Dick Mallaby obviously did not take it well.

With great sensitivity, Roseberry sent him a personal letter dated 11 May 1945 from his headquarters, trying to console him and highlighting the exceptional nature of his deeds and his good fortune in coming out of it alive. From the tone of this very interesting, unpublished and revealing letter, we can sense the disquiet generated by the results of Mallaby's second mission even within SOE, as well as the agent's frustration in the aftermath of *Edenton Blue*:

Dear Dick,

Thanks for your note of the 1st ... and fed up as you appear to be, I'm damn glad that you are in a position to write. You seemed determined to cause me headaches from the time your name was first put forward to me from Cairo – and that's a long time back.

I spent the whole of the Easter weekend thinking out ways and means of getting you out of your latest 'bag' or at least of ensuring that you were treated only as a minor miscreant. I still wonder whether you realise how lucky you were. The first time it was one in a million and this time it was one in 100,000, yet I still feel that you think the whole business is easy. I do, at least, congratulate you on your resource in 'telling a frank story' and one which, as it happened just fitted in with what the hun was looking for. Pity you got held up at the frontier and so the subsequent fun was handled by OSS. It would have been great to have been in the middle of two surrenders. Anyhow, now you are safe and even though bored, you should be damned thankful. Sorry to hear you are feeling bitter. I did my best to have you sent straight back from V-land to U.K., but somebody was afraid of losing a little reflected glory and said that AFHQ were dying to see you at once. It's up to you to persuade them that you are more than due for a spot of home leave – others seem to wangle it without the same amount of justification. If I hear nothing on the subject by the time GM gets back, I'll take it up with him. He should be here in about a week. Had Teddy here wuite [sic] a time waiting for his passport. He was a bit shy with me at first, which did not surprise me but worked back into the 'J camp' before very long. It is worth remembering that whatever has been achieved by M'land, the foundation was laid in the old 'Impero' days and that events have justified my refusal to alter the lines of policy on which we had started. Although everybody is delighted with the way things have gone, there is no doubt that they could have been vastly better with some forward vision and elimination of personal likes and dislikes. However, that's only for those 'inside' to know. Chris drops in when she is in town and I pull her leg to keep her morale up. I haven't quite convinced her that you found a better substitute in V-land and definitely better substitutes back where you are now. Have told her she had better buck up and get a decent job so as to be able to support a husband properly. Don't worry – she's looking well and seems devoted to you. I haven't attempted to cut you out – yet. Try to get back before I vacate my chair, so that I can do what there may be to do to try to get you fitted in somewhere for the rest of the war. Be sure I'll do whatever can be done. Once again congratulations on being free again.

Mallaby's personal testimony contributes to clarifying and illustrating, after more than 70 years, a fundamental and controversial episode in the history of World War II, which, as he correctly noted, 'was a point of confusion in the treatments of Operation *Sunrise*'.[27]

But this confusion was not, as the foregoing and the following shows, a result of the misunderstanding that 'Tucker', 'Drucker', 'Wallaby' and 'Tucker-Wallaby' were in fact one person: Dick Mallaby.

I have tracked down the documentary source containing the 'original sin', and, most importantly, the reason for its creation.

On 20 March, one of the readers of an internal memo circulated among the British leadership declared himself 'horrified when I saw the suggestion that Mallaby should return in any circumstances to N. Italy.'

A confidential message sent to Bern on 22 March 1945 shows that the oblivion and confusion surrounding the affair were far from coincidental.

This message, penned by an anonymous author, communicated (in familiar terms) the following to an unspecified recipient:

1 In view circumstance of Mallaby's release consider it essential for security reasons to his cover story for circulation in S.O.E. circles here.
2 suggest you work out story with Mallaby based on his straight forward exchange for German prisoner in our hands.[28]

Thus, knowledge of the details of Dick Mallaby's second mission was limited to a few people, and McCaffery himself forced Mallaby to confirm to everyone else that he was captured and then released following an exchange of prisoners.

Given that behind every situation there is always someone at work, some important personal profiles of the key figures involved are useful at this point. First of all there's Wolff, who, in his sharp tactical thinking, had wrongly assumed a key element. Among the many poorly reasoned and erroneous suppositions of the Germans who believed they needed to negotiate with the Allies, there was the one that considered the Americans to be better disposed towards them than the British.

Next, it should not be forgotten that McCaffery did not think highly of his American colleague Dulles and his methods (even going so far as to avoid meeting him, at least initially), considering him, along with all his fellow countrymen, a naive amateur to whom he could hand out presumptuous instructions. From the archival documents relating to Mallaby's missions, numerous compromising messages emerge sent by and to McCaffery concerning the management of Italian affairs and relations with the Americans. They indicate a relationship that was anything but collaborative and transparent between SOE and OSS (at least in Switzerland), and with time this attitude became mutual.[29]

Besides this, any evaluation of McCaffery's work must always bear in mind the widespread and heavy infiltration of SOE effected by Italian counterespionage, demonstrating that, in this world, nemesis sometimes takes concrete form in a specific and inexorable way.

Regarding Dulles' intimate motives over the operation, his political evaluation of the future role of post-war Germany was in anti-communist function. Thus Dulles and his team, according to British presuppositions, probably were meant to behave like 'useful idiots', but in fact gained long-lasting results.

The definitive version of what took place is revealed by a very important document, signed by Cecil Roseberry and sent to Sir Orme Sargent, deputy Under-Secretary at the Foreign Office. This message, dated 23 March 1945, is proof of and formalizes the handing of the baton by the British to the Americans for contact with Wolff and, in practical terms, the official version of the crucial phase of Operation *Sunrise*.

In this rather mystifying and carefully crafted message, Roseberry stated that OSS was approached directly by General Wolff, and 'so as to avoid duplication our representative was told not to pursue the contact and to leave everything to OSS unless he were [sic] asked by them to take a hand'. Beyond the sanitized version of events given, this crucial document, which bears witness to the doubts and fears about the explosive affair, also states: 'Wolff's first attempt at contact was apparently through Mallaby, but it seems (although the elements are not sufficiently defined on this point) that Wolff later contacted SOE directly.'[30]

It is also to be noted that, while:

> initial contact with OSS took place the day before Mallaby was taken into German custody, news of it did not reach Wolff until two or three days after he had interviewed him, when indeed Mallaby was already on his way back to Switzerland bearing Wolff's message to Alexander. Had Mallaby succeeded in delivering this message to McCaffery in Bern on 1 March, two days before Dollmann saw OSS, it is possible that Operation *Sunrise* might have taken a somewhat different course – but without necessarly significantly altering the eventual outcome.[31]

Evidently, even though the war was now ending, SOE's leadership believed that a negotiation with Wolff would not have been welcome.

In other words, the decision not to follow up what was begun by Mallaby was imposed by SOE's leadership, not only due to the sensitivity and uncertainty that existed in that embryonic phase of the negotiations, but also due to the fact that the British leadership decided to avoid any contact with an important and well-known member of the SS. Had the latter happened, in countries like neutral and free Switzerland, any form of contact could have been disseminated and twisted, even at the level of the press, with extreme ease.[32]

In fact, added to the embarrassment of the British, who had put about the false, bland reconstruction of developments activated by Mallaby's mission, was the bad feeling generated in neutral Switzerland.

An encoded, urgent telegram from SOE Bern to SOE London, dated 7 April 1945, in revealing that a morning newspaper the previous day had reported the news of negotiations between the German leaders in Italy and the Allies through Parri (allegedly released for this purpose), stated that the source of the article was the United Press correspondent in Zurich. This information had been censored in Great Britain, but could not be restricted beyond its borders. This telegram requested that Allied Headquarters take immediate action to avoid such dangerous leaks.

The following day, a further message emphasized the point. It suggested that there were doubts and suspicions about the situation, given that a Swiss informant in British service, in reporting the news of the peace negotiations beginning to circulate, interpreted Wolff's actions as a manoeuvre attempting to create post-war alibis in order to justify the surrender to the German people, and crediting it to a small group of generals. The informer also reported that the interests of Switzerland and Great Britain were identical, and, therefore, the potential and feared destruction of the industrial plants of northern Italy would not have been too high a price to pay in order to counter the cunning tactics of Hitler's henchmen, who were 'destined to lie and to incite new German generations through the falsification of contemporary events'. The author of the confidential message wisely concluded that only those who were fully up to date with everything that had gone on between the Germans and the Allies could have commented on the validity and genuineness of the German approaches.[33]

And so, Britain's diplomatic and political leaders chose to prevent Dick Mallaby from attempting to deliver his masterstroke in person. However, the conclusion of the war in Italy essentially sprang from Mallaby's impromptu stimulus.

Dick Mallaby thus broke his promise and wasn't able to meet Karl Wolff again. For his part, Wolff must have always wondered, in contrast to the actual intentions of the British agent, whether he was just a clever liar who had cheated him across the board, even though he positively reinforced his decisive determination.

Perhaps this is why even in his 1985 memoirs, *Der Adjutant*, edited by Jochen von Lang, Wolff curiously does not mention his contact with Mallaby and the agreements made between them. However, during his imprisonment Wolff confirmed that Mallaby swore that he really had been sent by Alexander, stating that he 'seemed to me a good boy'.[34]

The story told by Mallaby to avoid being shot was more easily accepted by the supreme commander of the SS in Italy, perhaps because Wolff wanted to believe it, than by the uneasy special service members. Wolff's conversation with Mallaby was to spur him into opening his own personal, and deceit filled, negotiations with the Allies.

According to a statement by Pino Adriano, author of *L'intrigo di Berna*, in April 1945 Wolff told Parrilli (the Italian intermediary in Operation *Sunrise*, whose recollections have not proved to be fully reliable) that 'in Genoa, a so-called British major had made contact with German intelligence. He had presented himself in civilian clothes, as the bearer of a verbal message from Alexander to forward to the commander-in-chief of the southern front', seeking to persuade the Germans to abandon negotiations with the Americans and conclude them with the British. According to historian Attilio Tamaro, Wolff even complained that a British captain 'had brought a message from Alexander to Graziani but no news had been given to the Germans'.[35]

By mid-April 1945, the German Army Group C in Italy was facing a desperate situation, and lacked the arms, ammunition and supplies to continue fighting. The final Allied offensive across the Po River, which was launched by the 15th Allied Army Group on 6 April, had forced them to abandon large numbers of heavy weapons and vehicles south of the river. As commander of Army Group C, General Heinrich von Vietinghoff had already taken the decision not to carry out Hitler's scorched earth policy in Italy; surrender was now the only option. Thus Vietinghoff too became actively involved in the negotiations with Dulles and the OSS.

The Instrument of Surrender of what became known as the Surrender of Caserta, the first surrender signed by Germany, was finally signed at the Royal Palace in Caserta, in Campania, at 2.17pm on 29 April 1945 by Wehrmacht Lieutenant-Colonel Victor von Schweinitz, on behalf of von Vietinghoff and Graziani, and SS-Sturmbannführer Eugen Wenner, on behalf of Wolff. The war in Italy was finally over.

———

The 'surrender of the 800,000', as the Italians named it, was a great success both qualitatively and quantitatively for the Allies, and was highly positive for Italy and the Italians, even if the thorny issues of Alto Adige, Friuli and Venezia Giulia, Istria and Dalmatia remained unresolved. This, unsurprisingly, is indirectly attested to by the attempts made by many in Italy and even Germany almost immediately to claim credit for their supposed important role in the operation.[36]

Evaluating its cost-benefit ratio in concrete terms, Operation *Sunrise* could be considered a profitable example of the pragmatic and dynamic interaction between espionage, diplomacy and military activities, resulting from the action of special forces.

It is clear that the decision of the United States to agree to negotiate with one of the most important members of Germany's most criminal military organization helped avoid further Nazi crimes, wanton destruction and violence.

Dick Mallaby, for the second time, had been at the centre of the most secret and historic negotiations. In the first mission, he was decisive strategically, though by chance, and his role, however fundamental and remarkable, was essentially a passive one. In his second mission, what Mallaby achieved in an improvised manner was decisive and was the fruit of his abilities, enlivened by the desperation of the moment.

Winning is hard enough, but turning two disasters into triumph is a very rare achievement.

Furthermore, analysis of Mallaby's last mission brings out further testimony regarding the German betrayal of the RSI, and the contrastingly loyal behaviour of Italy's leaders, who, after Mallaby's capture and initial interrogation, handed him over to their allies.

In Erich Kuby's *Il tradimento tedesco* (*The German Betrayal*), the deceptions perpetrated by the Germans against the Italians are summarized, as further reflections of the Mallaby–Wolff affair: Mussolini's suspicions, following news of the release of Parri on Wolff's order (labelled the 'ultimate limit of infamy' against Il Duce); the launching of various enquiries and of the surrender negotiations, with the Italians kept completely in the dark; and Wolff's overriding of the attempts to negotiate based around Cardinal Schuster and his right-hand man, Monsignor Giuseppe Bicchierai.[37]

Wolff and his family ran great risks. In the atmosphere of the general decay of the Third Reich, which pitched all against all even within the monolithic structure of the SS, his negotiations, which were more or less known to Himmler and SS Obergruppenführer Ernst Kaltenbrunner, could have brought him before the firing squad.

Adding confusion to confusion and danger to danger in those days, crude opportunistic moves were also made by those taking advantage of the moment for their own unrealistic purposes. A further, well-documented threat to achieving the 'surrender of the 800,000' came from the head of the autonomous Tyrol/Vorarlberg Province, Franz Hofer, who risked wrecking the negotiations between the Germans and the Allies in order to further his own unrealistic aim of creating an enlarged Tyrolean state including parts of Austria, Alto Adige and Bavaria.[38]

The Americans, to all intents and purposes, repaid Karl Wolff following the German surrender. He was first helped to escape and then received very favourable treatment in the post-war trials. In fact, he should by right have been one of the defendants, and convicted, at the Nuremberg trials.

According to Smith and Aga-Rossi: 'On the basis of the recently declassified documentation, it is now possible to state that Allen Dulles, who until that time seemed to have lost interest in Wolff, played a crucial role in the decision taken by the Commission to exclude him from the Nuremberg list.'

Thus, in a telegram to the head of the OSS, Donovan, sent on 23 August 1945, Dulles wrote: 'I think it is possible that Wolff will be included in some list for the trials against war criminals. Instead, I propose that he not be included in the first group, so as to prevent him from using his version of *Sunrise* to defend himself.'[39]

Thus, the Nuremberg trials, against Göring, Hess, von Ribbentrop and the others, saw Wolff appear only as a witness, as a result of the fear instilled deliberately and cunningly by Dulles that Wolff could reveal too much about the surrender negotiations. Wolff, however, was kept in protective custody by the Americans while other countries requested his extradition, and was interned in a psychiatric hospital for acute paranoia until the spring of 1946. Subsequently, he managed to escape trial even when investigations by the British started for the crimes that took place in Italy between 1943 and 1945.

The former SS-Obergruppenführer was finally charged in June 1949 in a fairly minor trial in Hamburg. His defence benefitted from sworn affidavits (sanitized so as not to create diplomatic embarrassment with the Soviet Union) from the main Allied protagonists of Operation *Sunrise*, as well as the in-trial testimony of Allen Dulles' colleague Gero von Schulze-Gaevernitz.[40]

Despite his high rank and his clear knowledge of and participation in the criminal activities of the SS in Italy, Wolff was sentenced to the minimum term of four years and then released, his period in custody having already been taken into account.[41]

But in January 1962, just when the heavy responsibilities of the past seemed to have been lifted from his shoulders, Karl Wolff suffered an interruption to his business career and was arrested for trial once again, for his active participation in the Holocaust. This time, out of his former collaborators in Operation *Sunrise*, only one, Gero von Schulze-Gaevernitz, came forward to testify in his favour.

Wolff was sentenced to 15 years in prison for collaborating in the murder of 300,000 Jews. He was released after six years for health reasons. He continued to live in the German Federal Republic, where he died in 1984.

Dick Mallaby's last mission has also been explored by other authors, highlighting some interesting details about the overall situation in Italy in the final part of the war.

In Giuseppe Parlato's *Fascisti senza Mussolini*, the author explains why Rodolfo Graziani refused to meet Dick Mallaby. Based on comments by Junio Valerio Borghese, a hard-line fascist and RSI naval commander, Parlato records that Graziani did not consider it appropriate to have contact with Mallaby 'due to excessive loyalty'. Moreover, on the basis of OSS documents, held in the United States, the author reveals that Borghese 'had ordered that the British officer be tracked down, in order to continue the negotiations that, nipped in the bud by Graziani, were then concluded with the Germans; unfortunately, contact was not possible since the British officer had already reached Switzerland.'[42]

Sergio Nesi provides details on Junio Valerio Borghese's assessments and proposals (and also his erroneous information and assumptions). According to Nesi, Graziani informed the Germans and Mussolini of the arrival of Mallaby-Tucker, and the Germans 'took over the British officer, forced him to speak and precluded any possibility of him contacting the head of the Armed Forces of the Repubblica Sociale Italiana'. Borghese commented:

> The failure to meet with Tucker, which was due to German prevarication and, it must be said, to the questionable behaviour of Graziani, was fatal. In fact, the armistice agreement signed in Caserta between Wolff and Alexander, which excluded representatives of our Armed Forces, had witnessed, among the intermediaries, the same Captain 'Tucker'.[43]

Moreover, on the basis of specific statements made by Borghese in the post-war period, it is clear that he knew from Wolff, with whom he was in constant personal contact, about his negotiations with the Allies.

In all this, the not so well informed (albeit suspicious) Mussolini remained loyal to the Germans, but finally had a rude awakening on 25 April in the Archbishopric of Milan, when he officially learnt of the German betrayal.

Rodolfo Graziani, the Minister of Defence in the RSI, recalls the events in his published memoirs as follows:

Captain Tooker [sic], who spoke excellent Italian, declared that he had been tasked with an important mission involving me by Field Marshal Alexander, but he was not allowed to disclose it to anyone other than me … He confirmed the plan of Field Marshal Alexander, to make contact with me, to get the Germans to withdraw from Italy to avoid destroying the industrial infrastructure, works of art and more. In truth this was superfluous, because its object was the same as one of my principal purposes. Di [sic] Leo, having completed the first interrogation, had to direct the officer to Colonel Helferik [sic], a German liaison officer in the SID, who put him in contact with General Haster in Verona. General Wolff later announced that he had been sent back to Switzerland with a special mission, which he did not specify.[44]

Cesare Rossi, one of the original fascists, and Mussolini's former press officer in the 1920s, in his *Trentatré vicende mussoliniane* (*Thirty-Three Mussolini Episodes*) provides some interesting points on what Mussolini actually knew of the affair:

One day, between February and March 1945, the Lecco Brigate Nera arrested at the Swiss border a guide, a priest and a British officer, who gave his name

as Captain Toocker [sic] and claimed to be on a mission
from Field Marshal Alexander to Graziani ...

Mussolini also learned of the capture of the
two and on that occasion complained that neither
Ambassador Rahn nor Wolff had ever informed him
about their movements. He added: 'Yet I know that
they are negotiating with the CLN', a suspicion that
he should not have found to be completely unknown
and defenceless. On the afternoon of April 25, in
Schuster's antechamber, he learned the unwelcome
news of the agreement reached for the surrender of
German troops.[45]

A secret message, undated but clearly from February
1945, reveals further key details. It was written by Paolo
Porta, Commander of the Brigate Nere Cesare Rodini
di Como, and is among the declassified documents in
the British archives. It also helps us to understand the
atmosphere of 'dog eat dog' that dominated the final
months of the RSI. Porta's message was stimulated by
Mussolini himself, as it starts with the phrase: 'Duce in
accordance with your request'. According to Porta's
message, following his capture, Mallaby's urgent request
for a meeting with Rodolfo Graziani was immediately
reported to Brigadier-General Facdouelle, who, after
his meeting with Mallaby, was told to inform Mussolini
about the matter.[46]

According to Vincenzo Alberto Mellini Ponce de
León, Foreign under secretary of the RSI, Mussolini
later commented with bitterness: 'I've learned that the

infamous British captain about whom – when he was in our hands – a big fuss was made, has been set free and tasked with communicating messages from the Allied Supreme Headquarters. Neither Rahn nor Wolff mentioned anything to me about this either.'[47]

Dick's father, Cecil Mallaby, had been officially informed on 22 March 1945 that Dick was safe and well, although it would take a little over a month before father and son were reunited. Eventually, after a long period of absence, Dick was able to return to his Tuscan home, to spend his birthday with his family.

A precise reconstruction of the closing stages of Dick Mallaby's wartime service is made possible by his father's diaries. Dick's own private memoirs, after a detailed summary of his second mission, end by recalling: 'after a few more weeks in Bern I was sent to France and then to Naples and our base in Siena', evidently not wishing to mention the most bitter phase of his wartime service.

In the euphoric spring of 1945, the Mallaby family's properties in Asciano, given their proximity to Siena, became a kind of after-work club for No. 1 Special Force's personnel. Often, as on 26 April, marking Mallaby's 26th birthday, large-scale dance parties were organized, and among the participants were numerous famous figures from SOE and the Italian resistance, many of whom mentioned the place in their memoirs.

SOE agent Henry Boutigny, who was perhaps the most frequent visitor to the Mallaby house, met his future wife at one of these convivial gatherings.

But this time Dick Mallaby's efforts were not recognized: he received no award or honour for the results of his second mission.

Roseberry, now no longer a part of SOE, sent another letter to Mallaby on 28 August 1945, in which, among other things, he informed him that his successor (caustically known as 'Pipsqueak') had not been best pleased to read the history of SOE's Italy department, which Roseberry himself had penned. Roseberry concluded: 'Pity you didn't call in at the office; they might have let you read a copy and see how much space I gave to your little escapade'.

Roseberry's letter ended on a note of bitterness that he decided to share with Mallaby:

> Strange, but I feel almost a relief that in the case of most of the old crowd, I need never bother to see them again. I think I stayed on too long. While the work was hot, one did not have time to observe all the petty intrigue and jockeying for personal advancement. It stood out miles when it became necessary to reduce staffs.

A few months later, by which point the tensions and paranoia of the time had mostly dissolved, it was the turn of Dick Hewitt, head of No. 1 Special Force in the final months of the war, to send a heartfelt, unconventional note of personal thanks to Dick

Mallaby. The handwritten letter, dated 12 September 1945 and on a No. 1 Special Force letterhead, began:

My dear Dick.

I wanted to send you a few lines, now that the unit has broken up, to thank you very much indeed for all that you did for us both in the field and at base. It was a contribution quite unsurpassed by anybody, and I want you to know that I am deeply grateful to you for all the support you gave me.

On 23 June 1946, Hewitt handwrote a reference letter for Mallaby, in which he highlighted the following:

Captain C. R. Mallaby, M.C., served under my command for nearly two years in Italy, from September 1943 to August 1945, and during this time I came to know him well and to appreciate his fine qualities. He was employed in Italy on special service, and he performed two missions behind the enemy lines which called for the greatest courage, endurance, and initiative, with high success. Although he was continually pressing to be allowed to proceed on operational work, he was in fact engaged on the staff for some months; and there he showed real ability in administrative and office duties. He was, however, most happy when undertaking outdoor work of a hazardous nature. He speaks fluent Italian and good French and has a home in Italy. He is also a fully qualified signals officer, and he has a highly developed artistic sense. In addition to this, he is easy to get on with and was always well liked by his fellow officers and men.

Captain Mallaby has an extremely distinguished war record, an attractive personality, and many of the qualities which should make him successful in civilian life. He fully deserves, and would amply repay, assistance of any kind.

Eight days prior to this, Gerard Holdsworth had penned a similar reference for Dick Mallaby:

Captain Mallaby, M.C., served under my command for upwards of three years. He volunteered for service behind the enemy lines and in due course was parachuted into Northern Italy some little while before the Allied Forces assaulted the European mainland. He was arrested by the Italian authorities, was taken to Rome for interrogation where he behaved magnificently under most rigorous handling. At this time secret armistice negotiations with Badoglio and his followers were commenced. They were handicapped by lack of direct and speedy communication. Mallaby is a highly skilled W/T operator and on the off chance that he still survived his name was passed to the Badoglio party as one suitable for the establishment of direct communication between Italy and A.F.H.Q. The Badoglio party discovered and released him from prison, and provided him with the necessary equipment with which he was quickly able to establish contact with A.F.H.Q.

From that time onwards Mallaby was responsible for the receipt and transmission of all message between the Allied authorities and the armistice-seeking Italians. Weeks of the most arduous work followed, culminating in the Armistice and the Allied landings on the Italian mainland.

I met Mallaby in Brindisi, and was amazed to find that, in spite of the great mental and physical ordeal through which he had passed, he remained the same calm, efficient and cheerful young officer I had despatched from a North African airport months before.

He continuously volunteered for further service in enemy territory, but it was not until close on the final collapse of the Germans that I finally consented to his carrying out another mission. Through no fault of his own he was again arrested and would have undoubtedly been executed had he not conceived a brilliant stratagem which caused a member of the German High Command to send him to Switzerland as an emissary between himself and the Allied Authorities.

The courage, resourcefulness and general ability of this young officer made an incalculable contribution to the Allied war effort in the Mediterranean. Such astonishing achievements by one so young might well have turned his head, but Mallaby has not changed. He remains a quiet, self-effacing Englishman of the highest quality.

The positive testimonies of those who knew Dick Mallaby were not, therefore, mere formalities, nor were they taken for granted, but coolly emphasized his qualities and the exceptional nature of his wartime activities, as well as his human gifts and artistic talents.

Dick and Christine met up once again, but this time without the risk of losing each other, and began the journey of their life together...

6

Aftermath

(Family – The end – Scattered and repressed memories)

> Truth is the daughter of time.
>
> Aulus Gellius (*c*. AD 125–180)

> Men occasionally stumble over the truth, but
> most of them pick themselves up and hurry off
> as if nothing ever happened.
>
> Sir Winston S. Churchill (1874–1965)

Cecil Richard Dallimore-Mallaby was officially promoted to captain for services rendered to his country on 17 August 1946, according to the War Office's notification. By that date, his military escapades had long been over.

His post-war life was certainly less adventurous, but was still lively and unusual, and still featured the odd special mission.

Between 1945 and 1948, Mallaby lived mainly in Reading, where on 30 March 1946 (his mother's birthday) he married Christine, who had left the FANY with the rank of sergeant. After the birth of their first child, Caroline Mary (in Milan on 24 April 1947), from 1949 to 1951 the Mallaby family lived in Southampton, where Dick attended the faculty of engineering from October 1949. It was there, on 19 June 1951, that their second daughter was born, Elizabeth Spray, whose unusual middle name reflected Mallaby's passion for sailing.

On 25 June 1950, at a time when Mallaby, at least officially, was a university student, the Mallaby couple recorded the BBC radio programme *Now it Can Be Told*, broadcasted three days later.[1]

Dick Mallaby, meanwhile, had been diagnosed with a testicular tumour. After an operation to remove it in Southampton on 13 March 1951, the doctors informed him that he was now sterile.

The path of Dick Mallaby's journey through life now led him back to Italy. And Italy turned out to bring him good fortune once again, offering him the chance to execute a pair of seemingly impossible missions.

Despite what the doctors had told him, in fact the Mallaby family continued to expand and Christine gave birth on 19 June 1952 to Christopher John and on 1 December 1955 to Richard Arthur (known as 'Vaky'), at Poggio Pinci and Verona, respectively. What Mallaby did for almost a decade after the end of the war remained shrouded in mystery and was unknown even to his children.

Mallaby senior, a wealthy landowner, who was able to support Dick and his family, noted down all his son's job interviews in this period. Cecil's diary also shows that he even attended the local 'Festival dell'Unità' (Festival of Unity) of the Partito Comunista Italiano (Italian Communist Party) in Asciano, calling it in his diary 'nice and quiet, almost a society event'.

The first concrete information about Dick Mallaby's activities dates from 1953, when he began working for NATO, initially at their offices in Florence. That same year, he was transferred to Naples, where he also joined the prestigious Circolo Canottieri sailing club. He remained in Naples until early 1955. That same year, he was finally transferred to NATO's Allied Land Forces Southern Europe (LANDSOUTH) headquarters in Verona.

According to the local registry office records, on 14 May 1957, 32 years after his first registration, Dick Mallaby ceased to be a resident of the town of Asciano, being 'cancelled due to emigration to England'.

Dick Mallaby and his family had actually moved to Verona. Mallaby's NATO work was based in Via Carmelitani, where, as previously noted, Mallaby himself had been threatened with execution, and close to the current Corso Porta Nuova (formerly Corso Vittorio Emanuele), where, in February 1945, the SOE agent had been held prisoner by the Germans. Dick Mallaby and his family lived a pleasant, routine life over those years, based in their apartment in No. 12 Via Giberti and then No. 18. They spoke mainly Italian at home, although Dick and Christine preferred English for their quarrels. Their apartment was filled with all sorts of animals, including a Java macaque named Noel, who was a family member for 17 years, and a black poodle named Jet.

The family enjoyed frequent sailing trips on Lake Garda and summer holidays in Cornwall, Castiglione della Pescaia and, of course, Asciano. They would travel to Tuscany in huge American cars – purchased by Dick Mallaby second-hand from NATO's American personnel – always avoiding the motorways.

Mallaby's family recall Dick's friendship with the former paratrooper and then actor and sculptor Nicola Morelli, whom in all likelihood he met during his time in Monopoli. Dick Mallaby's British friends were rather peculiar individuals too, one of whom was Anthony Smith, a famous popular writer and fan of hot air balloons and sailing adventures.

The only recurrent acts of eccentricity by Dick in those years were his behaviour when watching boxing matches, during which it was wise to retire to a distance of several metres, as he enjoyed mimicking the encounters from beginning to end, and his entrance into the Tuscan heartland, which immediately made him highly talkative in thick Sienese vernacular.

Dick Mallaby, in obedience to the bond of confidentiality, despite his sunny and easy-going nature, maintained his absolute silence on what had taken place during the war. Communications in Morse code and parachute drops no longer interested him, and no one in his family remembers him commenting on the war itself, news stories, or national and international politics. Thus, nobody, apart from his wife Christine, some former colleagues in SOE and his father Cecil, was party to the details of Dick Mallaby's extraordinary adventures during the war. Moreover, despite several minimal and inaccurate references to his role in articles and historical publications, Mallaby did not allow himself, or was not allowed, to be drawn in to correct them on what had actually taken place. Apart from the restrictions imposed by confidentiality, Mallaby's employment with NATO, officially in the role of interpreter and translator, obviously forbade any media exposure, even if this did not preclude him from taking part in the occasional commemorative event.[2]

Dick and Christine Mallaby's four children and their grandchildren went on to lead interesting lives. Vaky became a leading, well-respected Steadicam specialist. Elisabeth was one of the founders of the famous musical-cabaret group 'I gatti del Vicolo Miracoli' ('The Miracle Alley Cats'). By a further twist of fate, Elisabeth married Filippo d'Acquarone, a television journalist and grandson of Arturo Toscanini, who is also directly descended from Pietro d'Acquarone, the Minister of the Royal Household, who was a travelling companion of Dick Mallaby aboard the *Baionetta* from Ortona to Brindisi on 10 September 1943. Christopher, known as Gocky (who passed away in 2011), devoted himself mainly to antiques; one of his daughters, Elettra, is an actress.

On 16 April 1972, Dick Mallaby lost his father Cecil, and around that time, he began to have heart problems, possibly due to the stress of his wartime service, as well as his enjoyment of tobacco products. At the end of the 1970s, what seemed to be his first heart attack revealed that he had already suffered a previous, hidden one. He began a period of treatment that mainly resulted in the appearance of a poster in Mallaby's office on the dangers of heart disease, but did not induce him to abandon his harmful habits.

On 1 April 1981, at the end of a few hours of suffering and inadequate medical assistance, a third heart attack took the life of this nearly 62-year-old brave Englishman, who had spent only a few years of his life in Great Britain.[3]

Usually, death leads to some form of posthumous recognition, occasionally excessive, accompanied by the revelation of previously unrecounted facts and details.

After Dick Mallaby's death, the BBC, probably in the wake of the first release of classified documents relating to SOE's activities, became interested in him once again. However, a planned television documentary never saw the light of day, much to the annoyance of Mrs Christine Mallaby.

Previously, straight after the end of the war, Mallaby had been approached on numerous occasions to see if he was interested in publishing his wartime memoirs. Even his direct superior, Cecil Roseberry, had made known his intention to do this as early as 1945 (which was evidently then supressed). Dick Mallaby, fortunately for posterity, certainly harboured a desire to leave behind his testimony, as the papers set aside in his personal archive show.

Despite the fact that he never yielded to the temptation of revealing the truth of the events he had personally taken part in and the people he had encountered, the former special agent known as Olaf, Tito, Norris, Squarzina, Tucker, Tooker, Drucker, Wallaby, Dino Malerba, Bernardo Francini and Riccardo Riccio left a precious personal testimony for posterity.

In fact Mallaby had gathered documents and reconstructed his two missions; privately, he had begun almost immediately after the war to draft a memoir recounting his extraordinary experiences. Entitled 'My experience of war and adventures', this was first handwritten and then typed up in English. It was discovered by his wife after his death, and was carefully kept along with the other precious documents relating to the near 62 adventurous years of Dick Mallaby's life.[4]

Mallaby's private memoirs have played a fundamental role in the present work and have helped to clarify details and issues not documented in official papers, which have remained mysterious and inexplicable for 70 years.

Among the documents kindly supplied to me in their entirety by the Mallaby family, there is a black and white photo, taken at Faggeto Lario. It's almost postcard-like, with a leafy tree branch framing the sky, illuminated by the sun hiding behind two mountain chains that, from opposite sides, plunge into the south-western branch of Lake Como, where, in the foreground, a boat can be seen floating on its waters. Beneath the photo, in English, Dick Mallaby wrote: 'This is roughly the place where I dropped into Lake Como.'

In the Mallaby archive there are other photos of the locations around Como where the initial phases of his two missions took place as well: a clear sign that the former SOE agent felt the need to revisit and record those places, having come through the bad times there.

There is also the original and famous Monkey cryptographic code, via which, in August and September 1943, Mallaby conveyed the crucial communications that established the fate of Italy, but also that of the other nations at war and the many soldiers of the two coalitions. Evidently, for Mallaby this cipher plan was a secret souvenir to which he was more attached than the many others that passed through his hands.

The full details of everything that Dick Mallaby achieved remained unknown to all, even his family, until I had completed this book. Even his closest relatives were surprised when they read it.

Despite the unforgivable official lack of recognition of Mallaby in his home country, those who knew him personally and who risked their lives with him, when offered the opportunity, did not fail to recall and emphasize his courage and the importance of what he achieved – a valid recognition even for those who only knew of his deeds later, myself included.

Henry Boutigny, who shared many wartime experiences with Dick Mallaby as well as a love of the Tuscan countryside, and who managed to settle down just a short distance from Asciano, much as Mallaby would have liked to do, always referred to him as 'a true hero', both privately and officially.[5]

Furthermore, Boutigny and Richard Hewitt made a passionate presentation covering Mallaby's missions and his style of operating at the important conference held in Bologna on 28–30 April 1987 entitled 'No. 1 Special Force in the Italian Resistance'. The conference saw the participation of important SOE members, eyewitnesses, historians and subject experts, and a speech delivered by HRH The Prince of Wales.

On that occasion, Hewitt's contribution was entitled, 'Captain Dick Mallaby: A Tribute', in which, before describing his two missions, he recalled the following memories of Mallaby:

It is nearly six years since Dick Mallaby died, and I believe no tribute has been paid to his memory nor any account of his remarkable service with SOE put on record. Dick was a close personal friend in North Africa (at Massingham), in Italy (at Maryland) and then in this country after the war.

With most of the events recorded, I am familiar from memory, but I am indebted for them in large measure to Christopher Woods who himself served behind the lines in Italy and who has worked subsequently as SOE Adviser at the Foreign and Commonwealth Office, and so is in a position to verify the facts.

I believe you will recognise from my account of his two missions that Dick's SOE career was unique. To have acted as an intermediary in the Italian surrender negotiations was the result of an extraordinary series of coincidences. To have brought off the 'double', as he very nearly did, of playing a similar role in the German surrender negotiations, would have been even more remarkable! In the event OSS chose to send in a Czech to act as W/T operator for General Wolff. I do not know whether anyone ever asked General Wolff after the event whether Mallaby had any influence on his decision to pursue surrender negotiations through OSS, but it is clear both from Dick's account of his interview with Wolff and from Allen Dulles' *The Secret Surrender* (New York, 1966), that the idea of entering into negotiations was in his mind at the time that Mallaby came into the hands of the SS, and Wolff's interview with Mallaby took place two days before he received news of a line to OSS Switzerland. Mallaby gave his parole to Wolff to return, and the records make clear that he was specifically relieved of this undertaking in the talks in Switzerland between Dulles and Wolff. He was in the end deprived of an opportunity of playing a similar role in the German surrender to that which he played with the Italians in 1943. However, it may be noted that Mallaby's meeting with Wolff took place two days before, according to

Dulles' account, news reached Wolff of the existence of a line to OSS in Switzerland.

These short accounts of Dick's two missions demonstrate sufficiently aspects of his character which his easy-going nature did not always suggest to those who knew him only casually: his quiet but almost reckless courage, his initiative, his determination, his loyalty and his natural probity. He was most certainly one of those who, even by the exacting standard of SOE, served honourably and beyond the call of duty to the very end.[6]

Christine Mallaby did not attend the event.

In Asciano, many years on from the events, Dick Mallaby is associated with two distinct memories: the first is that of the daring little blond boy who used to ride his bike on the parapets of the bridges, which led to mothers warning their children 'not to hang around with that English rascal'; the other is of his mysterious wartime activities, which, however, prevented the area from being bombed by the Allies 'because he was the one who laid down the guidelines'.[7]

As for the second memory, it is possible that Mallaby was consulted and gave directions, but he certainly would never have boasted about this.

In the closing phase of his life, Dick Mallaby, according to his youngest son Vaky, was:

… an exceptional person, loved by all, and with a character that was splendid, selfless and uncomplicated. He was good company to be with, he had many friends and our house was a busy one; at Christmas it was brimming with people, and every year the number of people who came to visit us increased.

He never talked about the past and never boasted about anything, not even when people asked directly.

He had a special twinkle in his eyes, a light that perhaps belongs to those who have seen many things and who understand that simplicity, love and living in harmony with everyone are the fundamental things of life.

As a father he was a fundamental figure and a very important point of reference for all of us. He was a man belonging (unfortunately) to another time, who could make himself understood and gained respect with merely a simple look.

The body of Cecil Richard Dallimore-Mallaby was laid to rest in April 1981 in Poggio Pinci, in the town of Asciano, in a small country cemetery, at the foot of a wooded hill, stretching east to west and looking onto the beautiful Crete Senesi south of Siena, an area that has captivated three generations of Mallabys.

The community in Asciano felt it right to commemorate their quasi-fellow citizen Dick Mallaby. As a result, on 23 September 2016, in the presence of the military attaché to the British embassy in Italy, Colonel

Lindsay MacDuff, and also myself, his children were honoured with the presentation of a gold medal.

The news was prominently reported by the British press and, in a very curious 21st-century way, subsequently bounced in the Italian media.[8]

Dick Mallaby, who had managed to turn two disasters into triumphs, had not even begun the most important mission of his life: retiring to his beloved Tuscany and dedicating himself to sailing and little else.

Christine, Mallaby's wife, from the day of his death, constantly wore around her neck the Military Cross that her beloved Dick had so deservedly won.

BIBLIOGRAPHY

Primary sources

Archivio Centrale dello Stato, Rome, Italy
ACC microfilm, Public Safety, item: Cecil D. Mallaby, reel 166 C

Archivio dell'Ufficio Storico dello Stato Maggiore dell'Esercito, Rome, Italy
Diari Storici 2 G.M.: 'Mancata difesa di Roma', 2235, 3000, 3000 bis, b. 3000/III

The National Archives, London, UK
Government archives
Admiralty
Submarine Logs (ADM 173)
War History Cases and Papers, Second World War (ADM 199)
Naval Intelligence Division and Operational Intelligence Centre Intelligence Reports and Paper (ADM 223)

Air Ministry
Records of the Air Historical Branch (AIR 20)

Foreign Office
Political Departments: General Correspondence 1906–1966 (FO 371)

Ministry of Defence
Combined Operations: Records (DEFE 2)

Prime Minister's Office
Correspondence and Papers, 1951–1964 (PREM 1)

Special Operations Executive
(HS 3)
(HS 6/ 775-776-779-780-809-869-870-871-872-873-874-889)
(HS 7/ 58-236-262-265)
(HS 8)
(HS 9)
(HS 15)
(WO 169-193-201-204-373)

National Archives and Records Administration, College Park, USA
Office of Stategic Services records: RG 226

Dwight D. Eisenhower Presidential Library, Abilene, USA
Walter Bedell Smith collection: *Capitulation of Italy – Messages*

Other
My interview with Mrs Anna Maria Rusconi
My interview with Mrs Pia Teresa Mallaby
My interview with Mrs Christine Northcote-Marks Mallaby
Diary of Mary Beatrice Schofield and Cecil Mallaby, from the first
     volume: 19 April 1919–30 November 1920, onwards
Diary of Cecil Mallaby: 1 July 1942–31 December 1953
Interview with Don Giovanni Barbareschi by Vaky Mallaby, 27
     November 2012
Mallaby family papers
Private memoirs of Dick Mallaby

Original transcript of the BBC radio programme *Now it Can Be Told*, aired on 25 June 1950, in the Mallaby family papers/ author's archive

Federal Bureau of Investigation, Washington, DC
Bureau files relating to Max Salvadori

Imperial War Museum (Department of Documents), London
'No Pipes or Drums' Memoirs of J. McCaffery
Papers of Major-General Sir C. McV. Gubbins

Liddell Hart Centre for Military Archives, King's College, London
Paper of Lieutenant-Colonel Count J. A. Dobrski

Magdalen College, Oxford
Papers of Sir Douglas Dodds-Parker

Newspapers and Periodicals
Corriere della Sera, *La Sera–Il Secolo*, the *Daily Telegraph*, the *Evening Standard*, *The New York Times*, *The Times*

Published works

Books

Adriano, P., *L'intrigo di Berna*, Mondadori: Milan, 2010
Aga Rossi, E., *L'inganno reciproco: L'armistizio tra l'Italia e gli Angloamericani del settembre 1943*, Ministero per i Beni Culturali e Ambientali: Rome, 1993
Amè, Cesare, *Guerra segreta in Italia*, Gherardo Casini Editore: Rome, 1954
Bailey, R., *Target: Italy – The Secret War Against Mussolini, 1940–1943: The Official History of SOE Operations in Fascist Italy*, Faber and Faber: London, 2014
Barneschi, G., *Balvano 1944. Indagine su un disastro rimosso*, LEG: Gorizia, 2014

Barneschi, R., *Frau Von Weber, Vita e morte di Mafalda di Savoia*, Rusconi, 1982

——, *Elena di Savoia. Storia e segreti di un matrimonio reale*, Rusconi, 1986

Beevor, J. G., *SOE Recollections and Reflections 1940–1945*, Bodley Head: London, 1981

Berrettini, M., *La Gran Bretagna e l'antifascismo italiano: diplomazia clandestine, intelligence, operazioni speciali, 1940-1943*, La Lettere: Florence, 2010

Bolla, N., *Il segreto di due re*, Rizzoli: Milan, 1951

Butcher, Harry Cecil, *Three Years with Eisenhower*, Mondadori: Milan, 1948

Carboni, G., *Memorie segrete, 1935-1948: Più che il dovere*, Parenti: Florence, 1955

Castellano, Giuseppe, *Come firmai l'armistizio di Cassibile*, Mondadori: Milan, 1945

——, *La Guerra Continua*, Rizzoli: Milan, 1963

——, *Roma Kaputt*, Gherardo Casini Editore: Rome, 1967

Churchill, W.S., *The Second World War. Volume V: Closing The Ring*, Cassell: London, 1951

Corvo, M., *The OSS in Italy, 1942-1945: A Personal Memoir*, Praeger: New York, 1990

Costantinides, G. C. *Intelligence and Espionage: An Analytical Bibliography*, Westview Press: Boulder, CO, 1983.

Craveri, Raimondo, *La Campagna d'Italia e i servizi segreti: La storia dell'ORI (1943–1945)*, La Pietra: Milan, 1980

Crosswell, D.K.R., *Beetle: The Life of General Walter Bedell Smith*, University Press of Kentucky: Lexington, KY, 2010

Davis, M. C., *Chi difende Roma? I quarantacinque giorni: 25 luglio–8 settembre 1943*, Rizzoli Editore: Milan, 1973

Deakin, Frederick W., *Storia della repubblica di Salò*, Vol. 2, Einaudi: Turin, 1963

Degli Espinosa, A., *Il Regno del Sud*, Editori Riuniti: Rome, 1973

De Leonardis, Massimo, *La Gran Bretagna e la resistenza partigiana in Italia (1943–1945)*, Scientifiche Italiane: Naples, 1988

De Risio, Carlo, *Generali, Servizi Segreti e Fascismo 1940-1943*, Mondadori: Milan, 1978

De Risio, C., *La tenda di Cassibile*, Editrice Science Technology History: Rome, 1993

Di Benigno, J., *Occasione mancate*, S.E.I.: Rome, 1945

Dodds-Parker, D., *Setting Europe Ablaze: Some Account of Ungentlemanly Warfare*, Springwood Books: Windlesham, 1983

Dollmann, E., *Roma nazista*, Longanesi & C: Milan, 1951

Dulles, A., *The Secret Surrender*, The Lyons Press: Guildford, 2006

Ehrman, J., *History of the Second World War: Grand Strategy. Volume V*, HMSO: London, 1956

Eisenhower, D. D., *Crusade in Europe*, Heinemann: London, 1948

Foot, M. R. D., *S.O.E.: The Special Operations Executive 1940–46*, Arrow Books: London, 1984

Gallegos, A., *From Capri to Oblivion*, Hodder & Stoughton: London, 1960

Garland, A. N. and Smyth, H. M., *Sicily and the Surrender of Italy*, Government Printing Office: Washington, DC, 1993

Giacomozzi, C., *Un eccidio a Bolzano*, Città di Bolzano: Bolzano, 2011

Gleeson, J. and Waldron, T., *Now It Can Be Told*, Elek Books: London, 1954

Graziani, R., *Ho difeso la patria*, Garzanti: Milan, 1947

Holt, T., *The Deceivers*, Weidenfeld & Nicolson: London, 2004

Howarth, P., *Undercover: The Men and Women of the S.O.E.*, Routledge & Kegan Paul: London, 1980

Kuby, E., *Il tradimento tedesco*, Rizzoli: Milan, 1987

Jakub, J., *Spies and Saboteurs*, Palgrave Macmillan: London, 1999

Lamb, R., *War in Italy, 1943-1945: A Brutal Story*, John Murray: London, 1993

Lanfranchi, F., *La resa degli ottocentomila*, Rizzoli: Milan, 1948

Lembo, D., *I servizi segreti di Salò: Servizi Segreti e Servizi Speciali nella Repubblica Sociale Italiana*, Grafica Ma.Ro srl Editrice: Copiano, 2001

Macintosh, C., *From Cloak to Dagger: An SOE agent in Italy 1943-45*, William Kimber: London, 1982

Mackenzie, W. J. M., *The Secret History of SOE: The Special Operations Executive 1940-45*, St Ermin's Press: London, 2000

Marchesi, L., *Come siamo arrivati a Brindisi*, Bompiani: Milan, 1969

——, *1939-1945 Dall'impreparazione alla resa incondizionata*, Mursia: Milan, 1993

——, *Per la libertà. Il contributo militare italiano al servizio informazioni alleato (dall'8 settembre 1943 al 25 aprile 1945)*, Mursia: Milan, 1995

Marks, L., *Between Silk and Cyanide: The Story of SOE's Code War*, Harper Collins: London, 1998

Masci, M., *I Savoia. L'ultimo giorno*, Editrice Italica: Pescara, 1966

Mellano, P., *Da Roma a Brindisi (via Pescara)*, unpublished: Rome, 1967

Ministero degli Affari Esteri, *I Documenti Documenti diplomatici italiani, Nona serie: 1939–1943*, vol. X *(7 febbraio – 8 settembre 1943)*, Istituto Poligrafico e Zecca dello Stato: Rome, 1990

Moore, Bob and Fedorowich, Kent, *The British Empire and its Italian Prisoners of War, 1940–1947*, Palgrave: Basingstoke, 2002

Murphy, C. J., *Security and Special Operations: SOE and MI5 During the Second World War*, Palgrave Macmillan: London, 2006

Nesi, S., *Junio Valerio Borghese: Un principe un comandante un Italiano*, Lo Scarabeo: Bologna, 2004

Palermo, Ivan, *Storia di un Armistizio*, Mondadori: Milan, 1967

Parlato, Giuseppe, *Fascisti senza Mussolini*, Il Mulino: Bologna, 2006

Parri, Ferruccio, *Due mesi con i nazisti*, Carecas: Rome, 1973

Pawley, Margaret, *In Obedience to Instructions: F.A.N.Y. with the SOE in the Mediterranean*, Leo Cooper: Barnsley, 1999

Peniakoff, Vladimir, *Popski's Private Army*, Reprint: London, 1953

Piffer, T., *Il banchiere della resistenza. Alfredo Pizzoni, il protagonista cancellato della guerra di liberazione*, Mondadori: Milan, 2005

Pizzoni A., *Alla guida del CLNAI*, Il Mulino: Bologna, 1995

Richards, B., Secret Flotillas. Volume II: Clandestine Sea Operations in the Mediterranean, North Africa and the Adriatic, 1940-44, Frank Cass: London, 2004

Roatta, M., *Otto milioni di baionette*, Mondadori: Milan, 1946

Rossi, C., *Trentatré vicende mussoliniane*, Ceschina: Milan, 1958

Rossi, F., *Come arrivammo all'armistizio*, Garzanti: Milan, 1946

Smith, Bradley F. and Aga Rossi, Elena, *Operation Sunrise: La resa tedesca in Italia 2 maggio '45*, Mondadori: Milan, 2005

Sogno, E., *Guerra senza bandiera*, Rizzoli: Milan, 1950

——, *La Franchi: Storia di un'organizzazione partigiana*, Il Mulino: Bologna, 1996

Stafford, D., *Mission Accomplished: SOE and Italy 1943–1945*, Vintage Books: London, 2011

Strong, K., *Intelligence at the Top*, Cassell: London, 1968

Tamaro, A., *Due Anni di Storia 1943–1945*, Tosi: Rome, 1950

Taylor, M. D., *Swords and Plowshares*, W.W. Norton: New York, 1972

Tompkins, Peter, *A Spy in Rome*, Simon and Schuster: New York, 1962

——, *Italy Betrayed*, Simon and Schuster: New York, 1966

——, *L'altra resistenza*, Rizzoli: Milan, 1995

Torsiello, M., *Settembre 1943*, Istituto Editoriale Cisalpino: Milan-Varese, 1963

Toscano, M., *Dal 25 luglio all'8 settembre*, Le Monnier: Florence, 1966

Ufficio Storico della Marina Militare, *Le memorie dell'Ammiraglio de Courten (1943–1946)*, Stabilimento Grafico Militare: Rome, 1993

Vailati, Vanna, *L'armistizio e il Regno del Sud*, Palazzi Editore: Milan, 1969

——, *La Storia Nascosta*, GCC: Turin, 1986

various, *N. 1 Special Force nella Resistenza italiana*, Editrice Clueb: Bologna, 1990

von Lang, J., *Der Adjutant: Karl Wolff, der Mann zwischen Hitler und Himmler*, Herbig: Stuttgart, 1985

von Plehwe, F. K., *Il patto d'acciaio*, Longanesi: Milan, 1970

Wagg, A. and Brown, D., *No Spaghetti for Breakfast*, Nicholson and Watson: London, 1943

West, N., *Secret War: The Story of SOE, Britain's Wartime Sabotage Organisation*, Hodder & Stoughton: London, 1992

Wilkinson, P. and Astley, J. B., *Gubbins and SOE*, Leo Cooper: Barnsley, 1993

Zangrandi, R., *1943: 25 Luglio-8 Settembre*, Feltrinelli: Milan, 1964.

Articles, Book Chapters, Theses

Barneschi, G., 'La misteriosa (e curiosa) vicenda di Ettore Bastico, Maresciallo d'Italia', *Nuova Storia Contemporanea*, 4/2004

———, 'Misteri, equivoci e ambiguità del tragico settembre 1943: Le radiotrasmissioni dell'agente speciale Dick Mallaby, l'inglese che viaggiò con il re e con Badoglio', *Nuova Storia Contemporanea*, 3/2013

———, 'La verità sulla resa dei tedeschi in Italia', *Nuova Storia Contemporanea*, 5-6/2016

Campbell, A. E., 'Franklin Roosevelt and Unconditional Surrender', in E. Langhorne, *Diplomacy and Intelligence during the Second World War: Essays in Honour of F. H. Hinsley*, Cambridge University Press: Cambridge, 1985

Deakin, Frederick W., 'Lo Special Operations Executive e la lotta partigiana', in F. Ferratini Tosi, G. Grassi, M. Legnani, *L'Italia nella seconda guerra mondiale e nella resistenza*, Franco Angeli: Milan, 1988, pp. 93–126.

Manaresi, F., 'I tedeschi dietro la "fuga" del Re: Un colloquio e una corrispondenza con Eugenio Dollmann', in *Nuova Storia Contemporanea*, 6/2009

Seaman, M., 'A Glass Half Full: Some Thoughts on the Evolution of the Study of the Special Operations Executive', *Intelligence and National Security 20/1*, 2005

Wales, T. C., 'The "Massingham" Mission and the Secret "Special Relationship". Cooperation and Rivalry between the Anglo-American Clandestine Services in French North Africa, November 1942-May 1943', *Intelligence and National Security 20/1*, March 2005

Williams, D., 'An Interview with Miss Paddy Sproule', *FANY Gazette*, 1999

Woods, C., 'A Tale of Two Armistices', in K. G. Robertson (ed.), *War, Resistance & Intelligence: Essays in Honour of M. R. D. Foot*, Leo Cooper: London, 1999

——, 'SOE in Italy', in M. Seaman (ed.), *Special Operations Executive: A New Instrument of War*, Routledge: London, 2006

ENDNOTES

PREFACE

1 David Stafford, *Mission Accomplished: SOE and Italy 1943–1945*, Vintage Books: London, 2011, p. 10.
2 Ibid., p. XVI; on this point, see also the views in Patrick Howarth, *Undercover: The Men and Women of the S.O.E.*, Routledge & Kegan Paul: London, 1980, pp. 188–89.

CHAPTER 1: MALLABY'S EARLY YEARS, 1919–39

1 Private diary of Mary Beatrice Schofield and Cecil Mallaby, first volume: 19 April 1919–30 November 1920.
Unless specified, all information comes from the personal diary of Mary Beatrice Schofield and Cecil Mallaby (then only Cecil Mallaby), as well as from the papers and memoirs of Dick Mallaby, the consultation and custody of which was kindly and faithfully permitted by Dick Mallaby's wife, Mrs Christine Northcote-Marks Mallaby, their son Vaky Mallaby and Dick Mallaby's half-sister, Mrs Pia Teresa Mallaby (depending on the relevant diary years). Without access to such documents, the consistency, details and overall value of this work would have been greatly inferior.
2 Archivio Centrale dello Stato – Rome (henceforth abbreviated to ACS): Allied Control Commission (henceforth ACC) microfilm, Public Safety, item: Cecil D. Mallaby, reel 166 C.

CHAPTER 2: SPECIAL OPERATIONS EXECUTIVE

1 SOE activities were minimal or non-existent in Germany and Japan, as well as in Italy until 1943.

2   In a memorandum dated 28 September 1943 on SOE activity in Italy in the preceding years, it was reported that, with regard to Operation *Avalanche* (the Allied landings at Salerno), Allied HQ had requested information on Italy: 'SOE responded to this request and although gathering and transmitting information is not our function, considerable appreciation was expressed in relation to the prompt way in which we were able to provide complete answers to their questions.' The National Archives, London (henceforth TNA), HS 6/775.

3   Michael R. D. Foot, *S.O.E.: The Special Operations Executive 1940–46*, Arrow Books: London, 1984, p. 17. William Mackenzie, *The Secret History of S.O.E.: Special Operations Executive 1940–1945*, St Ermin's Press: London, 2002, p. XIX.

4   According to Foot 1984, King George personally awarded a well-deserved DSO to a known burglar, for reasons obviously unspecified. Also, among the agents recruited was the owner of a chain of brothels.

5   A photo of Hitler was found in the luggage of a newly arrived recruit at a training base. This person 'was discreetly dismissed and classified as "missing, probably killed"' (Foot 1984, p. 176).

6   In a similar vein, classified British documents provide evidence of correspondence between Gubbins and the head of Italian Affairs, Cecil Laurence Roseberry, concerning a detailed plan to eliminate Mussolini and prominent fascist Roberto Farinacci (TNA: HS 7/265). They also contain a Most Secret message dated 14 July 1943 between Foreign Minister Eden and Churchill, in which the former rejected the proposal to bomb Mussolini's residence, or his 'office' at Palazzo Venezia, given the lack of certainty of total success, and the consequent risks of increasing Mussolini's stature and creating civilian casualties. The prime minister agreed.

7   See (among others): Peter Tompkins, *A Spy in Rome*, Simon and Schuster: New York, 1962, p. 10; Raimondo Craveri, *La Campagna d'Italia e i servizi segreti: La storia dell'ORI (1943–1945)*, La Pietra: Milan, 1980, p. 41. Craveri was a top figure

in the Italian resistance movement. In this book, he also notes (p. 66) the typically Italo-American tale of the Sicilian anti-Fascist exile Biagio Massimo (later Max) Corvo, who went from being a common soldier to OSS Director of Italian Operations.

8   Foot 1984, pp. 81 and 89.

9   See (among others) Stafford 2011.

10   Douglas Dodds-Parker, *Setting Europe Ablaze*, Springwood Books: Windlesham, 1984, p. 86, confirms this type of use, reporting that he had heard that stink bombs were very popular in Greece, where they were used in cinemas frequented by Axis troops. The same author reveals that their manufacture had been contracted to the main perfume companies 'using predominantly traditional ingredients'.

11   Dodds-Parker 1984, p. 87.

12   Raimondo Craveri called Roseberry the 'éminence grise of the English government with regards to Italy ... An important man, surrounded by a halo of reverential mystery, he had performed delicate duties in India and in the Middle East, which were mentioned in whispers' (Craveri 1980, p. 139).

13   The Italian Social Republic, the state set up by Mussolini in northern Italy following ther armistice with the Allies in 1943.

14   A rich and lively collection of accounts and memories relating to SOE missions in Italy from 1943 to 1945, witnessed from a particular standpoint, is also contained in: Margaret Pawley, *In Obedience to Instructions: F.A.N.Y. with the SOE in the Mediterranean*, Leo Cooper: Barnsley, 1999, *passim*.

15   Craveri 1980, pp. 38–39; he also emphasizes (p. 76) that: 'SOE peppered northern Italy with missions led by brave British officers, even in Garibaldine formations, who knows? Perhaps more to control them than to genuinely help them.'

CHAPTER 3: OPERATION NECK, 14 AUGUST 1943

1   TNA: HS 6/775.

2   Ibid.; Bob Moore and Kent Fedorowich, *The British Empire and its Italian Prisoners of War, 1940–1947*, Palgrave: Basingstoke, 2002, pp. 109–10 and 259 (note).

3 TNA: HS 6/872-889.

4 SIM – Military Information Service – Italian military espionage and counterespionage.

5 Cesare Amè, *Guerra segreta in Italia*, Gherardo Casini Editore: Rome, 1954, pp. 163–64.

6 For further details, see: Stafford 2011, pp. 92–94, 99 and 100–01; TNA: HS 6/775–776–809; and National Archives and Records Administration (henceforth NARA) RG 226, Entry 215, Box 4.

7 Deakin, Frederick W., 'Lo Special Operations Executive e la lotta partigiana', in F. Ferratini Tosi, G. Grassi, M. Legnani, *L'Italia nella seconda guerra mondiale e nella resistenza*, Franco Angeli: Milan, 1988, pp. 93–126. Stafford 2011 and Thadeus Holt (in *The Deceivers*, Weidenfeld & Nicolson: London, 2004, p. 14) emphasize this notion.

8 TNA, HS 7/263. Bailey 2014, p. 201. The same author (ibid., pp. 356–57) observes that many historians wrongly shared Roseberry's glossing version of the Italians' successes, revealing (ibid., p. 355) that, after the official disclosure of the infiltration: 'When word was dispatched to SOE's outpost in Bern, care was taken to break the news gently to Jock McCaffery. A few weeks earlier he had ended up in a Lugano clinic suffering from nervous exhaustion from overwork and "cerebral commotion" from a spot of concussion. Unsurprisingly his first reaction to the report was one of shock and disbelief.'
Edgardo Sogno, in *La Franchi Storia di un'organizzazione partigiana* Il Mulino: Bologna, 1996, p. 123, pointed out that even in July 1944, in Monopoli, there took place 'something similar to what happened in the previous April in Bern with Mc Caffery', because British officials, with 'fundamental pragmatisms', kept on welcoming Italian resistance organizations 'the way they were, just because they worked, even if what we were doing was in part contrary to their standards of security'.

9 'It is important the groups are not aware of this, and since everything will be in code, it should not be difficult' (TNA: HS 6/869).

Craveri 1980 emphasizes (p. 76) that even after 1943: 'SOE peppered northern Italy with missions led by brave British officers, even in Garibaldine formations, who knows? Perhaps more to control them than to genuinely help them.'
An important, neglected truth.

10   TNA: HS 6/871.

11   TNA: HS 6/869.

12   TNA: HS 6/871.

13   Ibid. The simple 'double message' method was used for correspondence that contained place or personal names. The first message would give single letters (or less commonly numbers) in place of names; subsequent messages would provide keys to the meaning of these. The first message, for example, might read: 'X has volunteered to go in Kelly's place'. A second message transmitted shortly after would specify that X was 'an Englishman named Mallaby', adding that 'we will refer to him as Y', while a third message specified that 'Y is agent Olaf'.

14   Ibid.

15   According to Howarth 1980 (p. 189), Mallaby had become one of the best radio-telegraphy instructors, and among his students was Christine Granville (codename of the famous and celebrated Polish SOE agent Krystyna Skarbek, who conducted missions in Eastern Europe and France during the war).
Howarth describes Mallaby as a man 'with kind, almost whimsical ways', while according to McCaffery, Mallaby 'possessed the kind of courage known as the cold, two o'clock in the morning type. But his appearance prompted a Swiss friend who met him later to say that one of the great strengths of England lay in its being full of fresh-faced pleasant youngsters like Dick, who were capable of going out and doing the man-sized jobs that he did'. John McCaffery, 'No Pipes or Drums' (unpublished memories: Imperial War Museum, London).

16   ACS: ACC microfilm, Public Safety, item: Cecil D. Mallaby, reel 166 C.

17   According to Pawley 1999 (p. 36), FANY Dorothy Temple had also developed a code plan, called Muscat (continuing the alcohol theme), for the Italian agents whom Mallaby was tasked with contacting.

18   Stafford 2011, p. 100. Bailey 2014, *passim*. When Giacomino Sarfatti learned that SIM had controlled his nine-month stint in Milan, he had to admitt that, despite Klein's strange behavior, he didn't rumble that Klein was in effect an enemy agent either, inferring that he was 'handicapped by two things: (a) [by] my age (22 at the time) and my very little experience of life and men generally; [and] (b) by the fact that I had been repeatedly told both in London and Bern that I could trust [Klein] and rely completely on him. I was actually told he was [a] wonderful man and that I was going to be quite safe as long as he was looking after me' (Bailey 2014, p. 327 and TNA: HS 9/1313).

19   TNA: HS 6/872.

20   Ibid.

21   TNA: HS 6/870.

22   Ibid.

23   Stafford 2011, p. 12; Dodds-Parker 1984, pp. 118–19.

24   The Most Secret report dated 28 September 1943 (entitled 'The Olaf Story') stated that Mallaby was sent to Massingham in part to avoid the risk (which appeared to be real) of him backing out due to the repeated postponements: 'Once his morale was restored, plans were made to drop him "blind" over one of the northern Italian lakes and let him find a way to settle in one or other of the safe addresses provided to him' (TNA: HS 6/775). This kind of statement, a rarity in the services, helps us understand the level of tension that constantly filled the lives of SOE agents.

25   Moore and Fedorowich 2002, pp. 107 and 258 (note). Attempts to recruit Italian prisoners captured in Africa and those resident abroad had very poor results, both quantitatively and qualitatively; on this point, see Bailey 2014, *passim*. The

recruitment of prisoners for military purposes was obviously prohibited by international convention.

26 TNA: HS 6/870. This detailed memorandum specified that the toiletry bag, and above all the money, were the property of the administrative powers and were to be returned, subject to the issue of a specific receipt, if not used within the scheduled time frame for the operation. A request for this does not appear to have been issued.

27 TNA: HS 6/870-872.

28 Ibid.

29 Ibid.

30 Ibid.

31 As John Le Carré recalls in *Tinker, Tailor, Soldier, Spy*, even the best undercover agents were often betrayed by their footwear, it being difficult to change them, especially in winter. One of the most common mistakes by those involved in clandestine missions was providing agents working together or in the same area with identical clothing, as if they were school pupils or part of a sports team.

The clothing items for Mallaby's mission were provided by an SOE-based workshop, the so-called G Topo unit, commanded by Malcom Munthe.

32 TNA: HS 6/870.

33 Ibid.; TNA: HS 6/872.

34 Ibid.

35 TNA: HS 6/870.

36 TNA: HS 6/872.

37 For security reasons, as already indicated, it was established that Mallaby and his technical equipment should travel separately. At Cairo station, concealment work was carried out so well that on 15 July Massingham was forced to enquire by means of a special message where the photographic films with the cryptographic codes had been hidden (TNA: ibid.).

38 Ibid.

39 For a description of the strains that agents were under on operations, see Foot 1984, p. 235 and Pawley 1999, p. 59. As

noted by Foot 1984 (p. 235): 'Besides the agent who is said to have died of fright, there were several more who were more or less violently disturbed by the strains they had to undergo: the strain of being one person while seeming to be another; the strain of keeping silent while everyone round them gossiped; the strain of not correcting the under-informed; the strain of being important but being thought a nobody; the strain of remembering strings of addresses too secret to be written down and too important to be forgotten; the unforgettable threats of arrest and torture if discovered; the lack of time, the lack of any chance entirely to relax; the perpetual uncertainty; the perpetual lack of sleep. The first thought of an important agent, pulled in at a shop control but not yet identified by the enemy, when he had been out there receiving arms for eleven nights in two weeks and other agents parachuted in, was not for his safety, nor for those for whom he was responsible – it was, "Finally I can sleep".'

Pawley 1999 (p. 59) recalls the case of a wireless operator working in Yugoslavia who became convinced he was St Paul.

40 TNA: HS 6/870.

41 TNA: HS 6/872.

42 Ibid.

43 TNA: HS 6/870-872.

44 Ibid.

45 Ibid.

46 Ibid.

47 In a communication dated 11 August from Bern, the city names were omitted from the addresses, so that initially, at Massingham, it was believed that the Via Calvi safe house was in Como. A further exchange of messages was needed to clear things up. The building in Via Calvi was destroyed a few days later by bombing, at the same time as the beginning of Operation *Neck*.

48 TNA: HS 6/870. According to the final reports, Mallaby would have arrived in Italy with a total of 210,000 lire – a truly remarkable sum.

49 Ibid.

50 TNA: HS 6/775.

51 TNA: HS 6/872. Other reports provided slightly different coordinates. However, what matters (and what is certain) is the actual place where Mallaby was brought back to land: Carate Urio.

52 On the night of 12/13 August 1943, Milan suffered perhaps the most violent of its many wartime raids. According to Christopher Woods in 'A Tale of Two Armistices', in K. G. Robertson, *War, Resistance and Intelligence: Collected Essays in Honour of M.R.D. Foot*, Leo Cooper: Barnsley, 1999, p. 3, due to the bombing the owner of the Milanese safe house known to Mallaby would have fled the city, and in panic would have destroyed the radio apparatus intended for agent Olaf. This lacks credibility, given that the apartment and the apparatus were managed by SIM, and I have found no documentary evidence to support this.

53 My interview with Mrs Anna Maria Rusconi.

54 Carate Urio is in the area where, on 28 April 1945, Benito Mussolini and Clara Petacci were shot, and where, after the war, Winston Churchill holidayed with his artist's brushes.

55 My interview with Mrs Anna Maria Rusconi and local newspaper *La Provincia*, 29 September 2016.

56 Malcolm Tudor, *SOE in Italy: The Real Story*, Emilia Publishing: Newtown, 2011, p. 17.

57 Around this time, on 18 August 1943, the leadership of SIM passed from General Cesare Amè to General Giacomo Carboni.

58 Daniele Lembo, in *I servizi segreti di Salò* (Grafica Ma.Ro srl Editrice: Copiano, 2001, *passim*) states that in 1942, SIM, despite having discovered a radio base in Milan and identified its operator, did not arrest the agent in question, but instead aided his activities, since the information he transmitted was not only carefully monitored, but was in fact provided by the British network in northern Italy that was being manipulated by SIM itself. Each transmission was monitored by an Italian listening station, which had its own cypher. Evidently, this

station was the one managed by agent Galea (Sarfatti), under the full control of SIM, and was the one that agent Olaf – equipped with ad hoc ciphers for his mission – intended to use.

59 TNA: HS 6/872. Quite surprisingly SIM even knew Mallaby's SOE codename for the mission (i.e. Olaf): NARA RG 226.

60 TNA: HS 6/776-780-872.

61 TNA: HS 6/872.

62 The Italian secret reports relating to Mallaby's capture recorded that, according to confidential information, two additional parachute drops had taken place in the Lake Como area. Furthermore, according to other unconfirmed reports, two individuals wearing life jackets had been spotted in the Bellagio area in the early hours of the morning, and between Torriggia and Careno lights had been seen and aircraft engines heard. This had led to multi-agency search operations.
Following careful searches, all that was found was a rowing boat near Villa Frigerio at Nesso (TNA: ibid.)

63 Ibid. According to the accompanying note, this dossier was drawn up on the basis of the 'Italian documents requisitioned' and obtained by 'C.I.' (possibly referring to an agent from SIS's Italian branch), through his contacts in Rome.

64 Ibid. Article 35 of the Instrument of Surrender signed at Malta on 29 September 1943 stated: 'The Italian Government will supply all information and provide all documents required by the United Nations [i.e. the Allies]. There shall be no destruction or concealment of archives, records, plans or any other documents or information.'

65 Ibid. The concluding comment of the SOE report reveals an unsurprising detail. Mallaby's false identity documents were 'furnished by Cairo under general authority, but without express authority from "C" [i.e. SIS]'. Thus, it was recommended: 'the least said the better'.

66 Ibid.

67 TNA: HS 6/870. In October 1943, as mentioned above, the levels of accumulated stress resulted in McCaffery suffering a nervous breakdown that required a four-week convalescence.

68 TNA: HS 6/872. This message also noted the embarrassing situation of having to wait until the Friday following Mallaby's drop (i.e. six whole days) before attempting any contact.

69 Ibid.

70 Ibid.

71 Ibid.

72 Ibid. The codename Partito possibly referred to a member or a group of members of the Partito d'Azione (which had close ties with the British and SOE). This hypothesis is reinforced by an urgent message dated 23 August sent by London that indicated that some initiatives being considered to secure Mallaby's release might expose the links between this party and SOE. This is another proof of the misplaced confidence gained by the group managed by SIM, just reflecting that even if the Fascism was gone in that moment in Italy, political parties were not legitimized.

73 Ibid.

74 Ibid.

75 TNA: HS 6/870. The RAF's operating procedures for dropping *matériel* and people were often criticized by SOE agents, as they considered them crude and dangerous, both for those on the ground in reception committees, and for those who had to jump (see Stafford 2011, p. 286).

76 TNA: HS 6/872.

CHAPTER 4: FROM DISASTER TO TRIUMPH

1 In a confidential memorandum dated 28 September 1943, SOE's Department J recorded that a member of the Italian mission to Allied HQ in Africa had complained that the disinterest of British officials in considering the first Italian attempts to negotiate surrender had delayed the fall of Fascism by several months (TNA: HS 6/775).

2 For further details on Montanari, see Peter Tompkins, *Italy Betrayed*, Simon and Schuster: New York, 1966; Craveri 1980, p. 123.

3 Elena Aga Rossi, *L'inganno reciproco - L'armistizio tra l'Italia e gli Angloamericani del settembre 1943*, Roma – Ministero per i Beni Culturali e Ambientali – Ufficio Centrale per i Beni Archivistici – 1993, *passim*. *Una nazione allo sbando. L'armistizio italiano del settembre 1943 e le sue conseguenze*, Il Mulino: Bologna, 1993, *passim*. *A Nation Collapses: The Italian Surrender of September 1943*, Cambridge University Press: Cambridge, 2000, *passim*.

4 Giuseppe Castellano, *Come firmai l'armistizio di Cassibile*, Mondadori: Milan, 1945, *passim*; *La Guerra continua*, Rizzoli: Milan, 1963, *passim*; *Roma Kaputt*, Gherardo Casini Editore: Rome, 1967, *passim*.

5 Sir Kenneth Strong, *Intelligence at the Top*, Doubleday & Company: New York, 1969, p. 147; Castellano 1945, p. 152 (note); Ruggero Zangrandi, *1943: 25 Luglio-8 Settembre*, Feltrinelli: Milan, 1964, *passim*.
   Regarding Castellano's behaviour and beliefs, the following psychoanalytic explanation by Allied Force HQ on 10 September 1943 appears to be spot on, as Castellano's bluffing became more evident: 'Why had Castellano brought the negotiations to a head? Probably, AFHQ speculated, it was "chiefly due to his treatment by the Germans who apparently ignored the Italians militarily and told them nothing about operations"' (Albert N. Garland and Howard McGaw Smyth, *United States Army in World War II Mediterranean Theater of Operations: Sicily and the Surrender of Italy*, Center of Military History, United States Army: Washington DC, 1993, p. 541 and note 4).

6 The message document features a prominent handwritten addition, including the words 'My God!', a clear indication of the reader's surprise at some positive or unnerving aspect as reported. The anonymous amender of this message also underlined the part in which it was asked whether the proposed ideas on how to free Mallaby should be referred to 'J.Q.' (i.e. McCaffery).

7 A summary of the military and other discussions between Brigadier-General Castellano and General Eisenhower's General Staff in Lisbon on 19 August 1943 can be found in Castellano 1945, pp. 217–18; Ministero degli Affari Esteri, *Documenti diplomatici italiani, Nona serie: 1939–1943*, vol. X (7 febbraio – 8 settembre 1943), Istituto Poligrafico e Zecca dello Stato: Rome, 1990, pp. 851–57; and Aga Rossi, *L'inganno reciproco*, 1993, pp. 288–89.

8 Strong 1969, pp. 151–52.

9 TNA: HS 7/58 and TNA: 6/776. In his secret diary, written years after the events, Dick Mallaby wrote that the set and the signal plans were handed over to Montanari by 'the Colonel in charge of the Italian section SOE in London'. Even if his recollections were private, Mallaby still felt the need not to reveal details about SOE organization.

10 Castellano 1945, pp. 116–17, 122–23 and 172. Tompkins' version of events (Tompkins 1962, p. 110) matches this in most details – unsurprisingly, given the post-war contacts between the two authors.

During his interrogation before the Commission of Inquiry into the failure to defend Rome on 17 December 1944, Brigadier-General Castellano noted the following on this point: 'After having made the arrangements about my trip and having been equipped with a radio and cypher, I rapidly headed for Rome'. He fails to mention (as normal in his official statements) the role of Dick Mallaby (Archivio dell'Ufficio Storico dello Stato Maggiore dell' Esercito – henceforth AUSSME – Diari Storici 2 G.M., 'Mancata difesa di Roma', b. 3000).

11 The British–American versions of the events during this period are mildly contradictory and partially conflicting. See Marks 1998, p. 359; Dodds-Parker 1984, p.137; Bailey 2014, pp. 310–11; Melton C. Davis, *Chi difende Roma? I quarantacinque giorni: 25 luglio–8 settembre 1943*, Rizzoli Editore: Milan, 1973. p. 283.

12   Castellano 1945, p. 123. A. Wagg and D. Brown, *No Spaghetti for Breakfast*, Nicholson and Watson: London, 1943, p. 126. Ivan Palermo, *Storia di un Armistizio*, Mondadori: Milan, 1967, pp. 156–57.

13   Marks 1998, p. 359.

14   The secrecy of the Castellano mission and the lack of coordination with the Italian structures in Portugal had a positive consequence, as Ambassador Prunas had no need to lie when his German counterpart asked him for an information on intelligence about an Italian mission in Lisbon charged with surrender negiotiations.

15   Marks 1998, p. 359. TNA: HS 6/779.

16   TNA: HS 6/779. A message from a few days before (22 August) reported the unfounded opinion of Castellano that his leisurely return to Italy did not matter, as an Allied landing on mainland Italy was not considered imminent. It was the beginning of a catastrophic misunderstanding.

17   TNA: HS 6/872.

18   Ibid. As for American reactions, see Max Corvo, *The O.S.S. in Italy 1942–1945: A Personal Memoir*, Praeger: New York, 1990, p. 131; later (p. 167).

19   TNA: HS 6/872.

20   Ibid.

21   TNA: HS 6/775.

22   TNA: HS 6/872 In 1943, SIM had managed to install one of its agents as Osborne's butler. He was able to remove and photograph the cypher used by the British diplomat, but this was discovered by the British, who began using this unorthodox channel to spread false information to the Italians.

23   TNA: HS 6/775-779-780-870-871-872.

24   Ibid.

25   Ibid.

26   Ibid.

27   TNA: HS 6/775.

28   TNA: HS 6/872.

29 Castellano 1945 states (p. 123): 'I did not encounter difficulties, as soon as I arrived in Rome, in tracking down the officer, who was immediately freed.' This clearly shows he was led to believe that Mallaby was an officer (a fictitious promotion) and that the Italian leadership had no qualms about using a British agent.

30 TNA: HS 6/775.

31 Mallaby's private memoirs confirm the controversial existence of this letter and the writer's identity: 'I was handed a letter from my Colonel, which from its contents left me in no doubt'.

32 Beyond cryptographic techniques, the touch on the key of each operator is like a fingerprint, which becomes recognizable to those who usually receive the transmissions. This allowed a rapid identification of who was actually transmitting (and even some idea of their psychological state). The most experienced operators soon learned to distinguish whether the transmitting agents, who in any case often worked in highly tense conditions, were operating under duress (see Marks 1998, pp. 601–02).

Luigi Marchesi, who at the time was a major seconded to the Supreme Command and right-hand man of the Chief of the General Staff Vittorio Ambrosio and Castellano (and, in those days, the chief guardian angel of Dick Mallaby), confirms that operators known to Mallaby were used in the transmissions so that he could 'recognize the rhythm of the key' (Luigi Marchesi, *Come siamo arrivati a Brindisi*, Bompiani: Milan, 1969, p. 62; and also Luigi Marchesi, *1939–1945 Dall'impreparazione alla resa incondizionata*, Mursia: Milan, 1993, p. 52).

In his memoir, *La guerra continua*, Rizzoli: Milan, 1963, p.78, Castellano recalled: 'At first [Mallaby] refused, but the reward I had promised him, freedom, led him to start work, albeit with considerable mistrust. However, when he received the conventional phrase "Tie Rock" from Algiers, he was reassured and, from that point on, renamed "Squarzina", he served the Supreme Command.' Castellano is the only one to refer to this confirmation phrase used by Massingham.

33 In common with almost all radio-telegraphists, on several further occasions Mallaby interspersed brief personal or playful statements in his messages. These often got the intended recipients (mainly Christine Marks) into trouble and disciplinary sanctions (see also Bailey 2014, p. 316).

34 TNA: HS 6/779.

35 Marchesi 1969, pp. 61–62 and Marchesi 1993, p. 52. From Marchesi's recollections, we can infer that Castellano did not make clear to his collaborators that the radio had arrived in Italy with him and not Mallaby.

In his secret diary Dick Mallaby states that 'Maresciallo Baldanza was placed at my side to operate and to keep an eye on me ... I instructed in how to use the device, so that I could rest while he continued.'

Between the September 1943 surrender and the arrival of Allied troops in the Italian capital (4 June 1944), Baldanza was in charge of the transmissions from a secret transmitter called 'Centro X'.

36 Mrs Christine Joyce Northcote-Marks Dallimore-Mallaby's statement on this, and others besides, were compiled and recorded by me on 19 June 2008 in Milan.

Marks 1998 (p. 335) describes the Quirinale event; whereas, according to the detailed report contained in Palermo 1967 (p. 157), at least until the morning of 5 September, Mallaby operated from the Supreme Command HQ.

37 Stafford 2011, p. 15.

38 Ruggero Zangrandi, in *1943: 25 luglio – 8 settembre*, Feltrinelli: Milan, 1964 (p. 335), hypothesizes that the secret radio traffic managed by Mallaby was also used by Ambrosio and Castellano to exchange important confidential messages. There is no proof of this.

39 In his interrogation dated 27 February 1945, Lieutenant-Colonel De Francesco confirmed that 'all the secret radio messages were brought to me' (Palermo 1967, p. 410). Otello

Griffoni, in his unpublished memoir (in my possession), states that due to Castellano's and Marchesi's commitments, De Francesco entrusted him with the 'encoding and decoding' of the messages.

40 See: Zangrandi 1964; Toscano 1966; Palermo 1967; and Aga Rossi, *L'inganno reciproco*, 1993. In the latter work (p. 310) it is noted that the Monkey–Drizzle messages were destroyed at 7.30am on 9 September, as confessed in the diligent report of the following day, signed by the appointed, Major Mauro Aloni, complete with countersignatory confirmation by Lieutenant-Colonel Primo Peraldo of the General Staff, who authorized the destruction as 'head of the Exchequer'. In Annex I, point 11 of this report it can be read that the papers burnt included 'A collection of about 50 incoming and about 30 outgoing radio messages exchanged between the Supreme Command and the Allied commander in chief'. This provides a very useful quantification of the number of successful Monkey–Drizzle messages up to that point. This document can be found at AUSSME: N. 1-11, Fondo Diari Storici 2 G.M. b. 3000/III, and is reported in *I Documenti Diplomatici Italiani*, Istituto Poligrafico e Zecca dello Stato – Libreria dello Stato: Rome, 1990, pp. 957–58.
There were more destructions of documents relating to the Italian surrender (implemented by SIM and the Ministry of Foreign Affairs) during this period.

41 Castellano 1945 (p. 184, note) notes the unprecedented operational detail, stating that 'For security reasons all the telegrams, after deciphering and translation, were paraphrased and again retranslated.'

42 Carlo De Risio, in *La tenda di Cassibile* (Editrice Science Technology History: Rome, 1993, p. 82) refers to this message, but without a citation.

43 Castellano 1945, p. 128. AUSSME, n. 1–11, Diari Storici 2 G.M., b. 3000/III.

44 TNA: HS 6/779.

45 Ibid.

46 Aga Rossi, *L'inganno reciproco*, 1993, p. 397.

47 Ibid., p. 398.

48 The message is reproduced in its entirety in Castellano 1963 (p. 89). In Massingham the news was enthusiastically welcomed. The always very self-restrained Douglas Dodds-Parker gave Mary MacIntyre, the FANY who handed him the message, a kiss straightaway, then rushed the message to General Walter Bedell Smith, who commented: 'This is very satisfactory.' Eisenhower, on hearing the good news, declared himself 'very pleased'.

49 Castellano 1963, p. 88. AUSSME, n. 1–11, Fondo Diari Storici 2 G.M., b. 3000/III.

50 Aga Rossi, *L'inganno reciproco*, 1993, p. 210.

51 Castellano 1963, p. 90. AUSSME, n. 1–11, Fondo Diari Storici 2 G.M., b. 3000/III.

52 Ibid. See also Harry Cecil Butcher, *Three Years with Eisenhower*, Mondadori: Milan, 1948, p. 38; Vanna Vailati, *L'armistizio e il Regno del Sud*, Palazzi Editore: Milan, 1969, pp. 205–06; Castellano 1945, p. 157; and Castellano 1963, p. 90.

53 The 44-clause Long Armistice (the 'Instrument of Surrender of Italy') was eventually signed in Malta on 29 September 1943 aboard HMS *Nelson* by General Eisenhower and Marshal Badoglio, but kept secret until November 1945.

54 AUSSME n. 1–11, Fondo Diari Storici 2 G.M., b. 3000 bis.

55 Aga Rossi, *L'inganno reciproco*, 1993, pp. 310–11.

56 According to a secret message sent at the time from Rome to Berlin, Badoglio declared that the Italians would not necessarily attack the Germans or the Allies: 'It depends on who acts first.'

57 Aga Rossi, *L'inganno reciproco*, 1993, pp. 313–314.

58 Ibid., p. 217.

59 For both, see AUSSME: Diari Storici 2 G.M., 'Mancata difesa di Roma', b. 3000.

60 Aga Rossi, *L'inganno reciproco*, 1993, pp. 316–17 and Dwight D. Eisenhower Presidential Library, Abilene, Kansas, Walter Bedell Smith collection: *Capitulation of Italy – Messages*.

According to Dodds-Parker 1984 (p. 140), the message was dictated down the telephone to him by Eisenhower. The first two parts of the message were dictated at 11.30am, but there was then a two-hour delay before the last part was received. Eisenhower informed Dodds-Parker that the last part (evidently subject to careful drafting by committee with other Allied political, diplomatic and military leaders) would be sent by military courier with the utmost urgency. Someone, however, forgot to point out this urgency, as the courier only delivered the envelope to Massingham only after having eaten his lunch in the time between consignment and delivery.

61 Aga-Rossi, *L'inganno reciproco*, 1993, p. 317. Eisenhower Library, Walter Bedell Smith collection: *Capitulation of Italy – Messages*.

62 Eisenhower Library, Walter Bedell Smith collection: *Capitulation of Italy – Messages.*; TNA: HS 6/780; and Aga Rossi, *L'inganno reciproco*, 1993, pp. 311–12.

63 From the original transcript of the BBC radio programme *Now it Can Be Told*, which aired on 25 June 1950, in the Mallaby family papers/my archive.

64 Aga Rossi, *L'inganno reciproco*, 1993, *passim*.

65 AUSSME: Diari Storici 2 G.M., 'Mancata difesa di Roma', b. 3000. See also Marchesi 1969, pp. 110–11; and Marchesi 1993, p. 85.

66 Melton C. Davis (Davies 1973, p. 418) claims that Mallaby was accompanied by five officers, three non-commissioned officers and an Italian radio technician, as well as the radio. According to the same author (who does not indicate a source), the plane was piloted by Major Giovanni Battista Vassallo.
    Vassallo was in charge of the Supreme Command's air transport requirements, as well as being the personal pilot of Chief of the General Staff Vittorio Ambrosio. Although Vassallo's position might have allowed him to recall various interesting details (he even flew Castellano to Sicily

and back in those days), he has never been the subject of research, interviews or investigations. I have only managed to ascertain that Vassallo died in 1997.

67 TNA: HS 6/870.

68 Eisenhower Library, Walter Bedell Smith collection: *Capitulation of Italy – Messages.*

69 Ibid.

70 TNA: HS 6/780.

71 The transcription of this message bears the following note: 'Monkey went off the air at 2000 hrs GMT in spite of all our protests.' Eisenhower Library, Walter Bedell Smith collection: *Capitulation of Italy – Messages.* TNA: Ibid.

72 Practically all the accounts relating to this phase of the journey (one among many in Davis 1973, p. 449) refer to heated arguments, due to de Courten preventing some people from boarding (which was clearly the case), and the presence of an angry crowd on the harbour wall at Ortona (which is not true).

73 Both events are reported in Manlio Masci, *I Savoia. L'ultimo giorno*, Editrice Italica: Pescara, 1966, pp. 161–62 and pp. 168–69.

74 According to Luigi Marchesi's memoirs, his group (which also included the officers De Francesco, Adam, Marshal Baldanza and Sergeant Della Corte, plus Mallaby) was ferried across by boarding barge, together with King Vittorio Emanuele III, his consort and his son.

According to other eyewitnesses (Masci 1966, p. 167), the royal family reached the *Baionetta* on board the fishing boat *Littorio*.

Otello Griffoni, in his memoirs, refers to three transfers across: the first (with the members of the royal house, the leaders of the Supreme Command and Mallaby) was a calm affair, while the others were less so.

75 Luigi Marchesi, Edgardo Sogno, Carlo Milan, *Per la libertà: Il contributo militare italiano al servizio informazioni alleato*, Mursia: Milan, 1995, p. 10.

76 Zangrandi 1964 (p. 399) reports the presence of 'another British officer, assisting with the radio, soon no longer undercover'. This has no basis in fact.

77 Another eyewitness on board the *Baionetta*, Pietro Mellano, was the only one to report a further event, comprising a pair of German aircraft – a Ju 88 reconnaissance plane and another plane that flew very close to the ship. He also notes: 'We had requested a fighter escort from our airfields in Apulia, but none were ever seen. Perhaps they didn't exist anymore' (Pietro Mellano, *Da Roma a Brindisi (via Pescara)*, n.p., Rome, 1967, p. 78).

78 Zangrandi 1964, pp. 438–39; Agostino Degli Espinosa, *Il Regno del Sud*, Editori Riuniti: Rome, 1973, p. 10.

79 This particular 'non-event', which aroused suspicions among many alternative theorists, was actually stimulated by King Vittorio Emanuele III, who made the following surprising and slightly ambiguous statement on the matter: 'At 1.00 pm on 10 September, a German plane targeted our ship. I thought that it had been deliberately sent to bomb us, but *having identified us*, it flew off.', according to Nino Bolla *Il segreto di due re*, Rizzoli: Milan, 1951, p. 28.

One of the best-informed witnesses, Eugen Dollmann, made apparently conflicting and ambiguous statements on the matter. Having denied for decades the existence of an agreement, on 4 February 1984, during an interview in Munich, he asserted that a sort of tacit agreement was in place and also claimed credit for it. See Franco Manaresi, 'I tedeschi dietro la "fuga" del Re: Un colloquio e una corrispondenza con Eugenio Dollmann', in *Nuova Storia Contemporanea*, VI, November–December 2009, pp. 123–38.

80 TNA: HS 6/870.

81 See also Zangrandi 1964, p. 436; Vailati 1969, p. 308.

82 TNA: HS 6/780. Conversely, Mallaby at that time was asked to report to Algiers that the light cruiser *Scipione Africano* would remain in Brindisi at the king's disposal.

83 Ibid.

84 Ibid.

85 Ibid.

86 Ibid.

87 Ibid.

88 See TNA: HS 6/870 and Degli Espinosa 1973, pp. 53–78, for an accurate memory of the atmosphere existing in the autumn of 1943 in Apulia between the Italians and the British.

89 TNA, HS 6/775-872.

90 TNA: HS 6/779.

91 Dodds-Parker 1984, p. 136; Foot 1984, p. 296; Marks 1998, p. 397. Dwight D. Eisenhower, *Crusade in Europe*, Doubleday & Company: Baltimore, 1948, p. 183.

92 Foot 1984, p. 329.

93 Eisenhower Library, Walter Bedell Smith collection: *Capitulation of Italy – Messages*.

CHAPTER 5: THE SECOND MISSION

1   ACS: ACC microfilm, Public Safety, item: Cecil D. Mallaby, reel 166 C.

2   Private diary of Cecil Mallaby, 1 July 1942–31 December 1953: entries for 16 and 17 July 1944 (courtesy of Mrs Pia Teresa Mallaby).
    To understand what can happen to a father who has not seen his son return home, the following sad tale from Arezzo helps. Outside the railway station, or at the corner of the main street of the city, during the 1960s, stood a very distinguished man, tall and thin, getting on in years, staring into space, with a bicycle next to him. His clothes, as well as the bicycle, were completely coloured in gold. This man was waiting. He was waiting for his son, who left during World War II for the Russian Front and never returned. In his devastating, dignified and lucid delirium, he hoped that, after such a long time, his son would return. And so, to be easily spotted, he frequented the busiest places in the city, in that unmistakable colour, so that his son might recognize him after all that time.

3   According to Stafford 2011 (p. 152), Mallaby went with Henderson 'to liberated Macerata, to resume contact with

the partisans and assess the relevance of their activity, document their activities in the region, obtain elements that could be useful for northern Italy, recover weapons and *matériel*, which would have been used for "banditry", ensure that the partisan leaders now replaced by the Allies were well treated, and inform the Allied Military Government about the problems they might expect in the future, from partisan units that had been stood down. As the Allies advanced northwards and larger areas of Italy were liberated, the latter problem was emerging as one of the most pressing and complex.'

Carla Giacomozzi's *Un eccidio a Bolzano* confirms that Mallaby was simultaneously training Italian agents destined for missions in territory under RSI control (Città di Bolzano/ Assessorato alla Cultura, alla Convivenza, all Ambiente e alle Pari Opportunità Ufficio Servizi Museali e Storico-Artistici Archivio Storico: Bolzano, 2011, pp. 38, 103).

4 Mallaby was able to share his knowledge of the area with his colleagues, and so a group of FANYs began to attend the gymnasium of the famous fencing master Enrico Barbera. Mallaby had already practised the noble sport in his time in Modena before the war. Pawley 1999 (pp. 82–83) contains a photo taken after the end of Mallaby's second mission, showing Barbera and six FANYs holding fencing swords.

5 Demonstrating good taste, SOE's leadership had requisitioned Villa Scacciapensieri, near Siena, for the FANYs' accommodation. The name of the villa means 'banish thoughts', a highly appropriate choice.

6 Edgardo Sogno 1996, p. 295. Parri was arrested on 2 January and Sogno on the night of 27/28 January, which delayed the beginning of Mallaby's mission (Ferruccio Parri, *Due mesi con i nazisti*, Carecas: Rome, 1973, p. 27). TNA HS 6/785.

7 Don Giovanni (known as Giovannino) Barbareschi was born in Milan on 11 February 1922 and was ordained a priest on 13 August 1944. He was the son of Gaetano Barbareschi (a socialist parliamentarian of Genoese origin, who served

as Minister of Labour in the Parri government and in the first De Gasperi government after the war). Don Giovanni was a prominent member of the Catholic Brigate Fiamme Verdi, which between 1943 and 1945 formed one of the many Italian resistance bodies, but at war's end saved men and women of the RSI and German structures operating in Italy from reprisals. He was also a member of the Aquile Randagie and Organizzazione Scout Collocamento Assistenza Ricercati – OSCAR. I contacted Don Giovanni Barbareschi by telephone and letter, but he rather abruptly and enigmatically refused to discuss his contact with Mallaby. Fortunately, Dick Mallaby's son Vaky succeeded (like his father) in an impossible mission, interviewing Barbareschi on 27 November 2012. Don Giovanni Barbareschi passed away on 4 October 2018.

8   The report (drawn up six days after the events) by the Servizio Informazioni della Difesa (SID – Defence Information Service), signed by Colonel Collu, confirms that the arrest of the four occurred in Lecco (TNA: HS 6/873 and TNA: HS 6/874).

9   As reported by Don Giovanni Barbareschi in his aforementioned interview on 27 November 2012, the address in Via Sant'Agnese was where Barbareschi himself had lived.

10 Aloisio Bonfanti, in his 2008 research into the 75 years of the Opera Don Guanella institute in Lecco (private publication), wrote (p. 18) that Don Zanin 'managed to escape from his Lecco prison and finally came knocking on the door of a religious institute [most probably the Opera Don Guanella]. There, having tested him by making him recite the breviary, to make sure that he really was a priest, they gave him lodging.' Don Mario Zanin is also mentioned in Roger Absalom's *A Strange Alliance* (Leo Olschki: Florence, 1991, p. 106).

11 Ferruccio Parri recalls that his transfers as a prisoner from Milan to Verona and vice versa were always carried out at top speed, to avoid being hit by Allied airplanes (Parri 1973, pp. 65–74).

12 According to the Italian information in British possession, De Leo was 'very active, an expert in counterespionage, particularly good at investigations and the compilation of irreproachable denunciations' (Bailey 2014, p. 148). The important role played by De Leo in the RSI did not prevent his election as mayor of Bagnara Calabra in the post-war period, which he held for longer than any other person from 1958 to 1964 and from 1969 to 1977.

13 De Leo, captured a few weeks later by the Allies, revealed in his subsequent interrogation that he believed Mallaby's story. Rodolfo Graziani, however, took an interest in the matter again the following May after the war was over and asked De Leo himself for a detailed report. The note of reply from the latter (dated 5 May 1945) came into British hands and attests that Mallaby, as usual, had cleverly dropped into his interrogations truthful elements about his life and military career, as well as others that were quite fanciful. For example, in relation to his mission in the summer of 1943, he did not reveal how and why he arrived in Brindisi, but stated: 'In June of '43 I was transferred as an interpreter to Allied Headquarters in Algiers, where I remained until the beginning of September 1943. In the meantime I had been promoted to second lieutenant. On 12 September 1943, I was assigned to the Allied Command at Brindisi.' TNA: HS 6/870.

14 During their occupation, the Germans had, among other things, amassed machinery, requisitioned from factories in northern Italy, in various secure places (Parri 1973 cit., p. 26).

15 According to the minutes of his interrogation dated 18 February 1945, as well as inaccurate details of his entry into Italy and other imaginative information, Mallaby reported to De Leo that Field Marshal Alexander himself – whose organization he had joined the previous September – had entrusted him with the secret mission.

Mallaby stated that he reached Lugano by train from Bern on 13 February, and went to the offices of the British Vice Consul, to be presented to a person known as 'Avvocato' ('Lawyer'), who in turn introduced him to the three people who were to accompany him to Italy (a priest who had to take them to Milan to introduce him to Cardinal Schuster; a radio operator named Ricci, an expert in the use of British cyphers, needed for contacting Alexander; and a guide of unknown name and nationality who was to have accompanied them in RSI territory).

16 According to Mallaby's son Vaky, at a certain point the Germans, in an effort to test his truthfulness, passed from the 'carrot' to the 'stick', revealing preparations for his execution in the shooting range in Via Carmelitani Scalzi.

17 TNA: HS 6/870. Allen Dulles, head of the OSS, called Mallaby's extemporaneous idea an 'astute stratagem' (Bradley F. Smith and Elena Aga Rossi, *Operation Sunrise: La resa tedesca in Italia 2 maggio '45*, Mondadori: Milan, 2005, p. 89); Peter Tompkins, in *L'altra resistenza* (Rizzoli: Milan, 1995, p. 396), reports that the opportunity provided by Mallaby to Wolff was the latter's second attempt to open a channel of communication with the Allies; Frederick Deakin, on the other hand, states that Wolff had informed the German ambassador to the RSI, Rudolf Rahn, that he 'wanted to make use of the British captain to see if he could be considered as a liaison officer' (Frederick W. Deakin, *Storia della repubblica di Salò*, Vol. 2, Einaudi: Turin, 1963, p. 1033).

18 A report dated 28 March 1945 concerning dead or missing officers whilst on missions classified Mallaby in the second of the two categories, with effective date of 15 February 1945. On 8 May, it was officially communicated that he was no longer missing; on 1 April his pay scale had been reduced from special operations to standard military service, demonstrating that due to the outcome of his second mission, Mallaby had been retired from active service in SOE (TNA: HS 6/872).

19 See Alan Dulles, *The Secret Surrender*, The Lyons Press: Guildford, 1966, *passim*, for his account of *Sunrise*.

20 Wolff proved this by handing over a detailed map of the places where he had hidden – allegedly to protect them – important

Italian works of art and the famous coin collection of Vittorio Emanuele III.

21 A credible summary of US intelligence assessments of this matter is contained in the memoirs of Max Corvo, head of the OSS in Italy during the war (Corvo 1990, pp. 244–45).

22 On 10 March 1945, Field Marshal Kesselring was transferred to command the Army in the West (OB West), and General Heinrich von Vietinghoff was appointed as the supreme German commander in Italy, at the head of Army Group C.

23 Wolff had held a secret conversation on 8 March 1944 with Pope Pius XII at the Vatican, which undoubtedly influenced his later actions. For some new aspects on this event, see Manaresi 2009.

24 Smith and Aga Rossi 2005, *passim*; Dulles 1966, *passim*.

25 ACS: ACC microfilm, Public Safety, item: Cecil D. Mallaby, reel 166 C.

26 TNA: HS 6/873–874.

27 Smith and Aga Rossi 2005, p. 89.

28 TNA: HS 6/873.

29 Stafford 2011, pp. 91–92.

30 TNA: HS 6/873.

31 Woods 1999, pp. 15–16; Bailey's conclusions, 2014, p. 337, also match this.

32 TNA: HS 6/873.

33 Ibid.

34 Jochen von Lang, *Der Adjutant: Karl Wolff, der Mann zwischen Hitler und Himmler*, Herbig: Stuttgart, 1985. For Wolff's opinions about Mallaby, see: Foreign Office; Italian Documents, 032154; FO 371/46786.

35 Pino Adriano, *L'intrigo di Berna*, Mondadori: Milan, 2010, pp. 217–18. The author ignores or omits Mallaby's fundamental contribution to the events. Attilio Tamaro, *Due Anni di Storia 1943–1945*, Tosi: Rome, 1950, pp. 520–21. In *Memoria di sacerdoti 'ribelli per amore'*, written by Don Giovanni Barbareschi himself in 1986 (pp. 44–47), he states that after being arrested in Lecco, he was transferred to the

SS headquarters at Villa Carminati di Cernobbio. Here he met Karl Wolff, an SS general and Eugen Dollmann; then with a stratagem the Germans freed him from the Brigate Nere and sent him to Switzerland with a message about the negotiations under way with the Allies, about which the Fascist authorities were and had to remain completely in the dark.

36 First among these is the one by Cardinal Schuster. On this point see also Smith and Aga Rossi 2005, p. 283, mentioning industrialist Carlo Bianchi (previously involved with Fascism), who even claimed financial support for Operation *Sunrise*. Thus, Wolff would have replicated with Barbareschi what was implemented with Mallaby.

37 TNA: HS 6/873. E. Kuby, *Il tradimento tedesco*, Rizzoli: Milan, 1987, *passim*. Kuby's conclusions appear to be shared by Friedrich-Karl von Plehwe, *Il patto d'acciaio*, Longanesi: Milan, 1970, *passim*.

38 TNA: HS 6/873.

39 Smith and Aga Rossi 2005, p. 239.

40 Kuby 1987, pp. 403–04.

41 Smith and Aga Rossi 2005, pp. 240–41. Among the prosecution evidence collected against Wolff was his specific and willing involvement in the Holocaust, and experiments into the behaviour of the human body at low temperatures, and at extreme pressure, allegedly aimed at the development of safety and survival systems for aviators.

42 Giuseppe Parlato, *Fascisti senza Mussolini*, Il Mulino: Bologna, 2006, p. 88.

43 Sergio Nesi, *Junio Valerio Borghese: Un principe un comandante un Italiano*, Lo Scarabeo: Bologna, 2004, p. 505.

44 Rodolfo Graziani, *Ho difeso la patria*, Garzanti: Milan, 1947, pp. 488–89.

45 Cesare Rossi, *Trentatré vicende mussoliniane*, Ceschina: Milan, 1958, pp. 535–37.
Eugen Dollmann, one of the leading protagonists in Operation *Sunrise*, claimed to have been tasked with organizing the

meeting between Mallaby and also Barbareschi with Wolff by Temistocle Testa, an important RSI official. The latter was impatient with Graziani's unwillingness to deal with issues that were not strictly military, and was convinced of the usefulness of the 'Tucker card' (E. Dollman, *Roma nazista*, Longanesi & C: Milan, 1951, p. 427). Apart from the inaccuracy concerning the presence of Barbareschi, the testimony is plausible, and other accounts confirm that Testa, together with his right-arm man Giuseppe Cancarini Ghisetti, actually did this.

46   TNA: HS 6/869. This secret message reveals the identity of 'Anselmo': Everardo Galassini, an Italian soldier, a.k.a Carlo Ricci, Enzo Ricci, and Anselmo Montari, an SOE and No. 1 Special Force collaborator. According to Mallaby's statements and British reports, Galassini's behaviour was not particularly positive, especially during his interrogation.

47   Vincenzo Alberto Mellini Ponce de León, *Guerra diplomatica a Salò (ottobre 1943–aprile 1945)*, Cappelli: Bologna, 1950, p. 107.

CHAPTER 6: AFTERMATH

1   After its broadcast, Mallaby was contacted by the German newspaper *Frankfurter Illustrierte* with a view to serializing his story; nothing came of it, however.

2   In March 1965, Duilio Susmel, during one of the periodic revelations concerning the famous, secret 'suitcase papers' that Mussolini had with him at the time of his shooting, stated that some of them concerned the arrest and release 'of Captain Tucker, special envoy to General Alexander and British Prime Minister Churchill, tasked with making contact with Mussolini in order to shorten the duration of the war'. Susmel states that initially Mussolini did not believe Tucker-Mallaby, 'about whose arrest and whose statements he was immediately informed, so that he ordered him to be handed over to the Germans. But he changed his mind four days before his execution, when he tried to contact Churchill himself.' The resonance of this was significant, given that it was taken up by

the Florence newspaper *La Nazione* and even led to an official denial from Field Marshal Harold Alexander (reported in the papers with the headline: 'Alexander denies Captain Tucker's Claim' – as if it were Mallaby, and not Susmel, who had presented a misleading version of the facts).

Alexander affirmed the truth, by denying. Evidently, Dick Mallaby's ruse still produced effects 20 years later, like a war relic. Mallaby kept the newspaper clippings, hoping to one day reveal the truth.

3   Among those who attended Dick Mallaby's funeral was the commander of NATO LANDSOUTH in Verona, James Lee Dozier. He would be kidnapped by an Italian communist terrorist group a few months later, and then freed thanks to a commando action that would have been typical of SOE.

4   Mallaby, before joining NATO, had attempted to publish something about his experiences of war. His personal papers reveal a letter dated 3 August 1950 from a literary agent, containing a first encouraging evaluation of the proposed manuscript. Among its stylistic recommendations was the advice to write it in the first person, while among the suggested titles was 'From the vineyard to the battlefield'. The project probably hit a dead end due to the disclosure veto surrounding all things SOE.

5   Boutigny left a heartfelt testimony regarding Mallaby and his achievements in a piece of autobiographical writing that remains, unfortunately, unpublished, gathered by Mauro Taddei (who kindly allowed me to consult a transcript).

6   The proceedings of the conference are reported in *N. 1 Special Force nella Resistenza italiana*, Editrice Clueb: Bologna, 1990; the tributes of Hewitt and Boutigny appear on pp. 291–300 and pp. 313–24, respectively, while notes on Mallaby's first mission are contained in the contributions of Douglas Dodds-Parker (p. 20) and of Christopher Woods (p. 46).

7   See the interview with the Deputy Mayor of Asciano Fabrizio Nucci, available at: https://www.youtube.com/watch?v=7-Xot7HRW8Q.

8 'Real life James Bond who parachuted behind WWII enemy lines to be honoured by Italy', available at https://www.telegraph.co.uk/news/2016/09/22/real-life-james-bond-who-parachuted-behind-ww2-enemy-lines-to-be/; 'Italy honours the suave Briton who fooled Nazis', at https://www.thetimes.co.uk/article/italy-honours-the-suave-briton-who-fooled-nazis-dzh9ngpkz.

INDEX